Popular Punishment

Recent Titles in
STUDIES IN PENAL THEORY AND PHILOSOPHY
R. A. Duff, Michael Tonry, General Editors

Just Sentencing
Principles and Procedures for a Workable System
Richard S. Frase

Punishment, Participatory Democracy, and the Jury
Albert W. Dzur

Retributivism Has a Past
Has It a Future?
Edited by Michael Tonry

Popular Punishment

On the Normative Significance
of Public Opinion

EDITED BY
Jesper Ryberg &
Julian V. Roberts

OXFORD
UNIVERSITY PRESS

OXFORD
UNIVERSITY PRESS

Oxford University Press is a department of the University of Oxford.
It furthers the University's objective of excellence in research, scholarship,
and education by publishing worldwide.

Oxford   New York
Auckland   Cape Town   Dar es Salaam   Hong Kong   Karachi
Kuala Lumpur   Madrid   Melbourne   Mexico City   Nairobi
New Delhi   Shanghai   Taipei   Toronto

With offices in
Argentina   Austria   Brazil   Chile   Czech Republic   France   Greece
Guatemala   Hungary   Italy   Japan   Poland   Portugal   Singapore
South Korea   Switzerland   Thailand   Turkey   Ukraine   Vietnam

Oxford is a registered trade mark of Oxford University Press
in the UK and certain other countries.

Published in the United States of America by
Oxford University Press
198 Madison Avenue, New York, NY 10016

© Oxford University Press 2014

Library of Congress Cataloging-in-Publication Data
Ryberg, Jesper.
 Popular punishment on the normative significance of public opinion / Jesper Ryberg and
Julian V. Roberts.
    p.   cm.
 Includes bibliographical references and index.
 ISBN 978-0-19-994137-7 (hardcover : alk. paper)   1. Punishment—Public opinion.
2. Criminal liability—Public opinion. 3. Sentences (Criminal procedure)—Public opinion.
I. Roberts, Julian V. II. Title.
 K5101.R93 2014
 364.6—dc23
                                   2013038974

9 8 7 6 5 4 3 2 1

Printed in the United States of America on acid-free paper

CONTENTS

CONTRIBUTORS

Mirko Bagaric is Professor of Law and the Dean of Deakin Law School.

Christopher Bennett is Senior Lecturer in Philosophy at the University of Sheffield.

Thom Brooks is Reader in Law at Durham University.

Albert W. Dzur is Professor of Political Science and Philosophy at Bowling Green State University.

Jan W. de Keijser is Associate Professor of Criminology at Leiden University.

Matt Matravers is Professor of Political Philosophy at the University of York.

Richard L. Lippke is Professor of Criminal Justice at Indiana University.

Paul H. Robinson is Colin S. Diver Professor of Law at University of Pennsylvania Law School.

Julian V. Roberts is Professor of Criminology at Oxford University.

Jesper Ryberg is Professor of Ethics and Philosophy of Law at Roskilde University.

Frej K. Thomsen is Postdoctoral Scholar of Philosophy at Roskilde University.

Popular Punishment

Popular Punishments.

Introduction

Exploring the Normative Significance of Public Opinion for State Punishment

Jesper Ryberg and Julian V. Roberts

Should public opinion determine—or even influence—sentencing policy and practice? A simple question, perhaps, but one which conceals complex theoretical and methodological challenges. The present volume is evidence of the complexity of the issues and the importance of the topic to scholars of different disciplines and practitioners across a variety of jurisdictions.

A century ago, sentencing practices evolved without any apparent link to community values or opinions; politicians evinced little interest in consulting the public when devising penal policies. One explanation for this insulation of the system was methodological: Before the advent of systematic surveys using representative samples of the public, community views emerged only haphazardly—in letters to the editors of newspapers or to members of Parliament. The image of sentencing (and sentencers) may also have constrained public input: The determination of sentence was deemed to be the exclusive domain of professional judges appointed for their independence of community opinion, their detachment from society. Even in England and Wales, where sentencing was largely determined by lay magistrates, these individuals were often retired legal professionals or individuals who were very unrepresentative of the communities in which they sentenced. All this has now changed; by the beginning of the twenty-first century, public opinion has emerged as a significant force in the field of criminal policy and in particular sentencing policy.

When legislatures amend penal laws and practices, these amendments are rarely accompanied by substantial justifying arguments; principled reasoning is seldom a characteristic of decision making in the political arena. However, one of the arguments that has been advanced, and which has come to play a significant role in modern penal policy, is that societal responses to crime should reflect public views. Public

1

opinion, variously defined, has therefore become increasingly salient in penal political debate, and this is the case in all Western countries.

The theory and practice of sentencing varies widely around the world, although certain objectives and principles are common to many jurisdictions. One common element is the salience of public opinion: Community views emerge repeatedly as an influence—direct or indirect—upon sentencing policy and practice. The decisions of politicians and policy makers are often affected by perceptions of public opinion—thus creating an indirect and largely unseen influence. This effect is usually decried by scholars as malign: Public opinion has generally been invoked to justify unprincipled or needlessly punitive sentencing reforms such as mandatory sentencing, the abolition of parole, or the need to create more austere and aversive prison conditions. Judges also refer to the public in their judgments, citing the need to impose punishments which conform to, or at least do not clash with, community values.

The public also affect sentencing practices through participation in sentencing councils and commissions. Over the past decade, sentencing guidelines authorities in England and Wales have conducted public opinion research into the offence for which a guideline is being issued. The views of the public are then considered in determining the nature and severity of sentences recommended by the guidelines. For example, when the Sentencing Advisory Panel developed advice for sentencing driving offences causing death, it commissioned public opinion research to determine the levels of public acceptance for specific sentences. The report then noted that the public's views were used to devise the sentence levels for guidelines affecting these offences (Roberts et al., 2008; Sentencing Advisory Panel, 2008). More recently, the Sentencing Council has commissioned research into public attitudes to sentencing discounts for guilty pleas (Dawes et al., 2011), and this research will ultimately influence the council's guideline recommendations.

Community views also seep into the sentencing process in some jurisdictions through lay involvement in sentencing. In England and Wales, the vast majority (approximately 90 per cent) of sentences are imposed by lay magistrates, laypersons appointed to the magistracy with no formal legal qualification.[1] One of the putative benefits of a lay magistracy is that this infuses the sentencing process with community values in a way that is not possible with a small number of highly selected professional judges.[2] Over the past two decades efforts have been made to make the lay magistracies more representative of their communities, the argument being that this will enhance the degree of community input. In continental jurisdictions laypersons often sit in a panel with professional judges, thus fusing the lay and professional functions. Finally, in several US states sentencing is determined by juries,[3] and proposals have been advanced in other countries to increase the role of juries at sentencing.

The political economy of contemporary punishment cannot therefore reasonably ignore public opinion when accounting for current sentencing practices. The presence of the public—in one form or another—is clear enough. The justifications for incorporating public views—the normative significance—are far less apparent. Politicians often advert to the importance of ensuring a correspondence between public opinion and specific policies; sentencing reform proposals are often advanced with this very objective in mind. Yet this claim alone is insufficient; far more is needed to sustain a link between punishment policy and public opinion than merely appeals to populism.

Although politicians have for many years focused on crime and punishment—particularly at a time of elections—the prominence of public opinion-based arguments is a more recent development. For example, when Richard Nixon promoted tough law and order policies he—as pointed out by a recent theorist—did what he judged to be popular, important, or of concern to people. However, the public was not conceived as having any direct relevance or input into penal thinking and policy (Pratt, 2007). In contrast, over the last two or three decades, penal policy has often reflected the idea that the public should have an important influence on penal affairs. At least, so it has repeatedly been claimed. A typical argument was used by a former British Prime Minister (Blair) when he stated, 'There are more prison places, sentences are longer and sentences are tougher but if you look where the public is on this issue, the gap between what they expect and what they get is bigger in this service than anywhere else and we have got to bridge it' (Blair, 2006). Thus, the existence of a gap between courts and community was deemed problematic, and bridging the divide seen as unproblematic. Regardless of the political orientation of the government, penal policies in Britain have increasingly reflected what politicians believe that the public wants.[4]

Similar trends have been observed in other Western countries including New Zealand (Pratt, 2007), Canada (Roberts, 2011), and Australia (Pratt, 2007). Indeed, even in the Scandinavian countries, which have traditionally been regarded as moderate with respect to punishment policies and practices, public opinion has been influential. For instance, in Denmark the claim that punishment should reflect public opinion has driven all penal reforms over the last decade. Thus, the idea that public opinion constitutes a justification for policy initiatives regarding to state sentencing constitutes a general trend in modern penal policy. The opposing view—that legislation and individual sentencing decisions by the courts are supposed to educate or lead public opinion—has very little contemporary resonance (Freiberg & Gelb, 2008; Ryberg, 2010).

The political invocation of public opinion-based arguments has not passed unnoticed in academic circles. Scholars from various disciplines have seen such arguments as representing a new approach to democracy and have identified some of the underlying causes of this trend (see e.g. Pratt, 2007; Ryan, 2003). Moreover, the tendency to refer to or draw on public opinion has also been noted as one of the characteristics of 'populist punitiveness' or simply 'penal populism' (see Freiberg & Gelb, 2008; Pratt, 2007; Roberts et al., 2003). Anthony Bottoms originally coined the phrase 'populist punitiveness' to describe 'the notion of politicians tapping into, and using for their own purposes, what they believe to be the public's generally punitive stance' (1995, p. 40). The term has subsequently become standard terminology to refer to penal policies as 'populist' if they are advocated principally to attract votes and without regard to their effectiveness in reducing crime or promoting justice (Gelb, 2008). However, what is remarkable about the broader modern discussion on penal populism is that despite the rather pejorative use of the term 'populism', the questions as to whether public opinion *should* have a role to play and if so for what reason and to what extent are rarely addressed. This is also the case if we turn to penal philosophy.

Classical penal theory contains only a few stray references to the moral significance of public opinion. For instance, Bentham notes the public dissatisfaction to which a penal practice may give rise, by holding that a 'portion of superfluous pain is . . . produced when the punishment is unpopular: but in this case it is produced on the part of persons altogether innocent, the people at large' (1988, p. 198). Moreover, he notes the implications when the public is dissatisfied with the law: 'When people are satisfied with the law, they voluntarily lend their assistance in the execution; when they are dissatisfied, they will naturally withhold that assistance; it is well if they do not take a positive part in raising impediments' (p. 199). Hegel, as part of his philosophy of right, comments on why 'public opinion . . . deserves to be as much respected as despised', without, however, relating this specifically to the question of punishment (1967, p. 204). Contemporary penal philosophy has also failed to provide a comprehensive examination of the role of public opinion in legal punishment.

1. COMPETING APPROACHES TO PUBLIC OPINION

Three approaches can be identified with regard to the role that public opinion should play in relation to sentencing. The first may be labelled a direct importation model. According to this perspective, community values should be directly imported into sentencing practice; that is, sentencing policies (and hence practices) should strictly mirror the prevailing public opinion. Sentencing factors, principles, and policies would all be constructed to reflect the public's views, and policies inconsistent with community values would be modified or jettisoned entirely. No one has recently advocated this radical position. It is very hard to see how it could be theoretically sustained, and it is easy to imagine that it could lead to conspicuously unacceptable results (Roberts, 2011).

The other extreme is an exclusionary model, according to which community values are explicitly excluded from the evolution of any penal policies. If excluded from the determination of sentencing practices, for example, crime seriousness rankings would be determined objectively, by harm-based analyses or some other measure of gravity. Under an exclusionary model, factors influencing the offender's level of culpability would be derived from moral philosophy (and possibly the evolution of judicial practices). The resulting system would have universal application since it would be insensitive to local variation regarding the seriousness of specific offences or the relevance of various sentencing factors.

This exclusionary position has also attracted few advocates; however, the lack of attention paid to public attitudes when penal theoretical positions have been developed nevertheless suggests that this model has been implicitly assumed. Penal theorists clearly regard the public as an unreliable source of guidance. The model may be motivated by the belief that moral philosophical prescriptions must have universal application and that they can all be deduced from basic moral principles or perhaps by the general belief that public attitudes should carry no weight as a normative matter because they are unprincipled, prejudiced, based on a very limited degree of knowledge, or volatile (e.g. by changing rapidly in response to high-profile cases reported in the media; see Roberts, 2011).

A third model—qualified public input—represents an intermediate position between these two extremes of blindly following or totally excluding public views. That is, a community's views should be considered when shaping state punishment but with significant qualifications and subject to important limits. The idea of *via media* has been supported by reference to claims regarding the role of sentencing as a social practice or institution. For instance, it is asserted that sentencing practice must reflect the larger society within which it is embedded or that 'thinking of punishment as a social institution should change not only our mode of understanding penalty, but also our normative thinking about it' (Garland, 1991, p. 160). However, no matter whether one subscribes to one of the two extreme models or some intermediate position, few would disagree that more theoretical scrutiny is required to clarify and justify the role attributed to public opinion—and that is the principal purpose of our volume.

2. JUSTIFYING PUBLIC INPUT: CONSEQUENTIALIST ACCOUNTS

One way of justifying the qualified public input model is to defend the moral significance of public opinion by reference to consequentialist considerations. At first glance it appears that public opinion has no role to play within a consequentialist framework. It might be held that if there is a divergence between, on the one hand, what constitutes the right consequentialist answer as to how different crimes should be punished and, on the other, public attitudes to whatever the consequentialist answer prescribes, this does not constitute a reason for revising the answer. Considering the role of lay judgments in relation to sentencing, Bagaric and Edney argue, 'Seeking public views on sentencing is analogous to doctors basing treatment decisions on what the community thinks is appropriate or engineers building cars, not in accordance with the rules of physics, but on the basis of what lay members of the community "reckon" seems about right' (2004, p. 129). However, their answer is surely premature. When considering sentencing, the question from a consequentialist stance is not whether sentencing should be adjusted in accordance with public attitudes but rather whether public attitudes may affect what constitutes the correct consequentialist answer (Ryberg, 2010).

For instance, as the quotes from Bentham indicate, a mismatch between penal practice and the public opinion may have consequences which are relevant for the consequentialist calculus. It has thus been suggested—for instance, by Paul Robinson and his colleagues—that the credibility of the criminal law is essential to effective crime control and is enhanced if the sentencing process assigns punishment in a way that is consistent with 'shared intuitions of justice' (Robinson, 2007, 2008, 2009). Along the same lines, Roberts has suggested that 'if sentencing practices diverged widely and consistently from public opinion the legitimacy of the judicial system would be compromised' (2008, p. 211). What is unclear, however, is the extent to which perceptions of legitimacy would be affected and whether lower levels of perceived legitimacy would have demonstrable consequences in terms of compliance with the law or co-operation with the criminal justice system— to cite two claims made in the literature. Nor is it clear whether there are offsetting costs associated with greater alignment of community and courts—even if levels of legitimacy and compliance are enhanced. Several contributors to the present work pursue these arguments in greater depth.

To date, a more precise exploration of when, for what precise reasons, and to what extent public opinion is relevant from a consequentialist view has not been conducted. This may be because the answer is empirically underdetermined and because consequentialism has been overlooked in modern penal theory. Penal theorising has over the last few decades been dominated by retributivism and has witnessed a corresponding decline of the consequentialist approach that dominated it in earlier periods (Tonry, 2011). Thus, turning to retributivism, what role, if any, has public opinion been claimed from a desert theoretical perspective?

3. RETRIBUTIVE ACCOUNTS

Modern retributivism has evolved into many different versions. Most of the attempts that have been made to defend a desert-based view of sentencing pay scant attention to public opinion, although there are exceptions. Some retributivists advocate a limited degree of public input. For instance, following an expressive approach—constituting one of the dominant versions of modern retributivism—punishment should be seen as a way of communicating appropriate condemnatory messages to perpetrators (e.g. Duff, 1986, 2001; von Hirsch, 1993; von Hirsch & Ashworth, 2005). It has been suggested in relation to this approach that it 'would make little sense for the sentencing process of expressing censure on behalf of the community, yet pay no attention to public opinion regarding the kinds of offences and offenders, which in the eyes of the community are seen as being most worthy of condemnation' (Roberts, 2008, p. 85). More precisely, the few penal theorists who have addressed the question of the significance of public opinion within a retributivist context have done so in relation to considerations of punishment distribution.

Retributivist views of punishment distribution are based on the concept of proportionality. Proportionate sentencing presupposes a ranking of crimes in terms of their relative seriousness and a corresponding ranking of the severity of legal punishments. Constructing these rankings will suffice when it comes to observing the requirement of ordinal proportionality, that is, the purely relative requirement that one crime should be punished more harshly than another less serious crime and that two crimes of the same gravity should be punished equally harshly (see e.g. Ryberg, 2004; von Hirsch, 1993). However, the requirement of ordinal proportionality itself will not suffice as a complete theory of penal distribution; it leaves unanswered the question as to how severely a particular crime should be punished. Thus, further considerations are required. Several conceptualisations of the scaling of crimes and punishments have been developed. For instance, it has been suggested that the two scales should be connected on the ground of upper and lower anchor points (Kleinig, 1973; Scheid, 1997) or by applying a 'decremental strategy' combined with considerations of crime prevention (von Hirsch, 1993).

Neither of these proposals leaves any room for public attitudes to influence sentencing practices. However, it has also been suggested that public perceptions should be incorporated. Davies argues that 'with sentencing policy there is no ocean floor on which to anchor the system of proportionality. Ocean floors are variable in depth as well as out of sight to the spectator, but at sea level that which floats is visible. And this is where the tariff of sentencing should start—with what is visible and floats on a sea of public acceptability' (1993, p. 17). Although open to different interpretations, the essence of this metaphor is that to achieve a complete theory of proportional sentencing, the prevailing public view about sentencing levels must play a role in shaping policies. However, as noted, there is little agreement amongst modern retributivists with respect to this issue.

4. PURPOSE OF THE VOLUME

The purpose of the current work is to consider whether public opinion should play a role in shaping societal responses to offenders for three reasons. First, modern penal policy is dominated by the idea that community views are an important influence. Second, the role of public opinion has only been tentatively explored within modern penal theory. The third reason relates to empirical research and normative inquiry. Empirical research on public attitudes to sentencing has been conducted for more than a century now; as a result of the accumulated research, a great deal is now known about community views regarding legal punishment (for reviews, see Gelb, 2008; Roberts & Hough, 2005). Yet the implications of this research for the normative questions about public opinion and sentencing have not been fully explored.

The contributors address, for the first time in a volume, the normative significance of community views for the theory and practice of legal punishment. Contributions explore a range of potential justifications—some utilitarian, others deontological in nature. The authors explore the issue from different perspectives and reach a range of conclusions about the appropriate role of public opinion. Some scholars advocate a close fit between community views and sentencing practices while others are cautious of engaging the public and remain less or unconvinced of the normative significance of community views.

In addition to exploring the normative significance of community views, the volume also addresses the vexing question of methodology. If a justification exists for incorporating the public's views, how should public opinion be measured? The critical choice appears to lie between drawing upon raw, 'uninformed' views—which are closer to population norms—or the opinions of an elite or informed sample of the public. The choice creates a conundrum to which Jan de Keijser draws our attention: On the one hand, if we seek a correspondence between community views and sentencing practices, measuring the views of a small, select group of people provided with information about the issue under discussion is unlikely to promote widespread acceptance of the policy. On the other hand, if we take as a measure of public opinion the view of the average member of the public—expressed without additional information or reflection—the correspondence between community and courts will be achieved but in a way that is likely to guarantee unprincipled outcomes.

5. CONTENTS OF THE VOLUME

The opening chapter addresses the central question as to whether public opinion should play a role in penal theory. The affirmative answer given by Ryberg does not rest on a particular penal theoretical point of view. Rather, it is argued that insofar as moral intuitions should play a role in penal theorising—that is, in considerations for or against penal theories—public intuitions ought to be consulted. This means that even if, at the end of the day, the most plausible penal theory turns out to be one that does not require consultation of public opinion to guide penal practice, one would still have to draw on input from the public in the way that this theory is defended in the first place. While Ryberg does not subscribe to a particular penal theoretical position or a particular view on penal distribution, the next three chapters all relate to the idea of proportionality in sentencing, albeit from different theoretical perspectives and with very different implications with regard to the significance of public opinion.

Drawing upon the retributivist perspective, Matravers takes for granted a commitment to proportionality. What he suggests is that any plausible answer with regard to the rankings of crime gravity and punishment severity must be 'context sensitive' by which he means that judgments of seriousness and severity will reflect social conditions and practices such that what is deserved will be constituted by what is popularly believed to be—or what is implicit in current social practices as—serious, severe, and so proportionate.

When it comes to penal distribution, Robinson suggests that public opinion should play an even more significant role at sentencing. A criminal law, he holds, that distributes punishment in ways that the community perceives as just gains moral credibility, and this in turn results in greater support for and co-operation with the criminal justice system. Robinson draws attention to several empirical studies supporting this conclusion. In contrast, Bagaric is much more sceptical with regard to consultation of the public. He criticises several influential retributivist attempts to give content to the proportionality principle and suggests that the problems are best overcome by drawing, in different ways, on utilitarian considerations. He ends by rejecting any direct role for public opinion in shoring up the proportionality principle but underlines the importance of exploring the public's experiences about the effects of crime and of allowing such experiences to inform the seriousness component of the principle. Moreover, he suggests that through their links to the community, these experiences will help to dilute reflexive public demands for tougher sentences.

Bagaric's cautious attitude when it comes to the significance of public opinion also emerges in the de Keijser and Thomsen chapters. As noted, de Keijser's main focus is on the question as to 'what form of public opinion' one should be considering. However, he also notes that a mismatch between public opinion and sentencing practice does not necessarily significantly undermine the legitimacy of the criminal justice system. Despite the intense public criticism of courts in Western nations, the sentencing process has yet to collapse. He concludes that criminal justice should be left to experts such as the criminal policy elite and professional judges. But this does not necessarily imply that there should be no connection between public opinion and sentencing. There seems to be evidence that judges, much more so than a few decades ago, regard themselves as members of the larger community rather than as decision makers isolated from society.

Thomsen, for his part, attempts to examine what he takes to be the strongest possible version of an argument to the effect that we ought to punish in accordance with popular sentiment. More precisely, he explores three versions of the overall argument: epistemic, institutional, and instrumental. While Thomsen rejects the first two versions, he holds that the final one may provide *a* reason in favour of incorporating public opinion. However, he also believes that this reason is unlikely to prove satisfactory for most proponents of the view that public opinion should be taken into account.

Whether public input is justified constitutes the cardinal issue in a discussion of the possible role that public opinion should play in the criminal justice system. However, this is not the only question to address. Insofar as one believes—as most of the contributors to this volume do—that there should be at least some room for invoking community views in the sentencing process, another obvious question is *how* this should be done. The remaining chapters offer various ways of addressing the so-called democratic deficit. Bennett, against a background of considerations of reasons for giving the public input into sentencing matters, recommends a citizen jury system. According to Bennett, sentencing by jury has several advantages over other models of democratic control such as, for instance, a system that seeks to incorporate community views directly in the sentencing guidelines (as suggested by Robinson). For instance, it puts the public in a position where it can both endorse and indeed control sentencing outcomes. Moreover, a jury may be able to respond to an offender as a human being rather than as a party that should simply be sentenced in accordance with guidelines. This, Bennett suggests, may help reduce the likelihood of disproportionate sentencing decisions.

Another aspect of democratisation is addressed by the question as to whether democratic control is best obtained in a system that relies on the election of key criminal justice officials. This subject is discussed in the contribution by Lippke who evaluates the question of whether prosecutors should be elected rather than appointed. After having considered the respective strengths and weaknesses of electing prosecutors (compared with having them trained and promoted within professional bureaucracies), he concludes that public input of other kinds is preferable to the direct election of prosecutors. While Lippke leaves open the specific ways of ensuring public input, several proposals are advanced in the ensuing chapters by Brooks and Dzur.

Drawing on experiences from restorative justice, Brooks advocates a model referred to as 'stakeholder sentencing', according to which sentencing decisions should be made collectively by those who have a stake in the penal outcomes. He argues that this model may provide a solution to 'the problem of the public', namely that a greater public voice may secure higher confidence at the cost of abandoning evidence-based sentencing policy. An even more dramatic call for changes is advocated by Dzur who argues that contemporary criminal justice institutions are problematic because of the ways that they repel public responsibility for punishment. In his view, the institution of state punishment is so nondeliberative and exclusionary that profound change is required. Thus, although he is sympathetic to jury trials, restorative justice programs, and citizen advisory bodies, these models are—given the present dominance of the criminal justice institution—still too modest to offer the means through which the lay public can learn about criminal justice and help steer the institution acting in their name. Public engagement with punishment must, he suggests, be 'fostered beneath, outside, and all around the channels of criminal justice institutions'. For this purpose he believes that two arenas in particular stand out, namely primary education institutions and everyday networks of communication.

The volume closes with a contribution reconsidering both the 'why' and 'how' questions with regard to public consultation. Roberts acknowledges that a sentencing system which ignored public views entirely might ultimately suffer from lower compliance, diminished confidence, less co-operation and weaker penal censure. In other words, he believes that there are both deontological and instrumental reasons for public input into sentencing policy and practice. However, the

input, he underlines, should be strictly regulated. He reviews the arguments for
and research on sentencing by jury and concludes that the benefits are outweighed by the costs to principled sentencing. Having considered several models
for input including those advanced by other contributors—Roberts suggests that
a sentencing guidelines authority, conducting research into and then deliberating upon public opinion about crimes and punishments, constitutes a more
promising avenue for public input into sentencing practice and policy.

The role of the public in sentencing policy and practice will remain contested; it is unlikely that any jurisdiction or criminal justice agency will
soon implement a policy of determining sentencing by direct reference to
or explicit exclusion of the public's views. Contributors to this volume have
at least now laid bare many of the arguments on both sides of the debate.

REFERENCES

Bagaric, M., and R. Edney. 2004. 'The Sentencing Advisory Commissions and the
   Hope of Smarter Sentencing.' *Current Issues in Criminal Justice* 16: 125–139.
Bentham, J. 1988. *The Principles and Morals and Legislation*. New York: Prometheus.
Blair, T. 2006. 'Blair Argues Law Cannot Deal with Threats of 21st Century.' *Guard-
   ian*,   8   June.   http://www.theguardian.com/politics/2006/jun/09/ukcrime.
   immigrationpolicy
Bottoms, A. E. 1995. 'The Philosophy and Politics of Punishment and Sentencing.'
   In C. Clark and R. Morgan (eds.), *The Politics of Sentencing Reform*. Oxford:
   Clarendon.
Davies, M. 1993. *Punishing Criminals*. Westport: Greenwood.
Dawes W., P. H. Harvey, B. McIntosh, F. Nunney, and A. Phillips, 2011. *Attitudes to
   Guilty Plea Sentence Reductions*. London: Sentencing Council of England and
   Wales. http://sentencingcouncil.judiciary.gov.uk/docs/Attitudes_to_Guilty_Plea_
   Sentence_Reductions_%28web%29.pdf
Duff, A. 1986. *Trials and Punishment*. Cambridge, UK: Cambridge University Press.
Duff, A. 2001. *Punishment, Communication, and Community*. New York: Oxford
   University Press.
Freiberg, A., and K. Gelb (eds.). 2008. *Penal Populism, Sentencing Councils and Sen-
   tencing Policy*. Cullompton, UK: Willan.
Garland, D. 1991. 'Sociological Perspectives on Punishment.' *Crime and Justice* 14:
   115–165.
Gelb, K. 2008. 'Myths and Misconceptions: Public Opinion versus Public Judgment
   about Sentencing.' In A. Freiberg and K. Gelb (eds.), *Penal Populism, Sentencing
   Councils and Sentencing Policy*. Cullompton, UK: Willan.
Hegel, G. F. W. 1967. *The Philosophy of Right*. New York: Oxford University Press.
Kleinig, J. 1973. *Punishment and Desert*. The Hague: Martinus Nijhoff.
Pratt, J. 2007. *Penal Populism*. London: Taylor and Francis.
Roberts, J. V. 2008. *Punishing Persistent Offenders*. Oxford: Oxford University Press.
Roberts. J. 2011. 'The Future of State Punishment: The Role of Public Opinion in
   Sentencing.' In M. Tonry (ed.), *Retributivism Has a Past. Has It a Future?* New
   York: Oxford University Press.

Roberts, J. V., and M. Hough. 2005. *Understanding Public Attitudes to Criminal Justice*. Maidenhead, UK: Open University Press.

Roberts, J. V., M. Hough, J. Jacobson, A. Bredee, and N. Moon. 2008. 'Public Attitudes to the Sentencing of Offenders Convicted of Offences Involving Death by Driving.' *Criminal Law Review* 7: 525–540.

Roberts, J. V., L. S. Stalans, D. Indermaur, and M. Hough. 2003. *Penal Populism and Public Opinion: Lessons from Five Countries*. Oxford: Oxford University Press.

Robinson, P. 2007. *How Psychology is Changing the Punishment Theory Debate*. Philadelphia: University of Pennsylvania Law School.

Robinson, P. 2008. *Distributive Principles of Criminal Law*. Oxford: Oxford University Press.

Robinson, P. 2009. 'Empirical Desert.' In P. Robinson, S. Garvey, and K. Kessler Ferzan (eds.), *Criminal Law Conversations*. Oxford: Oxford University Press.

Ryan, M. 2003. *Penal Policy and Political Culture in England and Wales*. Winchester, UK: Waterside Press.

Ryberg, J. 2004. *Proportionate Punishment. A Critical Investigation*. Dordrecht, The Netherlands: Kluwer Academic.

Ryberg, J. 2010. 'Punishment and Public Opinion.' In J. Ryberg and A. Corlett (eds.), *Punishment and Ethics*. Basingstoke, UK: Palgrave Macmillan.

Scheid, D. E. 1997. 'Constructing a Theory of Punishment, Desert, and the Distribution of Punishment.' *The Canadian Journal of Law and Jurisprudence* 10: 441–506.

Sentencing Advisory Panel. 2008. *Causing Death by Driving. Advice to the Sentencing Guidelines Council*. London: Sentencing Advisory Panel.

Tonry, M. (ed.). 2011. *Retributivism Has a Past: Has It a Future?* New York: Oxford University Press.

von Hirsch, A. 1993. *Censure and Sanctions*. Oxford: Clarendon.

von Hirsch, A., and A. Ashworth. 2005. *Proportionate Sentencing*. Oxford: Oxford University Press.

NOTES

1. Magistrates do receive advice from a legally qualified advisor.
2. The number has declined in recent years, but there are still approximately 28,000 sitting lay magistrates. They are appointed to reflect the area in which they live, thus promoting both localism and community-based values.
3. In some jurisdictions juries are allowed to provide limited input into sentencing for certain very serious offences. For example, in Canada, juries who convict a defendant of second degree murder are allowed to make a recommendation to the sentencing judge with respect to the number of years that the offender should serve in prison before becoming eligible for release on parole.
4. It is interesting that in reconciling sentencing policy and community views, politicians generally favour modifying the former to accommodate the latter. If the public demand harsher sentencing, this usually results in get-tough legislative proposals. Yet current penal policy and public views can also be reconciled by changing the latter rather than amending the former. Seldom, if ever, do politicians change public views by encouraging people to recognise and accept the rationales underlying evidence-based criminal justice policies.

1

Penal Theory, Moral Intuitions, and Public Opinion

Jesper Ryberg

Should public opinion have an impact on criminal justice issues? For instance, should public attitudes be taken into account when the state makes decisions on such a significant moral question as to how criminals should be punished for their misdeeds?

The purpose of this chapter is to argue that the view—sometimes referred to as the exclusionary model (see Introduction)—that public opinion should not have any impact on penal law and penal practice is mistaken. In other words, public opinion should at least have *some* impact on what constitutes the proper state reaction to crime. However, this answer will be defended in a way that is very different from the way that the outlook has so far been advocated by penal theorists. In fact, it will be argued that, even if theorists adhere to penal theoretical positions according to which public opinion on sentencing should be regarded as totally irrelevant, they would still have to rely significantly on a particular sort of public attitude. Since this view may seem mysterious, if not contradictory and since mysticism is very much not a virtue in ethics, I hasten to outline, more clearly, the argument that is presented in the following.

Let us turn again to the question as to what role public opinion should play in penal law and practice. How should one determine what constitutes the correct overall approach to this question? If one examines how the question has so far been dealt with by penal theorists—or how applied ethicists work in general—the answer is simple. The way we, as penal theorists, would approach the question is by drawing on penal theoretical considerations. We will set forth what seems to constitute the most plausible moral theory of punishment and, on the grounds of this, consider whether there are any reasons for invoking public opinion when answers to concrete penal questions—such as how severely different crimes should be punished—arise. For instance, if one believes that punishment is justified on the grounds of an expressionist retributive theory, according to which what matters ethically is that a punishment should express or convey censure on behalf of the community, it seems to follow that public views should be consulted to determine how severely different crimes ought to be censured (see, e.g. Roberts, 2008, p. 84). Or, if one favours a particular consequentialist theory, one will engage in considerations of the possible effects which a match (or mismatch) between, say, the actual penal levels and the public view on these levels would have with regard to the promotion of what, according to the theory, should be regarded as valuable (see, e.g. Robinson & Darley, 2007). More generally, as these examples illustrate, the answer as to whether public opinion has any moral significance is answered by reference to normative penal theory. This approach could be referred to as *post-theoretical* in the sense that the relevance of public attitudes is considered on the grounds of a penal theory which is itself regarded as already settled when the question is addressed. If one takes a look at the literature, it is clear that the significance of public opinion has so far exclusively been addressed in post-theoretical terms (see also Ryberg, 2010a). However, there is another possibility. It might be the case that public opinion should have a role to play in the way that penal theories are formed in the first place. That is, it might be that public opinion should play what could be called a *pre-theoretical* role.[1] In fact, this is the view that is defended in this chapter. It will be argued that public attitudes should play a role when it comes to the development of penal theory.

While a post-theoretical approach to the question of the significance of public opinion, as indicated, operates fully within the framework of normative penal theory, this is not the case for a pre-theoretical approach. Rather, this approach concerns questions of how normative penal theories should be developed. That is, we are concerned with the methodology of penal reasoning or what would usually be regarded as a metaethical framework. As is well known, there exists a plethora of different—and very persistent—metaethical positions. However, the following considerations, although perhaps not consistent with all the theories in the field, do not rely on one particular metaethical theory. On the contrary, it is the belief that the argument will be relevant across different approaches to the method of ethics. Thus, I shall not introduce traditional metaethical positions and shall, to a large extent, abstain from drawing on standard metaethical terminology. But it should be kept in mind that what is going on is not penal theorising but considerations on penal theorising. Whether there exist post-theoretical reasons for consulting public opinion (say, on the grounds of consequentialist or retributivist theories, etc.) will be left open; this is a question on another level to the one addressed here. It is, thereby, also clear that there is nothing mysterious in the previous contention that, even if one favours a normative penal theory according to which public opinion has no moral significance (in post-theoretical terms), it might still be the case that public attitudes should be consulted (at the pre-theoretical stage).

To defend the significance of public attitudes as an element of penal theorising, the chapter will proceed in the following way. In Section 1, it is shown—and I take this as uncontroversial—that moral intuitions are in various ways involved when penal theories are defended or rejected. Subsequently, in Section 2, the main argument is presented. It is suggested that, given the fact that moral intuitions play a role in penal theorising, public opinion should be consulted. In Sections 3 to 5, a number of objections to this conclusion are addressed concerning, respectively, the expertise of penal theorists as moral intuiters, the truth of moral intuitions, and, finally, the triviality of the argument. The objections are rejected and, in relation to the final objection, it is argued that, even though the overall argument is neither controversial nor ingenious, it is nevertheless important both in terms of the way in which penal theory is discussed by philosophers and other theorists, and for the way that empirical studies on public opinion should be conducted. Section 6 summarises and concludes.

1. PENAL THEORY AND MORAL INTUITIONS

When penal theorists defend a particular theory concerning the justification of the punishment system or perhaps of some more detailed parts of the sentencing process or, alternatively, criticise theories that they regarded as implausible, it is usually not the case that the arguments advanced are preceded by more basic considerations of how a theory can be defended or rejected at all. The absence of more basic methodological considerations probably reflects the fact that there exists at least some degree of consensus on how penal theoretical research should be conducted. In the following, I will highlight the simple and, I believe, uncontroversial fact that references to moral intuitions play a significant role in penal theory. The theoretical significance of this fact will be made clear in the ensuing section. The point here is not to produce anything close to a complete overview of all the ways in which moral intuitions affect penal theory. More modestly, I shall simply outline a number of examples of how penal theorising in various ways draws on moral intuitions.[2]

The most comprehensive way of categorising penal theories—and theories in other branches of applied ethics—is to distinguish between *deontological* and *consequentialist* theories. While a consequentialist approach to punishment constituted the leading orthodoxy for most of the last century, it is an accepted fact that retributivism has dominated the penal theoretical field for the last three decades or so (see Ryberg, 2004; Tonry, 2011: 3–6;

Duff & Garland 1994: 1–43). Even though desert considerations might of course perfectly well operate within a consequentialist framework and, despite the fact that just desert theories have been defended in many different versions, it is a fact that retributivism is regarded as very much a nonconsequentialist theory. Retributivism is a deontological theory, in the sense that it operates with moral constraints. How has this aspect of retributive theory been defended? The standard answer since the 1960s has been to point to the unacceptable implications that are held to follow from a consequentialist approach to punishment. If punishing an innocent person produces the best outcome (e.g. the prevention of race riots), this is what consequentialism would prescribe. However, this—the argument runs—is morally unacceptable.[3] Why this is so is usually not explained (for an exception, see Duff, 1986, chapter 6). On the contrary, the punishment-of-the-innocent argument—as set forth in many different versions—is presented as a *reductio ad absurdum* argument in which a theory—*in casu* consequentialism—is rejected by pointing to a sufficiently counterintuitive implication. Thus, moral intuition has constituted the baseline in the penal theoretical consequentialism *versus* deontology dispute.

When it comes to the overall structure of a penal theory, moral intuitions also have a role to play in several other ways. For instance, it is a fact that consequences matter to most (if not all) modern penal theories. Not only consequentialist theories but several versions of retributivism explicitly rely on considerations of consequences. For instance, negative retributivism implies that criminals should not be punished too severely, that is, more than they deserve. However, as long as this proportionality constraint is observed, the actual punishment should be determined on the grounds of considerations of the consequences of punishing in one way or another (see, e.g. Murphy & Hampton, 1988). Likewise, so-called limiting retributivism implies that there are upper and lower limits of deserved punishment and that, within these limits, the proper punishment for a particular crime should be fixed on the grounds of consequentialist considerations (see Morris & Tonry, 1990; Tonry, 1993). In fact, even positive retributivism—according to which, criminals should receive punishment that is neither more *nor less* than they deserve—allows for consideration of consequences in several ways. For instance, some positive retributivists hold that proportionality constraints concern only the severity of the punishment, not the type of punishment, and that as long as the 'penal bite' is maintained there may be consequentialist reasons to prefer one type of punishment to another (see von Hirsch et al., 1989). Moreover, both positive retributivists and other, more relaxed retributivists have held that, even though it is not acceptable to punish a criminal more severely than he or she deserves, this prohibition is not absolute. That is, some retributivists explicitly reject the absolutist dictum *fiat justitia, et ruat mundus*.[4] If the consequences of observing justice in punishment become too terrible, justice may be overruled. Leaving aside the point that threshold deontology is clearly borne by the wish to avoid counterintuitive implications, the fact that one accepts thresholds constitutes another example of how respect to consequences plays a role even within a retributivist theory. But this means that consequentialists and retributivists are confronted with the challenge of specifying which consequences should matter. For instance, it needs to be made clear whether one should favour a monist or a pluralist value theory and what should figure on the list of intrinsic values. Moreover, in the case where one favours a pluralist value theory, one will also have to engage in considerations of how different values should be weighed against each other. It is very hard to believe that such value-theoretical questions can be answered without reference to moral intuitions. Thus, when it comes to the overall structure of a normative penal theory—that is, whether the theory is consequentialist or deontological, whether it is an absolutist or threshold version of deontological theory, or whether some or other consequences matter—moral intuitions seem to play a significant role.

The same seems to be the case if we move from the overall structure of a normative penal theory to the more detailed aspects of penal theory. This is most clearly seen if we turn to retributivist theories.[5] As noted, the retributivist view on penal distribution is captured by the idea of proportionality in sentencing, that is, the idea that the severity of the punishment should reflect the gravity of the crime. This view presupposes that it is possible to rank crimes in seriousness and punishments in severity. Although different theories have been developed on how this may be accomplished, it is, I believe, also the case that these theories in various ways draw on moral intuitions. Here, briefly put, are a few examples.

Consider first the ranking of crimes in seriousness. The standard view is that crime gravity should be determined on the grounds of harm and culpability (see, e.g. von Hirsch, 1993). Discussions of what should be regarded as harm in the relevant sense, and why harm matters, seem to a large extent (although not exclusively) to be based on intuitions. The same is the case in discussions of culpability. Consider the *mens rea* distinction between intentionally versus knowingly inflicted harm. Should this distinction reflect different degrees of culpability? Discussion of this question usually consists in the presentation of scenarios designed to appeal to the intuition that this distinction has (or has no) moral significance. And what about the intriguing question as to how different degrees of harm and different degrees of culpability should be combined into an assessment of the gravity of particular crimes? Despite the fact that considerations of retributivist penal distribution have often been presented under the heading 'principled sentencing', there exist no theories devising guidelines for the comparative ranking in gravity of crimes of different degrees of harm and culpability.[6] In the case in which a theory can be developed, it will probably draw heavily on intuitions. Or perhaps one should simply admit that we have here reached a point at which no further theories can be developed and that answers must rely directly on what intuitively strikes us as the most plausible way of giving weight to harm and culpability.

The same seems to be the case if one turns to another sentencing factor, namely the significance of a criminal's criminal record. Retributivists who believe that previous convictions should be taken into account have presented different justifications for why this is so and how it should be accomplished.[7] However, none of these theories are strictly determining in the sense of offering, by simple deduction, precise answers to the question of how criminals with different criminal records should be punished. Rather, the theories provide reasons that should be taken into account thereby leaving room for what seems intuitively the most plausible answer within the outlined theoretical framework. As this and the previous examples indicate, moral intuitions play a significant role in theorising on crime gravity. The same is the case—although I shall not endeavour to show this—if one turns to theorising on the comparison of punishment severity.[8]

As the above considerations indicate, moral intuitions play a significant role in penal theory. It is often the case that theories are defended, at least partially, by pointing to the fact that they are intuitively appealing. And theories are criticised or rejected on the grounds of *reductio* arguments in which intuitions serve as some sort of evaluative baseline. Moreover, as indicated, there are many cases in which penal theories leave a gap between the prescriptions that follow from the theories and the accuracy of the answers that are needed in penal practice (e.g. should the fine for theft be $200 or $210; should a violent criminal be imprisoned for 150 days or 151 days; should the recidivist premium for a criminal who has two prior convictions for assault be 65 days or 70 extra days in prison, and so on), and where this gap is not simply an epistemic question (i.e. a result of insufficient empirical knowledge) but rather a question of theoretical underdetermination. In such cases, the theories provide us with reasons that ought to be taken into account, but leave room for what strikes us as most plausible (i.e. intuitively appealing)within this theoretical framework.[9]

Even if one believes that this latter way of giving room for intuitions is questionable (or perhaps theoretically undesirable), it is still indisputable that intuitions are frequently invoked in the first-mentioned explicit sense in penal theory. In this respect, penal theorising is no different from what goes on in most other branches of applied ethics and in normative ethics in general, where it is frequently emphasised that justifications of substantive moral positions would not ever get off the ground without appealing to some moral intuition at some point.

2. MORAL INTUITIONS AND PUBLIC OPINION

How does the fact that moral intuitions constitute a basic ingredient in the cuisine of penal theorising relate to the initial question as to whether public opinion should have a role to play in criminal justice policies? The answer, as we shall now see, is simple. The obvious question confronting theorists who draw on moral intuitions is 'whose intuitions?' The answer to this question, I suggest, is that what matters is generally shared intuitions which, roughly, amount to intuitions shared by the public. In fact, this should not come as a surprise. Intuition-based theorising implicitly contains a *generality assumption*. For instance, when a *reductio* argument is presented, the purpose of the writer is not to assert that a particular implication simply strikes him or her as counterintuitive (although this is sometimes how arguments are put). On the contrary, the expectation of writers presenting such arguments is clearly that the implication is generally seen as counterintuitive. It is precisely this generality expectation that is supposed to provide the persuasive force of the argument. Thus, McMahan (1999, p. 94) is clearly right when he says that 'if a case fails to elicit the same intuitive response from most readers, it provides no basis for moral argument' where 'most readers' does not mean the contingent readers of the argument, but any member of the public at large.[10]

Then, what do these considerations imply for the question of the significance of public opinion? It is a fact that there are some philosophers who believe that intuitions have no proper role in reasoning about moral problems. They believe, for instance, that reasoning about a problem consists in determining what a particular moral theory implies about the problem and that such a theory can be developed without reference to moral intuition. In the context presented here, I cannot engage in a thorough metaethical discussion of the plausibility of this point of view. However, more modestly, the view can be accounted for by making a conditional premise. What we have seen in the previous section is that intuitions have a role to play in the way penal theory is actually carried out. It would, of course, be a fallacy to conclude from this that intuitions *should* have a role to play (i.e. that penal theory is carried out in the way it should be carried out). Thus, I shall here make the unsustained assumption that penal theory is carried out in the way that it should be carried out (an assumption which, unsurprisingly, penal theorists in general are most likely to accept). The argument that I have advanced can then be summarised in the following way: Assuming that penal theory is methodologically sound, moral intuitions should have a role in penal theorising. If moral intuitions should have a role to play then—to test whether the generality assumption implicit in intuition-based reasoning is satisfied—public attitudes ought to be consulted. Therefore,

assuming that penal theory is methodologically appropriate, public attitudes ought to be consulted.

Can this argument bear closer scrutiny? In the following sections, I shall
consider a number of objections that might be directed against the argument. As will be argued, I do not believe that any of these objections are
compelling.

3. LIMITING THE SCOPE OF THE GENERALITY ASSUMPTION

Even if one accepts the assumption that penal theorising, as it is carried out
by philosophers and other theorists, is methodologically on the right track
and consequently that moral intuitions should play a role in penal theoretical considerations, one might still be reluctant to accept the idea that the
intuitions of the public should have a place in penal reasoning. It might be
suggested that there are reasons to distinguish between, on the one hand,
the moral intuitions of philosophers or other penal theorists and, on the
other, the intuitions of people in general. What could sustain such a distinction? There are several possible answers.

A first possibility is to suggest that laypeople may not always fully grasp
the kind of cases—often highly hypothetical ones—which are used to support or reject particular positions in philosophical reasoning. Fully understanding such cases requires a certain level of abstraction and a way of focusing which is one of the skills of trained philosophers. For instance, a
view along these lines is defended by Kamm when she, reflecting on the
use of thought experiments, says, 'Having responses to complex and unfamiliar cases requires that one sees a whole complex landscape at once,
rather than piecemeal. This often requires deep concentration. Only a few
people may be able to respond to a complex case with a firm response. . . .
The princess and the pea' is the fairy tale best associated with the method I
describe: it tells of someone, despite much interference, who cannot ignore
a slight difference that others may never sense' (1993, p. 8). Thus, on this
view, the reason to exclude lay intuitions from the scope of the generality
assumption does not concern the validity of these intuitions but rather
whether people in general are able to fully grasp the cases one is supposed
to intuitively evaluate.

However, as a general argument for ignoring laypeople intuitions this
argument is clearly dubious. First, it is not correct that the cases in which
intuitions are invoked in penal theorising are highly complex and that they
cannot be understood by the general public. Surely laypeople are able to
grasp punishment-of-the-innocent scenarios or cases designed to assess
the distinction between acting intentionally or knowingly? Moreover, even

if there are some hypothetical cases which might at first be misunderstood by not philosophically trained respondents—for instance, some people might at first sight not fully understand the *ceteris paribus* clauses which are often part of hypothetical scenarios—all that this shows is that one has to be a little more careful when such cases are presented to people who are unfamiliar with such scenarios. That one should be careful to make sure that people respond to the question that one is posing and not to something different is of no surprise to scientists who are used to conducting surveys of public attitudes. Thus, the first reason for distinguishing between the intuitions of penal theorists and laypeople in general is clearly unconvincing.

Another possibility is to try to support the distinction by directing attention to the reliability of public intuitions. That is, even if laypeople fully grasp the cases in which intuitive judgments are supposed to play a role, it does not follow that their intuitive judgments are reliable. For instance, folk intuitions may be the result of prejudice or biases.[11] Moreover, recent studies in moral psychology have revealed that intuitive judgments may be affected in several ways by factors which are clearly morally irrelevant. For instance, intuitive judgments may be distorted by odours or by other circumstantial characteristics. Indeed, in a recent study it was shown that whether respondents washed their hands (or were simply placed close to a washbasin) before answering moral questions had an impact on some of their moral judgments (Helzer & Pizarro, 2011). Thus, there is evidence supporting the view that intuitions may be influenced by various kinds of extraneous factors. However, to sustain the distinction between the intuitions of laypeople and philosophers, it is not enough to establish that ordinary people's intuitions are unreliable because they may be influenced by extraneous features; it also has to be shown that the same is not the case when it comes to the intuitions of philosophers. The problem is that there is no empirical evidence supporting this claim. On the contrary, although the evidence is still scarce, two recent experiments on the intuitions of philosophers point in the opposite direction. In a study by Schwitzgebel and Cushman (2012), participants were given two hypothetical cases (the traditional bystander and footbridge trolley cases) in two different orders to see whether order of presentation influenced participants' judgments. It turned out that the judgments of both philosophers and laypeople were influenced by the order of the cases. Another recent study by Schulz et al. (2011) showed that philosophical expertise did not prevent influences on moral intuition of extraneous factors (i.e. the personality trait extraversion). Thus, there is no empirical support for the claim that laypeople's intuitions, but not the intuitions of philosophers, are affected by extraneous influences or that the vulnerability to such influences is higher for laypeople.

Moreover, even if it is the case that laypeople's intuitions are to a greater degree affected by extraneous factors, there is nothing to prevent one from controlling for such influences when intuitions are examined. Indeed, scientists conducting research on lay intuitions do as much as is possible to reduce such influences. Once again, it is of no surprise to scientists carrying out serious studies on public attitudes that responses may be influenced by extraneous factors. And there is no reason to believe that this cannot be addressed—or that the problem cannot at least be significantly reduced—by relying on an adequate methodology.

There is, however, a third way in which a distinction between lay and philosopher intuitions could be defended. It might be held that, irrespective of the question as to whether philosophers' intuitions are affected by or are immune from the sorts of distortions to which folk intuitions seem to be prey, there is still a strong reason to regard the intuitions of philosophers as more trustworthy. The reason is simply that philosophers are *experts* on moral issues. That is, contrary to laypeople, philosophers engaged in ethics have a wide experience of examining and reflecting on moral questions. By analogy, if confronted with a mathematical problem, whose intuitive judgment would you trust, the intuition of the mathematician or of the layperson? Or, if you are considering the next move in a game of chess, on whose intuition would you rely, the professional chess player's or the amateur's? The answers are obvious and likewise it seems obvious to suggest that, due to their expertise, much greater credence should be given to the intuitions of philosophers than to the intuitions of laypeople.

However appealing this may sound, the problem facing this argument is to provide firm support for the claim that philosophical expertise increases the validity of moral intuition (for a more detailed discussion, see Ryberg, 2013). Merely to draw on the general idea that training and experience is all it takes to get better at any given activity will not suffice. The step from experience to expertise presupposes both that the activity in question is assessable on some sort of quality parameter—that is, that it makes sense to talk of being better or worse at this activity—and that there is a relation between experience and an increase in the quality of the activity. Obviously this is not always the case. The fact that A walks much more than B does not demonstrate that A has more expertise in walking. There is simply no quality parameter for the activity of walking according to which a step taken by A can be assessed as better than a step taken by B. And if one imagines some sort of quality parameter assigned to walking—say, the beauty of walking—there is no reason to believe that A walks better (i.e. more beautifully) than B because he or she walks more. The beauty of a person's way of walking may not be a result of experience, that is, of more rather than less previous walking.[12] Both facts—that a quality parameter and a relation between experience and expertise are required—are precisely what make the suggested analogies questionable.

First, when it comes to intuitions of penal theorists there seems to be no quality parameter for the validity of intuitions.[13] The mathematician has prior experience of being engaged in *correct* mathematical proofs and the professional chess player has prior experience of moves in numerous of *successful games*. But the fact that the penal theorist is used to drawing on his or her intuition is not the same as holding that the expert is used to drawing on intuitions that have led to *correct* moral answers. To point out that philosophical reasoning of itself provides a quality parameter, in the simple sense that reasoning often leads to revision of intuitive judgments, will not do. Recall that the cases in which it has here been suggested that public attitudes should be consulted are those in which penal theorists themselves draw on intuitions and not the cases in which intuitions should be abandoned from the outset for theoretical reasons. Moreover, while there is an intuition-independent criterion for the assessment of mathematical proofs and success in chess, this is not the case with regard to moral theories. Rather, the intuitions themselves are part of what makes one theory more plausible than another. Thus, with regard to the existence of a quality parameter, the analogies do not seem incisive.

Second, and more important, while the intuition of the chess player is the direct result of thousands of moves in previous games stored by complex neural processes in the brain—which means that the novice usually has very few or most likely no intuitions of what constitutes the best next move—the same is not the case when we are considering the moral intuitions of philosophers. Such intuitions are not a direct product of engagement in early cases of moral reflection. For instance, the reason that it strikes some penal theorists as morally appalling to convict an innocent person, even if this could prevent a worse outcome, is not that these philosophers have previously considered hundreds or thousands of hypothetical scenarios. On the contrary, such intuitions probably have various sources (e.g. there is strong evidence that many intuitions can be explained in evolutionary terms; see, e.g. Green, 2008) which is also supported by the fact that laypeople apparently have just as many moral intuitions as trained penal theorists.

Thus, the lack of an independent criterion for judging what constitutes prior successful cases of drawing on intuitions and the fact that the intuitions are not the result of earlier cases of moral intuitioning, together seriously question the idea of expertise in this respect. It is not the case that the intuitions of penal theorists are simply a causal result in some condensed form of earlier experiences of correct moral judgments. In contrast to the mathematician or the chess player, expertise in ethics does not make the philosopher an expert intuiter. At least, pointing to totally general considerations on expertise or drawing on analogies to intuitions in mathematics or chess does not provide evidence for the idea of expertise in intuitioning.[14]

To summarise, the previous considerations indicate that the idea, on the one hand, of accepting the generality assumption while, on the other, holding that the scope of the assumption should be limited to penal theorists and should not include the *hoi polloi* is hard to sustain. The claim that people in general do not grasp the cases to which intuitions are applied or that lay intuitions are much more afflicted by distortions than are the intuitions of philosophers seems incorrect. And even if it is the case, this is something that serious scientists might well correct when researching public attitudes. Moreover, the idea that philosophical expertise implies that philosophers are expert intuiters seems doubtful. Thus, given the way that penal theorising is conducted, there is no reason—so far—to disregard public attitudes. However, as we shall now see, there is another way in which the generality assumption could be questioned.

4. REJECTING THE GENERALITY ASSUMPTION

The presented argument to the effect that pre-theoretical public attitudes ought to be consulted as a part of penal theoretical reasoning could be questioned in a more radical way, namely by straightforwardly rejecting the generality assumption. More precisely, it might be suggested that, even though it is correct that intuitions play an important role in penal reasoning, it is a mistake to believe that what matters is that such intuitions are generally shared. Rather, the objection might go, the important thing is that the intuitive judgments are true. However, the truth of a judgment is not in any way dependent on whether the judgment is widely shared. Therefore, the generality assumption should be rejected, which means that the argument in favour of consulting public attitudes is blocked.

As noted earlier, the present discussion prompts various methodological questions and this objection in particular gives rise to basic considerations of the truth and justification of moral judgments, which reach far beyond the limits of this chapter. However, what I shall do, more modestly, is to indicate why the fact that what matters is the truth of intuitive judgments does not suffice as a reason for rejecting the generality assumption.

Suppose that someone holds that penal theory T should be rejected because T has implication A and because A is counterintuitive. Suppose, further, that everyone else replies that A is not counterintuitive at all. In that case, the person who has advanced the *reductio* argument against T might respond that whatever other people hold about A is simply irrelevant because the intuitive judgment, that A is absurd, is true. Should we be satisfied with this reply? The answer is obviously in the negative. Merely insisting on the truth of an intuitive judgment does not contribute anything when it comes to establishing that the judgment is, in fact, true. Everyone seems to agree that even though a judgment strikes us as true, this may not be the case. Thus, the well-known epistemological question that arises is what might be—in Sidgwick's words—the 'conditions, the complete fulfilment of which would establish a significant proposition, apparently self-evident, in the highest degree of certainty attainable' (1907, p. 338). In short, how can we become as certain as possible that A is, in fact, morally absurd? A broadly accepted answer to this question is that it is a mark of truth that it commands convergence.[15] That is, consensus on a basic moral judgment provides justification for a high degree of certainty, while a widespread dissensus precludes certainty. This is precisely the reason why one should object if it is insisted—other sources of evidence being absent—that it is true that A is counterintuitive despite the fact that everyone else disagrees.

Thus, if we accept this view of truth and certainty, it is clear why the suggested objection against the generality assumption fails. It is correct that the widespread consensus on some intuitive moral judgment does not establish that this judgment is true. But given the fact that a judgment might be false, even if it strikes one as self-evident, what we need is evidence of the fact that the judgment is true and, insofar as consensus constitutes a truth mark, there is reason to accept the generality assumption and, hence, the view that public attitudes should be consulted. To avoid misunderstandings, the outlined epistemological position does not imply that the fact that someone disagrees with a particular moral judgment necessarily precludes certainty in the truth of this judgment. As is well known in the traditional metaethical discussion on whether moral disagreements constitute a problem for the existence of objective moral facts, there may well be cases in which disagreement can be explained away by reference to the epistemic position of those who disagree (they may not be fully informed, rational, or whatever). In other words, consensus is only a truth mark amongst epistemically similarly situated discussants. But, as noted in the previous section, there is no reason to hold that laypeople in general cannot (with sufficient guidance from those who conduct surveys) consider moral judgments from a position that is epistemically comparable to that of penal theorists.

In sum, what we have seen is that, even if one accepts the idea that what matters is the truth of intuitions in penal theory and that consensus does not in itself affect the truth value of a moral judgment, this does not imply that the generality assumption should be rejected.

5. THE BANALITY OF INVOKING FOLK INTUITIONS

The argument that I have presented to the effect that public attitudes ought to be invoked in penal theorising is, as should be clear by now, not in any way based on a methodologically revisionary position. On the contrary, the argument has been founded on the claim that penal theorising is carried out in a proper way. However, this may give rise to a final objection, very different from the ones considered in the two previous sections, namely that the conclusion is close to constituting a banality. Especially in the light of the fact that I have not sustained the view that penal theorising is methodologically on the right track, but merely accepted this as a precondition, it might be objected that the conclusion on the significance of public attitudes becomes uninteresting. In short, the problem is not that the argument is not valid but that the conclusion is trivial.

Depicting a picture of what is going on when philosophers and others engage in and develop penal theories will inevitably be somewhat rough in nature. But it seems to me that the fact that public opinion ought to be invoked in cases in which intuitions play a role in penal reasoning is not generally reflected in the way this type of reasoning is carried out by penal theorists. A possible explanation of this fact could of course be that conducting studies on public attitudes is something that falls far outside the scope of the work of philosophers. Thus, in the same way that the philosopher is not qualified when it comes to conducting studies of empirical facts in general, and thus ends his or her reasoning at the very point at which other empirical scientists will have to take over, it is also natural to expect that penal theorists leave the studies of public attitudes to scientists with the requisite skills.

Plausible as this may sound, it does not, however, constitute a fully adequate picture of what is going on in penal theory. Although penal theorists, as suggested, would usually accept the generality assumption, the realisation of the fact that generality includes not only other penal theorists but people in general is not reflected in the way penal reasoning is conducted. It is often the case that studies of public attitudes, when they are actually available, are not brought into or even referred to as a way of underpinning intuition-based penal reasoning. And explicit statements of the fact that it is left an open question—and thus a question that requires further empirical scrutiny—as to whether intuitions invoked in penal reasoning do have a general resonance in the public are pretty rare in penal theory. Thus, as this indicates, the recognition of the fact that public attitudes ought to be consulted in relation to intuition-based penal reasoning is not as widespread as the objection holds which means that the conclusion of the advanced argument may not be so trivial after all.

Moreover, the implications of the argument are relevant not only for the way in which penal theorising is carried out but also for those who conduct research on public opinion. Studies on public attitudes to penal issues are far from always supplied with considerations on why it is important to examine public opinion on a particular issue. Sometimes, broader formulations are presented along the line that to reach plausible decisions, it is important to know what people believe. But it is much less often the case that one is provided with a stricter argument as to why a study of a particular aspect of public attitudes needs to be examined to develop a principled answer to a penal theoretical challenge. If the argument of this chapter is valid, it shows that close collaboration between penal philosophers and public opinion scientists is required for the development of penal theory. Insofar as this is not fully acknowledged by public opinion researchers, there is another reason to believe that the conclusion which I have defended is far from trivial.

The foregoing considerations are somewhat difficult to sustain. They mostly consist of general reflections on the way that public opinion surveys are often motivated and on what constitutes the general tendency not to pay sufficient attention to public attitudes in penal theory. Since these considerations are hard to back up in a way that is fully satisfactory, it should be conceded that the answer to the suggested objection is somewhat speculative. However, it should be noted that the objection itself is equally speculative. To give the objection force, it would have to be shown that it is a fact that penal philosophers generally are fully conscious of the role that public attitudes should play in intuition-based penal theorising—that is, for instance, that the expertise objection considered above is not something that philosophers tend to subscribe to—and that public opinion scientists are generally well aware of the role which they should play in the development of penal theories. Given what I have said earlier, and in the absence of clear evidence for these claims, the objection is insufficient to show that the conclusion which has been defended here is trivial.

6. CONCLUSION

Finally, I sum up the previous discussion. First, however, it is important to emphasise what I have *not* argued. It has not been demonstrated that intuitions ought to play a role in penal reasoning. Moreover, neither has it been more thoroughly established that the generality assumption—the assumption that intuitions in intuition-based reasoning presuppose general acceptance—is correct. However, I have suggested that the drawing of intuitions and the command of generality is part of how penal theorising is conducted by philosophers and other theorists. Furthermore, I have assumed that in this respect penal theorists are methodologically on the right track. Although disputable, this assumption is not very controversial. Obviously, penal theorists would usually hold that they engage in penal theory in the very way one should engage in this sort of theorising. On the ground of this assumption, it was then shown that—since there exist no reasons, based on expertise considerations, to narrow the scope of the generality assumption to penal theorists and since the generality command is not proven irrelevant by the claim that it is the truth of intuitions that matters—public attitudes ought to be consulted when intuitions are invoked in penal reasoning. Underlining the conditional character of this claim, another way of expressing the conclusion of this chapter is to say that either penal theorising, as currently performed by penal theorists, is on the wrong track and ought to be methodologically revised or that public attitudes should be consulted as a part of the reasoning of penal theorists. Whether public attitudes to penal issues also ought to be consulted in the post-theoretical sense, that is, once a proper penal theory has been developed and is about to be applied to answer specific questions—such as, how seriously should a burglar be punished or how much (if at all) more severely than a first-time criminal ought a recidivist to be punished—obviously depends on the nature of this theory. However, as noted, even if there are no post-theoretical reasons—neither direct nor indirect—for consulting public opinion, this does not change the fact that public attitudes should be consulted, if penal theory is carried out as it should be—at the pre-theoretical level.

Finally, it has been suggested that this conclusion is not trivial; that is, that it ought to be more clearly realised by penal theorists and that the conclusion—in so far as the goal is to develop principled answers to questions on state punishment—calls for a closer future collaboration between penal theorists and public opinion researchers.

REFERENCES

Crisp, R. 2006. *Reasons and the Good.* Oxford: Oxford University Press.

Davis, M. 1990. 'The Death Penalty, Civilization, and in humaneness.' *Social Theory and Practice* 16: 245–259.

Doris, J. M., and A. Plakias. 2008. 'How to Argue about Disagreement.' In W. Sinnott-Armstrong (ed.), *Moral Psychology.* Vol. 2, The Cognitive Science of Morality: Intuition and Diversity. Cambridge, MA: MIT Press.

Duff, R. A. 1986. *Trials and Punishments.* Cambridge, UK: Cambridge University Press.

Duff, R. A., and D. Garland (eds.). 1994. *A Reader on Punishment.* Oxford: Oxford University Press.

Green, J. D. 2008. 'The Secret Joke of Kant's Soul.' In W. Sinnott-Armstrong (ed.), *Moral Psychology.* Vol. 3, *The Neuroscience of Morality: Emotion, Brain Disorders, and Development.* Cambridge: MIT Press.

Haidt, J., and F. Bjorklund. 2008. 'Social Intuitionists Answer Six Questions about Moral Psychology.' In W. Sinnott-Armstrong (ed.), *Moral Psychology*. Vol. 2, *The Cognitive Science of Morality: Intuition and Diversity*. Cambridge: MIT Press.

Helzer, E. G., and D. A. Pizarro. 2011. 'Dirty Liberals! Reminders of Physical Cleanliness Influence Moral and Political Attitudes.' *Psychological Science* 22(4): 517–522.

Kamm, F. M. 1993. *Morality, Mortality*. Vol. 1, *Death and Whom to Save from It*. New York: Oxford University Press.

McCloskey, H. J. 1962. 'The Complexity of the Concept of Punishment.' *Philosophy* 37: 307–325.

McCloskey, H. J. 1963. 'A Note on Utilitarian Punishment.' *Mind* 72: 509.

McCloskey, H. J. 1965. 'A Non-Utilitarian Approach to Punishment.' *Inquiry* 8: 249–263.

McMahan, J. 1999. 'Moral Intuition.' In H. LaFollette (ed.), *The Blackwell Guide to Ethical Theory*. Oxford: Blackwell.

Morris, N. and M. Tonry. 1990. *Between Prison and Probation*. New York: Oxford University Press.

Murphy, J. G. 1979. *Retribution, Justice and Therapy*. Dordrecht, The Netherlands: Reidel.

Murphy, J., and J. Hampton. 1988. *Forgiveness and Mercy*. New York: Cambridge University Press.

Roberts, J. 2008. *Punishing Persistent Offenders*. Oxford: Oxford University Press.

Roberts, J., and A. von Hirsch (eds.). 2010. *Previous Convictions at Sentencing*. Oxford: Hart.

Robinson P. H., and J. M. Darley. 2007. 'Intuitions of Justice: Implications for Criminal Law and Justice Policy.' *Southern California Law Review* 81: 1–68.

Ryberg, J. 2004. *The Ethics of Proportionate Punishment*. Dordrecht, The Netherlands: Kluwer Academic.

Ryberg, J. 2010a. 'Punishment and Public Opinion.' In J. Ryberg and J. A. Corlett (eds.), *Punishment and Ethics—New Perspectives*. Basingstoke, UK: Palgrave Macmillan.

Ryberg, J. 2010b. 'Punishment and the Measurement of Severity.' In J. Ryberg and A. Corlett (eds.), *Punishment and Ethics*. Basingstoke, UK: Palgrave Macmillan.

Ryberg, J. 2010c. 'Mass Atrocities, Retributivism, and the Threshold Challenge.' *Res Publica* 16: 169–179.

Ryberg, J. 2013. 'Moral Intuitions and the Expertise Defence.' *Analysis* 73(1): 3–9.

Schultz, E., E. T. Cokely, and A. Feltz. 2011. 'Persistent Bias in Expert Judgments about Free Will and Moral Responsibility: A Test of the Expertise Defense.' *Consciousness and Cognition* 20(4): 1722–1731.

Schwitzgebel, E., and F. Cushman, 2012. 'Expertise in Moral Reasoning? Order Effects on Moral Judgment in Professional Philosophers and Non-Philosophers.' *Mind & Language* 27(2): 135–153.

Sidgwick, H. 1907. *The Methods of Ethics*. 7th ed. London: Macmillan.

Sinnott-Armstrong, W. 2002. 'Moral Relativity and Intuitionism.' *Philosophical Issues* 12: 305–328.

Smilansky, S. 1990. 'Utilitarianism and the "Punishment" of the Innocent: The General Problem.' *Analysis* 50: 256–261.

Tamburrini, C., and J. Ryberg (eds.). 2012. *Recidivist Punishments: The Philosopher's View*. Lanham, MD: Lexington Books.

Tonry, M. 1993. 'Proportionality, Interchangeability, and Intermediate Punishments.' In R. Dobash, R. A. Duff, and S. Marshall (eds.), *Penal Theory and Penal Practice*. Manchester, UK: Manchester University Press.

Tonry, M. 2011. 'Can Twenty-First Century Punishment Policies Be Justified in Principle?' In M. Tonry (ed.), *Retributivism Has a Past—Has It a Future?* New York: Oxford University Press.

von Hirsch, A. 1993. *Censure and Sanctions*. Oxford: Clarendon.

von Hirsch, A., M. Wasik, and J. Green. 1989. 'Punishments in the Community and the Principles of Desert.' *Rutgers Law Journal* 20(3): 595–618.

Weinberg, J. M., C. Gonnerman, C. Buckner, and J. Alexander. 2010. 'Are Philosophers Expert Intuiters?' *Philosophical Psychology* 23(3): 331–355.

Wiggins, D. 1987. *Needs, Values, Truth*. Oxford: Blackwell.

NOTES

1. To avoid misunderstandings: By 'pre-theoretical' I do not mean that public opinion should be consulted prior to any kind of penal theorising but rather that public opinion should be consulted as a part of penal theorising, that is, before a particular penal theory is fully developed.
2. The phrase 'moral intuition' is used in somewhat different ways in the literature. However, in the following, I shall use the term to denote a moral belief that is not the result of conscious inferential reasoning (see, e.g. Sinnott-Armstrong, 2002, p. 310).
3. The earliest versions of this argument were presented by McCloskey (1962, 1963, 1965). For a more recent version see, for instance, Smilansky, 1990.
4. 'Let the world perish so long as justice be done' (for a discussion of threshold retributivism, see Ryberg, 2010c).
5. Obviously, the consequentialist will give the same normative answer no matter whether one is considering the overall justification of the punishment system or some detailed aspect of sentencing. However, retributivists have, in various ways, presented theories which are supposed to deal with many of the more detailed challenges of sentencing and which are supposed to supply an overall idea of just deserts.
6. For a more comprehensive discussion of this problem see Ryberg (2004, chapter 2).
7. For comprehensive discussions of the different retributivist theories, Roberts and von Hirsch (2010) or Tamburrini and Ryberg (2012).
8. Unsurprisingly, theories of what constitutes the proper measure of punishment severity draw, to some extent, on intuition judgments (for a discussion of different theories, see Ryberg, 2010b; for explicit intuition-based rejections of particular types of punishment, see Davis, 1990; Murphy, 1979).
9. There are many examples of this sort of theoretical underdetermination in modern retributivism. For obvious reasons, the same is not the case if one turns to consequentialist theories.
10. It might be asked how wide the scope of the generality assumption should be. Does it imply that intuitions are shared by all persons at all times? However, in

the present context I shall not engage in considerations of this (interesting) question. What matters here is the point that it is hard to defend the view that the generality assumption should be restricted to philosophers and other penal theorists. However, it should be mentioned that the question arises even if one holds it is only the intuitions of philosophers that counts: Is it the intuitions shared by all philosophers at all times?

11. A large number of studies on intuitions are presented in Haidt and Bjorklund (2008).

12. Obviously, the point is not to claim that the beauty of a way of walking cannot be practiced at all but simply that it is typically, to a major extent, determined by other factors (length of limbs, physical harmony, or whatever).

13. Or, as we shall see in the next section, if there are reasons to have more trust in some intuitions than in others, these reasons will probably include considerations of the possible consensus on these intuitions.

14. See also Weinberg et al. (2010). The authors argue that neither philosophical expertise when it comes to better conceptual schemata, mastery of entrenched theories, nor general practical know-how, provide good reason to support the assertion that philosophers are expert intuiters.

15. See, for instance, Crisp (2006, p. 90ff) or Wiggins (1987, p. 147ff). For a critical discussion of the possibility of rejecting convergence while maintaining moral realism, see Doris and Plakias (2008). However, I admit that this sort of metaethical position may be one according to which the argument defended in this chapter is questionable.

2

Proportionality Theory and Popular Opinion[1]

Matt Matravers

Many penal philosophers think that offering a justification of the state's right to punish is particularly urgent (and difficult) precisely because punishment involves doing things to people that would be gross rights violations were they to be done outside the practice of punishment. That is, punishment typically involves imposing some deprivation—for example, the removal of property or freedoms—on a person for committing an offence and to do these things to someone requires special justification. Yet, despite this motivation, many theories of the justification of punishment say surprisingly little about the detail of sentencing and penalties.

Now, this may be a matter of a sensible division of intellectual labour. As Stanley Benn put it in 1958, to address the justification of punishment is 'to ask why we should have the sorts of rules that provide those who contravene them should be made to suffer' (Benn, 1958, p. 326; cf. Hart, 1968, chapter 1; Matravers, 2000, pp. 2–3), and this is a different project from asking what justifies the infliction of particular quantities of punishment for particular kinds of behaviour on particular offenders. Yet, surely punishment theorists should have *something* to say about sentencing issues?[2]

Beyond questions of the division of labour, the explanation of the relatively small number of penal philosophers who link their accounts of the justification of punishment to sentencing issues may also lie with the pluralistic nature of sentencing. At the point of sentencing, judges in systems where there is discretion will often call upon many considerations (an intuitive notion of desert, the need to express the community's blame, deterrence, the risk posed by the offender, the offender's potential for reform, and so on), and such pluralism sits ill with philosophers of punishment who make their living defining terms and making distinctions.

In what follows, my aim is first to establish the parameters within which the argument operates. For reasons given there, my concern is with *proportionality*-based sentencing schemes and, in particular, with those who are committed to an expressive or communicative retributive justification of punishment that incorporates proportionality. Second, I argue that in the absence of a metaphysical account of desert, the critical elements that make up such a proportional scheme are constituted by popular judgements. In the light of the literature on penal populism, amongst other things, this result is worrying in that it appears to afford no perspective from which to declare popular judgements wrong or to engage with them critically. Thus, third, I consider how we might engage with these judgements. My conclusion is that they cannot be declared wrong in the usual sense, but that there are critical resources available that allow us to engage with the public to deliver an account of desert. Finally, I offer a few words to defend the conclusion against those who might think it unduly weak.

1. JUSTIFICATIONS OF PUNISHMENT AND SENTENCING

Above I noted that we can think of punishment theory in general as operating at three levels. At one level (Level 1), it offers—or purports to offer—a justification of there being rules the contravention of which leads to penal hard treatment; at another (Level 2), it offers an account of the kinds of acts and omissions that are governed by those rules, of their relative seriousness, and of the range and relative severity of hard treatments that can be imposed on offenders; and finally (Level 3), it offers accounts of the justification of imposing a particular penal sanction on a particular offender.[3]

This tripartite division is not meant to be definitive—the overall cake of punishment theory could be cut in many other ways[4]—nor does this division do substantive work; its function is simply to make the argument easier to follow. The focus of the argument is on Level 2 issues. Level 2 concerns criminalisation (what should be criminalised and why), penal hard treatment (what kinds of things can be done to offenders and why), and the relative ranking of these things both *within* each category—that is, amongst those things that are justifiably criminalised how should we scale them in terms of seriousness and amongst those things that are justifiably used as hard treatment how should we scale them in terms of severity—and *between* the categories—that is, how should we align offences of a particular seriousness with penalties of a particular severity—and it is this final question that takes up most of what follows.

2. GENERAL JUSTIFICATIONS OF PUNISHMENT (LEVEL 1)

Although the argument is concerned mainly with Level 2 issues, it is worth saying something about general justifications of punishment both to narrow the scope of the argument and to motivate (at least part of) it. One general justification—to be found in utilitarianism—might be thought to be an exception to the rumination with which the chapter began on the silence of philosophers of punishment when it comes to sentencing issues. Jeremy Bentham wrote at length about both and his account of sentencing stems directly from his overall hedonistic utilitarian framework (Bentham, 1843, 1970). This argument—and all utilitarian arguments in a similar vein—are not considered here. This is partly because given the overall justificatory framework, questions of offence seriousness and penalty severity become entirely technical and are best addressed by empirical, not philosophical, enquiry. As Brian Barry once remarked, 'Adherence to utilitarianism makes for very boring political philosophy, because once the goal has been postulated . . . everything else is a matter of arguing about the most efficacious means to that end' (1990, p. 35). It is also partly because insofar as there is empirical evidence—at least when it comes to marginal effects of sentencing changes—it is (at best) unclear (Bottoms & von Hirsch, 2011; von Hirsch, 1999).

Having put utilitarian justifications to one side then, one is left with forms of retributivism. There are of course many such forms (Cottingham [1979] gives nine), but for the sake of argument I shall take the defining claim to be that punishment is justified because it is deserved. For Kant, and in a different way for Hegel, the appeal is to some kind of ' "celestial mechanics" in which every criminal action . . . deserves an "equal and opposite reaction" in the shape of punishment' (Fleischacker, 1992, p. 204). In Hegel, punishment rebounds on the offender for his offence so as to 'annul' the wrong (Hegel, 1942, §§96–104). For both, the penalty imposed ought to reflect the value of the offence. For Kant, 'whatever undeserved evil you inflict upon another within the people, that you inflict upon yourself. If you insult him, you insult yourself; . . . if you kill him, you kill yourself. But only the *law of retribution* (*ius talionis*) . . . can specify definitely the quality and the quantity of punishment' (Kant, 1996, p. 473; emphasis in original). Hegel is less categorical about the matching of crime and penalty but is clear that the value of the penalty must match the value of the offence.[5]

With the exception of Michael Moore (1982, 1987, 1992, 1993, 1997), no contemporary theorist defends the 'celestial mechanics' needed for this sort of retributivist account. I have criticised Moore's account elsewhere—in particular with respect to his moral realism—and do not engage with it here (Matravers, 2000, pp. 81–87).

However, contemporary retributivists (and others) have defended—indeed, have made central to their accounts—the claim that the value of the offence must match in some way or other the value of the penalty. That is, although contemporary retributivists continue to maintain that they are committed to the idea that punishment is justified by desert, their accounts—or perhaps their understanding of desert—are best understood as involving a commitment to *proportionality* rather than to any prejusticial notion of desert (for a defence of this claim, see Matravers, 2011). That is, to the idea that the *severity* of the penalty must be proportionate to the *seriousness* of the offence.

Proportionality involves two discrete elements. One is *ordinal proportionality*, which concerns the ranking of seriousness and severity. The idea is that the most serious offence should attract the most severe penalty and lesser offences, less severe penalties in proportion to the degree that they are lesser. This captures an important sense of justice (that we should treat like cases alike and different cases differently). Two equally culpable offenders who commit offences of equal seriousness ought to receive equally severe penalties and a third offender whose offence is less serious ought to receive a less severe penalty.

The other element is *cardinal proportionality*, which concerns the overall magnitude of the penalties (the so-called anchoring points of the scale).[6] Issues of cardinal proportionality arise in particular when penalties are, or appear to be, unduly severe or lenient. However, as the idea of anchoring points makes clear, they are more important to the overall theory than that. For penalties to be arrayed along a scale so that we can begin to assess ordinal proportionality, the scale must be have at least one of a maximum and a minimum; it must be anchored.[7]

Proportionality has been key to much of the recent revival in retributivism (although, as discussed below, it need not be associated only with retributivism) and is of course a means to address issues at Level 2. Moreover, as noted above, it speaks to the values of justice and equality that are central to contemporary liberal political theory (and practice). Yet it is deeply unclear how the account is meant to be filled out. The problem is that it is very difficult to determine the upper (and lower) anchoring points when it comes to both 'seriousness' and 'severity'.

The argument from here takes for granted a commitment to proportionality as the guiding principle in addressing Level 2 questions of relative rankings within and between offence seriousness and penalty severity. It first asks how rankings can be achieved. The claim is that any plausible answer will be context sensitive. By 'context sensitive' I mean that judgements of seriousness and severity will reflect social conditions and practices such that what is deserved will be *constituted* by what is popularly believed to be—or what is implicit in current social practices as—serious, severe, and so proportionate. The final part of the argument then considers what critical resources philosophy might have to assess the beliefs and social practices that constitute that context sensitivity.

3. PROPORTIONALITY AND CONTEXT SENSITIVITY

As we have seen, proportionality—if it is to tell us which punishment fits what crime and in that sense is deserved—requires an ordinal ranking of offence seriousness and one of penalty severity. It also requires cardinal rankings for which anchoring points are needed. How can these things be fixed?

Seriousness of Offence

What are the most serious offences? It might be thought that this question can only be addressed by asking first for an account of what ought to be offences and then for an account of their relative seriousness. Moreover, the first of these subquestions will call upon the Level 1 account of the overall justification of punishment. That is, imagine that the Level 1 theory justifies punishment in part by reference to the autonomy of citizens and their rights and interests together with an accompanying account of what is legitimately a 'public wrong'. The theory of criminalisation that accompanies that account is then going to rest (at least in large part) on those rights and interests. Homicide, for example, will be subject to criminal regulation because it violates the rights, or sets back the interests, of the victim in a particular, permanent and noncompensable manner and it does so in a way that is legitimately the business of the public.

If this is right, it might be thought that the present argument cannot continue without returning to Level 1 and offering a full theory of punishment and, in addition, that any claim to the context sensitivity of offence seriousness must be rejected. That claim may be given additional support by the thought that such an account will allow us to criticise the criminalisation of conduct that is—or has been—regarded by the public as warranting criminalisation but where no rights or interests violations occur (e.g. the criminalisation of consensual atypical forms of sexual conduct between adults) or where rights or interests might be set back, but it is nobody's business (e.g. in cases of consensual adult sado-masochistic sex that involve actions that might otherwise be criminal assault).[8]

However, to vindicate the claim that offence seriousness is, at least in part, context sensitive, it is not necessary to consider each and every Level 1

theory and what it entails for criminalisation. To see why, consider the ordinal ranking of offences (on whatever account of criminalisation is endorsed). One claim—which I think true, but which I am not going to pursue
here—is that any plausible theory of rights and interests will be in part
context sensitive. However, that claim does not need to be vindicated to
show that offence seriousness is partly context sensitive.

Standards of seriousness have fluctuated over time not only because of
disputes over what rights and interests persons have but also because of
rankings of the relative importance of those rights *and* the relative importance of their protection in particular social and economic circumstances.
Thus, even if we grant a context-independent, 'moral philosophy-established'
account of the person, it is implausible to think that will give us a ranking
of offence seriousness that can simply be read off from that account *or* that,
were such a reading possible, it would be an adequate account for the purposes of the criminal law.

Famously, at the high point of England's 'Bloody Code' at the end of the
eighteenth centuy, there were over 220 offences that carried a potential capital sentence. Many of these were for crimes against property. Of course, to
some extent this reflects a consequentialist deterrence approach to punishment. As George Savile put it, 'men are not hanged for stealing horses, but
that horses may not be stolen'. And such an approach may be ruled out by a
Level 1 anti-consequentialism as failing to respect the demand that persons
not be treated as 'means' but only as 'ends'.

However, to understand the Bloody Code simply as resulting from the
application of (what would have had to have been rather misguided) deterrence theory is far too crude. Rather, the economic and social circumstances
of (amongst other things) the industrial revolution meant that while life
was relatively plentiful and cheap, establishing and securing property
rights was essential. Moreover, the influx of people into metropolitan areas
led to a fragile sense of stability. The fact that capital sentences were often
either not imposed or followed by mercy (Sharpe, 1990) was essential to
controlling public anger, but the seriousness of the code's protection of
property and its symbolic assertion of order are important components of
understanding what was going on.

The point here is not to defend the Bloody Code. Rather, to defend two
claims, which contrasting the Code with contemporary practices illustrate.
First, rankings of offence seriousness will reflect temporary agreement on
contested rankings of what 'really matters' in a human life (is the fact of
human psycho-physical existence so important that the interests and rights
that follow from it—the right to life and thus the criminalisation of
homicide—always of paramount importance even, for example, where life
is no longer 'worth living'?), and these rankings will reflect current beliefs

about what matters. In addition, they will reflect judgements about what 'really matters' in the socio-economic and cultural moment in which the question is asked. In the eighteenth century, the securing of property rights mattered and attacks on such rights threatened 'the public safety and happiness' (Blackstone, [1765–1769] 1966, vol. 4, p. 16).

Second, offence seriousness will reflect in part the stability of the society and of its government. This is a broader claim that is relevant to penalty severity as well. The point is that, as Hegel puts it, the 'magnitude [of the crime] varies . . . according to the *condition* of civil society' such that in unstable conditions minor acts that in happier times would not be offences at all may be (ranked as) serious (1942, §218R; emphasis in the original; see also §218, §218A).[9]

Severity of Penalty

If deciding on offence seriousness poses a challenge, making equivalent judgements of sentence severity is even more difficult. Take the ordinal question first: it may be possible to generate a ranking from a similar notion of rights, interests, and 'what matters' as underpinned the discussion of offence seriousness (although with analogous problems). That is, given that, for example, freedoms and property matter to human beings, the loss of, say, x units of property might be said to be half as bad as the loss of $2x$ (with possible adjustments to take account of changing marginal rates of loss). However, as with the discussion above, what matters and how it matters will be affected by social circumstance. To lose face in one culture may be much worse than to lose property in another. In addition, in the case of penalties most jurisdictions will be working not only with quantitative changes in severity (e.g. comparing a fine of £1,000 with a fine of £2,000), but also with qualitative ones (e.g. comparing a fine of £1,000 with a custodial sentence of six months). If proportionality is to have any chance at all, these qualitatively distinct forms of penalty must be commensurable. Each, for example, could be brought onto a single scale that tries to measure 'setback to persons' interests' (so that a fine of £1,000 would be said to setback interests by n units, a fine of £2,000 by $2n$, and a custodial sentence of six months by $4n$; for a sophisticated account of this type, see von Hirsch & Ashworth, 2005).

Any such account of penalty severity need not be 'subjective' in the sense in which von Hirsch and Ashworth (2005) mean (and object to) that term. A subjective account would rank penalty severity experientially; how severe a penalty is would depend on the experience of severity endured by particular offenders. In drawing up the setback-to-interests scale we need not refer to the experience of particular offenders in response to particular penalties, but we would have to refer to how severely different penalties *typically* affect individuals in a given society. That is, the account is not 'objective' either. Rather, it is conventionalist. A custodial sentence is severe because it restricts a person's 'freedom of movement, choice regarding his activities, choice of associates, privacy, and so forth' and these are things that typically matter *in our society at this time* (or as von Hirsh and Ashworth put it, they matter in relation to our 'living standard'; 2005, pp. 147–148).[10] Agreement on how and to what degree this is true will reflect temporary social agreements in this case as in the case of offence seriousness.

The challenges facing the construction of an ordinal ranking of penalty severity given plural methods of punishing are significant, but they are far fewer than those that are faced when considering the anchoring points for penalty severity. However, before moving on to those—which are of a slightly different kind, or so I will argue—it is worth offering a brief (and blunt) summary in relation to ordinal and cardinal offence seriousness and ordinal penalty severity.

In the case of offences, given that human beings share certain features— we lack exoskeletons, feel pain, and so on—it is likely that a proportion of what will be on the list (i.e. what will be criminalised) will be common across societies (hence Hart's claim that positive law and morality are likely to overlap with respect to such things as prohibitions on needlessly inflicting pain and so on).[11] What else is on the list and the ranking of offences in terms of seriousness will then (at best on this account) reflect the considered judgements of the society on both what matters in a human life and what matters to the society given its particular history and circumstances. It will, in these senses, be conventional.

Similarly, with respect to the ordinal ranking of penalties, we should expect there to be some overlap across jurisdictions for the same reason. The things that make human beings suffer are likely the things from which they need protection. However, the overlap will of course be far less given the fine-grained judgements involved. It may be that all jurisdictions are likely to have a prohibition on homicide—and that tells us something interesting (even if not exactly how such a prohibition will be formulated)— but that all punishing jurisdictions are likely to punish in ways that cause suffering is not informative (indeed, it is tautological). Nevertheless, again on the account offered above, we should expect that at best the kind or penalties used and their ordinal rankings will reflect the considered judgements of the society on both what matters in a human life and what matters to the society given its particular history and circumstances. It is then also conventional.

These results may not seem surprising. Surely, it is obvious that punishment systems are conventional? Sentencing schemes in particular reflect the values, needs, and histories of different criminal justice systems and are designed for those systems. As Hegel remarks, 'a penal code, then, is primarily the child of its age and the state of civil society at the time' (1942, §218A). Such a response raises a separate question about the degree to which 'conventionalism' is adequate. Before discussing that, however, what of the cardinal anchoring points in penalty severity?

The bottom anchoring point may be thought reasonably clear. Presumably in most jurisdictions the police are empowered to issue some kind of formal caution, warning, or reprimand that need not go any further. However, what of the upper anchoring point? Human history gives many ghastly examples of punishments beyond mere death. These include the punishment of relatives and extreme forms of torture prior to execution (see Berkowitz, 2012; for a range of capital punishments in Europe, see Evans, 1996; also the famous opening pages of Foucault, 1977).

We can put to one side punishments of relatives as inconsistent with the fundamental attraction of proportionality, which is that like cases are treated alike (and different ones differently).[12] Moreover, we do not need even to consider brutal penalties involving suffering in excess of, and prior to, execution. Even amongst contemporary developed liberal democracies there is a wide range of maximum sentences. The most obvious contrast is between those states that use capital punishment and those that do not. However, we might also consider the use of prison sentences. For example, in 2009 the financier Bernie Madoff was sentenced to 150 years in prison for running a ponzi scheme; in 2007, a Georgia judge sentenced two armed robbers to life in prison plus an additional 265 years each; and in 1981, Dudley Wayne Kyzer was sentenced to two life sentences plus an additional 10,000 years in prison in Alabama after murdering his wife, his mother-in-law, and a third person. Contrast this with the maximum sentence of twenty-one years given to the mass murderer Anders Behring Breivik in Norway in 2012.

Confronted by a US citizen who believes that 'death deserves death' or financial fraud deserves a sentence of 150 years, and by a Norwegian for whom twenty-one years is held to be the deserved sentence even for multiple homicide, there is nothing *within* proportionality theory that will resolve the issue. Of course, a sophisticated 'setback of interests' account may be able to determine on some scale what quantum of interests were setback by the fraud and will then be able to compare this with the quantum of interests set back by a prison sentence of 150 years. However, that does not tell us anything about what is deserved since there is no command that punishments must be *equal* to crimes. Indeed, as the name suggests, they must be *proportionate*. What we are left with once again are the considered judgements of the community. Assuming consistency in sentencing within each jurisdiction—that is, assuming the formal requirements of a proportionality-based sentencing scheme are respected—what is deserved for a given crime in Norway is very different to what is deserved for the same crime in the states of Georgia or Texas.

4. 'THE PROPER ROLE OF THE COMMUNITY'

I have argued that in the absence of a metaphysical account of desert there are no resources within proportionality theory to resolve the issue of how to anchor the scale of penalty severity. I have instead located the resource for anchoring the scale in the considered judgements of the community. This of course need not be the case. We could, for example, envisage a 'Socio-Penal Commission' of expert sociologists, psychiatrists, and psychologists (as proposed in Glueck, 1952) who would consider how to anchor the scale taking into account various criteria such as deterrence and resources as well as the need to express the community's response to crime.

The motivation for appealing instead to the judgements of the community is twofold. First, there are reasons in favour of so doing. These are considered below. Second, doing so allows an investigation of one possible role for the community in criminal justice. So, even if the argument above is unsuccessful, what follows could be taken as an intellectual exercise in thinking through one proposal for the use of public opinion in sentencing theory and policy.

Why the Community?

The idea that the community's considered judgements constitute the idea of desert has a number of attractions. In his chapter in this volume, Paul Robinson (who has done more than anyone to define and clarify what is popularly believed in relation to desert) offers the following claim:

> Criminal law protects us from the most egregious harms. It also allows government to wield the most serious intrusions on our personal liberties. Given these special responsibilities and special powers, it is particularly appropriate that criminal law reflect the people's shared values—their shared values on what conduct deserves the condemnation of criminal conviction and their shared views on when and how much a violation of the criminal law should be punished.

One response to this—we might dub it 'the Platonic response'—is to think that it is not at all obvious that when things matter a great deal it follows that they should be turned over to 'the people'. In many areas of public policy—for example, defence, the setting of interest rates, and other economic policies— we think that *precisely because they matter*, we should leave it to the experts.

However, the Platonic response relies on there being a right answer and on the claim that experts have some epistemic advantage in knowing what that answer is. That is, we think that there is an independent answer to the questions of, for example, which attack helicopter is best and what interest rate will allow economic growth while controlling for inflation. There is no such independent answer in the case of desert so the force of the Platonic response is blunted.

In addition there are positive reasons to think that determining desert is an appropriate role for the community. These reasons reflect the overall aims of sentencing. Thus, there may be consequentialist reasons such as that reflecting community values will have good consequences in terms of public obedience and co-operation and thus crime reduction. Alternatively, the claim might be grounded in a deontological commitment to democracy (both the above arguments appear in Robinson's work). However, perhaps the most compelling reason (for contemporary retributivists) is that punishment is meant to express the community's *censure* of the offender (see e.g. Duff, 2001; Matravers, 2000; von Hirsch, 1993) and to do this it must reflect the community's judgement of what is deserved. In this sense, a sentence of twenty-one years for Bernie Madoff would have failed to express the censure that he deserved.

Why Not the Community?

The above arguments present reasons in defence of using the community's judgement to determine desert—given that desert needs to be determined—grounded in efficacy, democracy, and philosophical justifications of punishment that are (in part) expressive or communicative. However, we might be cautious of such a conventional approach and indeed of the conventionalism that has been argued to be found across proportionality-based sentencing theory.

There are at least two kinds of reasons to be cautious. One is that in general the charge of conventionalism is damaging in morality or distributive justice. The other is that powerful arguments have been mounted against allowing popular opinion to determine desert (against 'empirical desert').

The general critique can be found, for example, in Brian Barry's response to Michael Walzer's conventionalist account of justice. Barry defines conventionalism as 'the view that justice (what really is just, not merely what is locally called just) is determined for each society by the shared beliefs of the members of that society about the meanings of the goods that are to be distributed amongst them. Since these meanings are socially defined, what is just is a matter of convention' (1995b, p. 75; criticising Walzer, 1983). As Barry notes, appealing to 'the way we do things round here' is hardly a satisfactory justification of, for example, the caste system or systemic sexism.

Punishment theorists should and do share this concern. As already noted, human history is replete with punishments that repel us—such as to be hanged almost to the point of death, emasculated, disembowelled, and beheaded (hanged, drawn, and quartered)—and the conventionalist risks having to endorse such punishments if they reflect the community's beliefs about desert. In this volume, Roberts, Thomsen, Bennett, and others all cast doubt on, or severely restrict, the role of public beliefs in sentencing. To incorporate public opinion directly, as Roberts puts it, would lead to 'chaotic, unprincipled' outcomes (this volume).

The worry of course is that the public might 'get it wrong', and this thought has been reinforced by many years of research into 'penal populism' (see e.g. Pratt, 2007; Roberts, 2003). However, the problem is that we need to be careful about what it is to be 'wrong' when it comes to desert within a proportional system (and, in particular, in a proportionality-based expressive retributive theory). I have argued that there is no independent answer—no so-called deontological desert—and that in such a system, desert must be conventionally determined. The question we are left with, then, is from where the resources can be found to allow for the critical assessment of communal beliefs.

5. JUDGING THE COMMUNITY

If desert is constituted by society's considered beliefs about what is deserved then what resources exist for sentencing theorists to stand back from these beliefs to assess, criticise, and revise them? That is, how can we escape the kinds of criticisms levelled by Barry against conventionalism and by penal theorists against the excesses of penal populism?

There are two ways in which we might respond to this challenge. One is to find independent constraints on what can be justified by appeal to popular beliefs. The other is to challenge the beliefs themselves. In what follows I shall first consider two plausible independent constraints (parsimony and dignity) and then second survey the possible grounds on which we might build a case to challenge and revise errant beliefs.

Parsimony

A wide variety of punishment theorists argue for a justified general commitment to *parsimony* in punishment. By 'parsimony' is meant that punishment levels ought in general to be set such that offenders receive 'the least severe sentence consistent with the governing purposes at sentencing' (Tonry 1994, p. 81). Hugo Adam Bedau offers a slightly different formulation of this as the 'Minimal Invasion Principle', which is glossed by Matthew Kramer (who uses the principle as an important criterion for judging accounts of penalties) as requiring that 'any significant exertion of legal-governmental power must satisfy two conditions: it must be in furtherance of an important public purpose, and it must employ the least invasive or restrictive means that is sufficient to achieve that purpose' (see Bedau, 1999, p. 47, 2002; Kramer, 2011, pp. 4–5, n3).

The argument for parsimony is easily understood. As noted at the beginning of the chapter, punishment involves doing things to people that would otherwise be gross rights violations and we should do as little of it as is consistent with the 'governing purposes' of criminal justice. However, the degree to which such a principle can be used in the current argument is restricted by the 'governing purposes' of punishment. To the degree that the main—or an important—purpose of punishment is to express appropriate censure of the offender, the appropriate level of punishment will be determined by what is thought to express that censure.[13] That said, the community's beliefs about desert are not precise and allow for punishment within a range (Robinson, this volume). This offers the prospect of slowly ratcheting down sentencing levels by on each occasion choosing the lowest penalty within the range with the expectation that the new penalty will become the norm and a penalty slightly lower than that will then be included in the range in the future, and so on. The degree to which popular beliefs permit this will of course be an empirical matter, but the possibility is nevertheless an important one (and one that clearly overlaps with 'limiting retributivist' theories; see, e.g. Frase, 2004).

Dignity

A second independent constraint to which the sentencing theorist might appeal is human *dignity*. Dignity can be understood in a number of ways depending on the grounding it is thought to have. For Kant, and neo-Kantians, it is a moral claim that human beings in virtue of some capacities that are normal to the species possess some kind of equal value, or instantiate some kind of equal status, such that there are things that are always wrong to do (other than perhaps under very extreme, 'ticking bomb' type scenarios). For those, including me, who are sceptical of the (spooky) metaphysics needed to sustain this Kantian picture, dignity is a socio-legal construct that, together with notions like human rights, prove useful in arranging human life in the 'circumstances of justice'.[14]

Whatever the origins and authority of the commitment to human dignity, it needs interpretation. For sceptics, one of the oddities of (neo)Kantian thought is the confidence with which things are declared to be incompatible with respect for human dignity. This can include not only the death penalty—despite Kant's own commitment to the use of that penalty—but also corporal punishments of all kinds. Of course, in this neo-Kantians are not unusual. Throughout human history various things have been thought to conflict with human dignity and on occasion when confronted by such things, death was thought to be the only dignified alternative to living in shame (Williams, 1993).

Any sensitivity to the socio-legal interpretation of dignity, of course, undermines our confidence that the concept can by itself tell us anything very much about the range of penalties that might be inflicted on our fellow citizens. The German constitutional court may think that capital punishment is clearly incompatible with respecting human dignity, but the US Supreme Court equally clearly disagrees. Singapore, and many other countries, operate systems of corporal punishment that seem not to exclude them from the fraternity of legitimate states. The notion of dignity may, however, tell us something about which of our fellow citizens are eligible for punishment. Dignity is, as we have seen, closely tied to agency and thus provides a constraint on punishing those who are not agents such as children and the severely mentally ill.[15]

In short, in terms of sentencing what human dignity allows will in practice—and in my view, must in theory—be a matter of judicial interpretation, which will take place in the context of local and global political and social change and in the context of particular histories. As such, it is more likely simply to relocate the debate (so that discussions of sentences become discussions of dignity) than it is to provide a critical constraint on popular beliefs about desert.

A Critical Perspective

The worry—one surely shared by any critical theorist—is that the above account of desert leaves popular beliefs not merely unchallenged but unchallenge*able*. The constraints of parsimony and dignity may be able to rein in some aspects of penal severity, but they do not themselves offer a critical stance from which the beliefs themselves can be challenged. Of course, for such a stance to be possible we have to have 'a view from somewhere' (cf. Nagel, 1986) other than from within our community's beliefs.

To consider this, imagine a society in which there is a widespread view that certain sexual practices (take your choice between incest, bestiality, and homosexuality[16]) are serious violations of the natural order and ought to be treated as serious criminal offences that attract severe penalties (say, a lengthy prison sentence). In this society, 'first-degree' murder is thought to be more serious, although only just, and attracts the death penalty. The society is otherwise democratic and its (independent) judiciary have upheld the positions described. From what stance might we assess these positions?

One way in which we might approach the critical assessment is by testing the reasoning in support of these beliefs against standards of truth. Cases of factual inaccuracy might include the belief that, for example, the death penalty is wrongly supposed to be essential for deterrence. It may also—depending on how one wishes to distinguish between criticism based on false beliefs and on superstition—allow the criticism of the regulation of sexual conduct on the grounds that there is no normatively significant thing that is described by the term 'natural order'.

However, the invocation of truth is tricky other than where there are straightforward empirical beliefs that can be corrected. This is particularly so in relation to normative beliefs in societies characterised by deep pluralism about values (it is contested—and in any case is not sensible for a liberal state to rule—that the belief that homosexuality is contrary to the will of God is straightforwardly false).

A different approach is to appeal not to truth but to consistency. That is, we might ask whether the use of the death penalty, or the imprisoning of sexual 'deviants' is consistent with other values implicit in the public political culture of the society. This route is often pursued by those who link abortion to the death penalty.

However, as the example of abortion and capital punishment makes clear, the use of consistency is problematic. For some who are (with respect to abortion) 'pro-life' there is no inconsistency in also being in favour of capital punishment since far from being (as their critics allege) 'pro-death' they see themselves as being 'pro-innocent life' with respect to (possible) victims of violent crime. Appeal to consistency just by itself, then, is insufficient. However, we should be more optimistic about its prospects if we consider it in the context of an ongoing public conversation about 'our' values. That is, consistency is unlikely to be a trump in a one off argument— individuals' normative judgements are seldom internally inconsistent in any straightforward way—but if we think instead of a long-term adjustment that results from engagement over time with what our values mean, consistency may have a greater role to play (although as with the abortion debate in the United States, there is no guarantee of this).

Finally, one might appeal to 'the liberal principle of legitimacy'. According to a powerful recent account of the liberal state, the use of public power is legitimate only if it can be endorsed by those who are subject to it, which in a pluralistic state means only if it can be justified in terms that do not appeal to one, or some set of, comprehensive conception(s) of the good.[17] This would, of course, be enough to rule out religious-based justifications of prohibitions of sexual conduct. However, it would not rule out the use of popular beliefs in determining deserved sentences as these need not appeal to any such comprehensive conception.

6. CONCLUSION

There is of course a great deal more than could be said about parsimony, dignity, truth, consistency, and legitimacy. Each can do some work in allowing a critical assessment of communal beliefs about desert in sentencing. However, even in the example given it is unclear just how much work they can do and the situation is worse still if we take a more commonplace example such as the twenty-one years given to Behring Breivik, given the very lengthy, including term-of-natural-life, sentences routinely handed down in the United States. It is just not plausible to think that the beliefs of United States and Norwegian judges and citizens with respect to desert can be immediately unmasked as based in false beliefs, clearly inconsistent with their other values, or in violation of the liberal principle of legitimacy.

Thus, to be a retributivist committed to proportionality in sentencing in the absence of a metaphysical (or 'deontological') account of desert is to accept a significant degree of conventionalism in one's theory. This is the space for public opinion—or at least public judgement—in sentencing. I have tried to argue that conventionalism is inescapable (to the degree that one has the above commitments) and is implicit in communicative and expressive justifications of punishment.

In arguing for this, I am in broad agreement with Roberts when he writes that

> Proportionality is not a culturally invariant concept, but one which reflects a societal element. Community views influence the ascribed seriousness of criminal acts, as well as ascriptions of blameworthiness; these concepts do not exist in a vacuum without some reference to the community in which such judgements are set (Roberts, this volume).

However, I have added penalty severity to Roberts's list (of crime seriousness and blameworthiness) and can see no reason not to do so.

Like all forms of conventionalism, this leaves in its wake the worry that it will licence local practices no matter how abhorrent and deny to the critically engaged any point from which criticism can take hold. This worry is real and serious. For Roberts, the way forward is in part to educate the public and in part to ensure that any public determination of desert is mixed with other 'objective indicia' (Roberts, this volume). I have argued that the second of these strategies is unavailable to the (expressive) proportionality theorist. Some may take that to be a reason to avoid such an approach, but then they would owe an account of punishment that plausibly avoids proportionality or shows *how* it can incorporate other aims of sentencing.

The other possibility is to think of public beliefs about desert as malleable and in particular as sensitive to information, factual correction, critical evaluation for consistency, and so on (that is, to pursue Roberts's first way forward). These are the tools with which legal and political philosophers and penal theorists and practitioners can engage in public debate with their fellow citizens. For reasons given above, I do not think these tools always quick and decisive, but that is not to say that they have no critical bite or that there is reason to despair.

REFERENCES

Barry, Brian. 1990. *Political Argument: A Reissue with a New Introduction*. Berkeley: University of California Press.

Barry, Brian. 1995a. *A Treatise on Social Justice*. Vol. 2, *Justice as Impartiality*. Oxford: Clarendon.

Barry, Brian. 1995b. 'Spherical Justice and Global Injustice.' In David Miller and Michael Walzer (eds.), *Pluralism, Justice, and Equality*. Oxford: Oxford University Press, 67–81.

Bedau, Hugo Adam. 1999. 'Abolishing the Death Penalty Even for the Worst Murderers.' In Austin Sarat (ed.), *The Killing State*. New York: Oxford University Press, 40–59.

Bedau, Hugo Adam. 2002. 'The Minimal Invasion Argument Against the Death Penalty.' *Criminal Justice Ethics* 21(2): 3–8.

Benn, Stanley. 1958. 'An Apporach to the Problems of Punishment.' *Philosophy*, 33: 325–341.

Bentham, Jeremy. 1843. 'Principles of Penal Law.' In John Bowring (ed.), *The Works of Jeremy Bentham*. Edinburgh, UK: William Tait.

Bentham, Jeremy. 1970. *An Introduction to the Principles of Morals and Legislation*. Edited by Fred Rosen and Philip Schofield. Oxford: Oxford University Press.

Berkowitz, Eric. 2012. *Sex and Punishment: Four Thousand Years of Judging Desire*. Berkeley, CA: Counterpoint.

Blackstone, William. (1765–1769) 1966. *Commentaries on the Laws of England*. 4 vols. Oxford: Clarendon.

Bottoms, Anthony, and Andrew von Hirsch. 2011. 'The Crime Preventive Impact of Penal Sanctions.' In P. Cane and H. Kritzer (eds.), *The Oxford Handbook of Empirical Legal Research*. Oxford: Oxford University Press.

Cottingham, J. 1979. 'Varieties of Retribution.' *Philosophical Quarterly* 29: 238–246.

Duff, R. Antony. 1986. *Trials & Punishments*. Cambridge, UK: Cambridge University Press.

Duff, R. Antony. 2001. *Punishment, Communication, and Community*. Oxford: Oxford University Press.

Evans, Richard J. 1996. *Rituals of Retribution: Capital Punishment in Germany 1600–1987.* Oxford: Oxford University Press.

Fleischacker, S. 1992. 'Kant's Theory of Punishment.' In Howard Williams (ed.), *Essays on Kant's Philosophy.* Cardiff, UK: University of Wales Press, 191–212.

Foucault, Michel. 1977. *Discipline and Punish: The Birth of the Prison.* Translated by Alan Sheridan; London: Lane.

Frase, Richard. 2004. 'Limiting Retributivism.' In Michael Tonry (ed.), *The Future of Imprisonment.* New York: Oxford University Press, 83–120.

Garland, David. 2010. *Peculiar Institution: America's Death Penalty in an Age of Abolition.* Cambridge, MA: Belknap.

Glueck, Sheldon. 1952. 'Principles of a Rational Penal Code.' In *Crime and Correction: Selectd Papers.* Boston: Addison-Wesley.

Hart, H. L. A. 1958. 'Positivism and the Separation of Law and Morals.' *Harvard Law Review* 71(1958): 593–629.

Hart, H. L. A. 1968. *Punishment and Responsibility: Essays in the Philosophy of Law.* Oxford: Oxford University Press.

Hegel, Georg Wilhelm Friedrich. 1942. *Hegel's Philosophy of Right.* Translated by T. M. Knox. Oxford: Clarendon.

Kant, I. 1996. 'The Metaphysics of Morals.' In Mary J. Gregor (ed.), *The Cambridge Edition of the Works of Immanuel Kant: Practical Philosophy.* Cambridge, UK: Cambridge University Press, 353–603.

Kleinig, John. 1973. *Punishment and Desert.* The Hague: Martinus Nijhoff.

Kramer, Matthew H. 2011. *The Ethics of Capital Punishment: A Philosophical Investigation of Evil and Its Consequences.* Oxford: Oxford University Press.

Matravers, Matt. 2000. *Justice and Punishment: The Rationale of Coercion.* Oxford: Oxford University Press.

Matravers, Matt. 2011. 'Is Twenty-First Century Punishment Post-Desert?' In Michael Tonry (ed.), *Retributivism Has a Past: Has It a Future?* New York: Oxford University Press.

Moore, Michael. 1982. 'Moral Reality.' *Wisconsin Law Review* 1982: 1061–1156.

Moore, Michael. 1987. 'The Moral Worth of Retribution.' In Ferdinand Schoemann (ed.), *Responsibility, Character and the Emotions.* New York: Cambridge University Press, 179–219.

Moore, Michael. 1992. 'Moral Reality Revisited.' *Michigan Law Review* 90: 2424–2533.

Moore, Michael. 1993. 'Justifying Retributivism.' *Israel Law Review,* 27: 15–49.

Moore, Michael. 1997. *Placing Blame: A General Theory of the Criminal Law.* Oxford: Oxford University Press.

Nagel, Thomas. 1986. *The View from Nowhere.* New York: Oxford University Press.

Nietzsche, F. 1956. *On the Genealogy of Morals.* New York: Doubleday.

Pratt, John. 2007. *Penal Populism.* London: Routledge.

Rawls, John. 1971. *A Theory of Justice.* Cambridge, MA: Harvard University Press.

Rawls, John. 2005. *Political Liberalism.* Exp. ed. New York: Columbia University Press.

Roberts, J. V., L. S. Stalans, D. Indermaur, and M. Hough, 2003. *Penal Populism and Public Opinion.* Oxford: Oxford University Press.

Sharpe, J. A. 1990. *Judicial Punishment in England.* London: Faber.

Tonry, M. 1994. 'Proportionality, Parsimony, and Interchangeability of Punishments.' In R. A. Duff, S. E. Marshall, R. E. Dobash, and R. P. Dobash (eds.), *Penal Theory and Penal Practice*. Manchester: Manchester University Press, 59–83.

von Hirsch, Andrew. 1993. *Censure and Sanctions*. Oxford: Clarendon.

von Hirsch, Andrew. 1999. *Criminal Deterrence and Sentence Severity: An analysis of Recent Research*. Oxford: Hart.

von Hirsch, Andrew, and Andrew Ashworth. 2005. *Proportionate Sentencing: Exploring the Principles*. Oxford: Oxford University Press.

Walzer, Michael. 1983. *Spheres of Justice: A Defence of Pluralism and Equality*. Oxford: Blackwell.

Williams, Bernard Arthur Owen. 1993. *Shame and Necessity*. Berkeley: University of California Press.

NOTES

1. I am grateful to the audiences at the seminar on Popular Punishment in Copenhagen and at the legal theory workshop at Pompeu Fabra University of Barcelona and to Jesper Ryberg and Julian Roberts and to José L Marti for the invitations to these two places. I am also grateful to Jesper and Julian for written comments, their invitation to think about these issues, and most of all for their patience.

2. Of course, some of those who offer justifications of punishment have also written on sentencing issues, and some—although a minority—have written on such issues as part of their overall accounts of punishment (see e.g. Duff, 1986; Kleinig, 1973; von Hirsch, 1993).

3. I am grateful to José L Marti for the suggestion that the overall argument of the paper would be more clearly stated by first making these distinctions.

4. Most obviously, Level 2 could be split into questions of criminalisation on the one hand and sentencing severity on the other. This split will in fact play a role below.

5. In one of the few light-hearted moments in *Philosophy of Right*, Hegel complains of the absurdity of 'specific equality' in crime and penalty: 'Furthermore, it is easy enough . . . to exhibit the retributive character of punishment as an absurdity (theft for theft, robbery for robbery, an eye for an eye, a tooth for a tooth—and then you can go on to suppose that the criminal has only one eye and no teeth)' (Hegel, 1942: § 101). Hegel's point one might think is amply demonstrated by reading Kant's comments on the appropriate penalties for those who murder fellow soldiers in a duel and for those who commit pederasty and bestiality (Kant, 1996, pp. 98, 476).

6. Kramer prefers the words 'commensurateness' or 'fittingness' for cardinal proportionality (2011, p. 74).

7. In an earlier draft of this paper, I claimed that cardinal proportionality requires both an upper and lower anchoring point. Jesper Ryberg correctly pointed out to me that that is not the case because if one defends a strict interval matching of the scales, one can make do with a single anchoring point. For independent reasons, I think such a matching implausible, but I do not defend that here. Instead, I take it for granted that proportionality requires both upper and lower limits on the scales.

8. The use of sexual examples here is not through prurience. Throughout much of post-Christian history some of the most severe punishments have been reserved for sexual misconduct. To give one current example, as of 2010 seventy-six countries across the globe criminalised homosexual sex and of these seven included the possibility of the use of the death penalty for convicted offenders (Berkowitz, 2012).

9. I am grateful to Thom Brooks for reminding me of this passage. I discuss it in Matravers (2000, pp. 246–247). As I note there, Nietzsche (a thinker otherwise very different from Hegel) makes the same point in characteristically more purple prose: 'The "creditor" always becomes more humane to the extent that he has grown richer. . . . It is not unthinkable that a society might attain such a consciousness of power that it could allow itself the noblest luxury possible to it—letting those who harm it go unpunished. "What are my parasites to me? It might say. May they live and prosper: I am strong enough for that!"' (1956, p. 72).

10. Note that we could construct the scale of severity using an experientialist measure such as suffering so that each penalty type was assessed for how much suffering it caused. In that case, the question would be how much suffering is proportionate for a given offence and then there would be an empirical matter of what penalty—a fine of £1,000 or a fine of £2,000 or a custodial sentence of six months—delivered that quantum of suffering for the particular offender. Aside from the empirical and epistemological difficulties, such a proposal would be likely to have unpleasant social consequences (in that those who are 'hardened' to life's experiences—or by prior punishment—would attract greater penalties).

11. 'Suppose that men were to become invulnerable to attack by each other, were clad perhaps like giant land crabs with an impenetrable carapace, and could extract the food they needed from the air by some internal chemical process. In such circumstances (the details of which can be left to science fiction) rules forbidding the free use of violence and rules constituting the minimum form of property—with its rights and duties sufficient to enable food to grow and be retained until eaten—would not have the necessary nonarbitrary status which they have for us, constituted as we are in a would like ours' (Hart, 1958, p. 623).

12. Historically, of course, the punishment of wives and children would not have been thought of as the punishment of 'third parties', but of the 'property' of the offender.

13. Thus, the communicative or expressive theory of punishment is much more constrained in its use of an independent principle of parsimony. For example, consider a (side-constrained) consequentialist (i.e. someone who thinks the general justifying aim of punishment is the reduction of future crimes but that this aim must be pursued in a manner consistent with respect for individual rights). In such a theory parsimony is likely to be able to do significant work. Exactly how much is of course an empirical question, but if we assume that marginal increases in pain above some threshold will be of rapidly declining deterrence value *and* combine that with Bentham's constraints on penalty levels, it is likely that parsimony would rule out some punishments at the upper level of severity.

14. The circumstances that give rise to the need for justice include, according to Rawls, that people coexist on the same territory, are of comparable strength and intelligence and that there is moderate scarcity such that there are benefits to co-operation for mutual advantage (Rawls 1971, p. 126).

15. Consider the ways in which the US Supreme Court has debated and dealt with the execution of the mentally disabled and of those who were minors at the time of their crimes (with reference to 'evolving standards of decency in a civilized society'; Garland, 2010, pp. 269–270).

16. To be clear, I am not asserting an equivalence between these three activities. What they have in common that matters here is only that they have been subject to criminal regulation and have attracted severe penalties.

17. The origins of this account lie in Rawls's 'liberal principle of legitimacy' which has it that, 'our exercise of political power is fully proper only when it is exercised in accordance with a constitution the essentials of which all citizens as free and equal may reasonably be expected to endorse in the light of principles and ideals acceptable to their common human reason' (Rawls, 2005, p. 137). The best articulation of what this requires in practice is Barry's (1995a) *Justice as Impartiality*.

3

The Proper Role of Community in Determining Criminal Liability and Punishment

Paul H. Robinson

Criminal law protects us from the most egregious harms. It also allows government to wield the most serious intrusions on our personal liberties. Given these special responsibilities and special powers, it is particularly appropriate that criminal law reflect the people's shared values—their shared values on what conduct deserves the condemnation of criminal conviction and their shared views on when and how much a violation of the criminal law should be punished (Kennedy, 2009, pp. 54–55).

But in this chapter I would like to talk about an alternative justification, aside from its democratic value, for consulting the community's judgements of justice. Recent social science research has revealed that there is practical crime-control value in having the criminal law reflect community views. A criminal law that distributes criminal liability and punishment in ways that the community perceives as just gains moral credibility with the community, which translates into greater deference to, support for, and co-operation with the criminal justice system. In contrast, a criminal law that is seen as regularly doing injustice or failing to do justice loses moral credibility with the community and thereby reduces its influence. People are less likely to defer to it, to support it, to co-operate with it, or to acquiesce in its commands (see, in general, Robinson, 2008, pp. 175–184; Robinson & Darley, 2007, pp. 18–28; Robinson, Goodwin, & Reisig, 2010, pp. 1995–2011). Add to these powerful forces of social influence the general deterrence and incapacitation of dangerous persons that is inherent in what is seen as a just distribution of criminal liability and punishment, and it becomes difficult to justify adopting rules that conflict with community views.

In this paper I will describe some of the research that has revealed this practical value in having criminal law track people's shared judgements of justice, but I also will describe the potential dangers that exist in considering community views in the adjudication of individual cases, especially when community views are assumed to be those contained in newspaper or Internet reports. Finally, I will say a word about the current debates on the subject in the United States and in China. The points of debate in the two countries are quite different and illustrate additional advantages and dangers of the approach.

This informal essay is drawn from the research and conclusions of my recent book, *Intuitions of Justice and the Utility of Desert* (Oxford, 2013). Its five hundred-plus pages and one hundred graphics bring together in an integrated whole my scholarship on the topic over the past two decades with nine co-authors. I urge readers to consult that volume for the details and documentation of the points that I discuss here.

1. THE PRACTICAL VALUE IN FOLLOWING THE COMMUNITY'S JUDGEMENTS ABOUT JUSTICE

The empirical studies examine two distinct questions. First, does knowledge that criminal law rules regularly do injustice or fail to do justice decrease respect for the criminal law? Second, if so, does such decreased respect reduce deference to the criminal justice system—specifically, reduced co-operation, compliance, and normative influence?

History certainly suggests such a dynamic, at least for dramatic levels of disrespect. For example, the early Soviet criminal justice system was notoriously arbitrary and corrupt with little or no moral credibility amongst the general population. The compliance that it gained was through the coercion of a brutal and extensive police power. When those power centres weakened with the collapse of the Soviet Union, the crime rate increased dramatically. It was only the coercive influence of the state's threat that had given the system effect, and once that was gone, so too went its control.

Empirical studies initially hinted, and more recent studies have confirmed, that this same relationship between the criminal justice system's moral credibility and its ability to gain deference applies not just to extreme situations but rather defines a general dynamic: the greater the system's moral credibility, the greater its ability to gain deference, influence, and co-operation.

We know that systems with public support have greater effect in gaining deference than systems with no public support and credibility with the community, such as the early Soviet system. (Obviously, there are many other examples that one could use of discredited criminal justice systems.) What the recent studies have shown is that a marginal decrease in credibility will produce a marginal decrease in deference. (This is represented by the dashed line in the lower left of Figure 3.1.) This suggests that a system with moral credibility might further improve its ability to gain deference by further improving its reputation for doing justice and avoiding injustice, as the community perceives it. (This is represented by the dashed line in the upper right of Figure 3.1. In reality, of course, none of the lines on the graphic would be perfectly straight; we do not yet know their shape.)

Why should it be the case that undermining the system's moral credibility undermines its crime-control effectiveness? The forces of social influence and internalised norms are potentially enormous. A criminal law that has earned moral credibility with the people can harness these powerful normative forces through a variety of mechanisms (for a more detailed discussion, see Robinson & Darley, 2007, pp. 18–31; Robinson, 2008, pp. 175–89).

First, a criminal law with moral credibility can harness the power of stigmatisation. Many people will avoid breaking the law if doing so will stigmatise them and thereby endanger their personal and social relationships. A criminal law that regularly punishes conduct that is seen as blameless or at least not deserving the condemnation of criminal liability will be unable to harness the power of stigmatisation. Second, a system that has

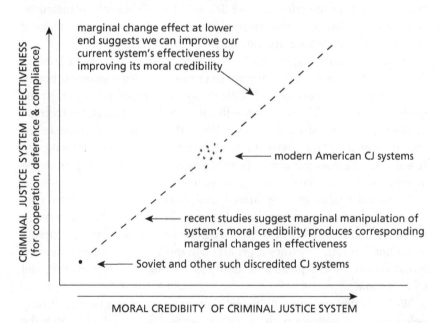

Figure 3.1

earned moral credibility with the people also can help avoid vigilantism. People will be less likely to take matters into their own hands if they have confidence that the system is trying hard to do justice. Third, a reputation for moral credibility also can avoid inspiring the kind of resistance and subversion that we see in criminal justice systems which have with poor reputations. Such resistance and subversion can appear amongst any of the participants in the system. Do victims report offences? Do potential witnesses come forward to help police and investigators? Do prosecutors and judges follow the legal rules, or do they feel free to make up their own? In systems with trial juries, do the jurors follow their legal jury instructions or substitute their own judgment? Do offenders acquiesce in their liability and punishment, or do they focus instead on the injustice that they think is being done to them? Finally, the most powerful force that comes from a criminal justice system with moral credibility is its power to shape societal norms and to cause people to internalise those norms. If the criminal law has earned a reputation for doing justice, when the law criminalises some new form of conduct or makes some conduct a more serious offence than it had previously thought to be, the community assumes that this action means the conduct really is more condemnable.

A variety of studies have this relationship (see Robinson & Darley, 2007, pp. 77–91), but let me show the results of just one recent study about this dynamic between the system's moral credibility and people's deference to it (see Robinson et al., 2010, pp. 1995–2011). Subjects were tested to determine their willingness to defer in the variety of ways just described: whether they would help investigators, or report an offence, or take criminalisation to mean that the conduct really was morally condemnable, and so on. With this baseline established, the subjects were then told of a variety of real cases in which the criminal justice system had done serious injustice or failed to do justice, not by accident but as the result of the liability rules formally adopted with the knowledge that they would have such unjust results. The testing confirmed that this information tended to disillusion the subjects about the criminal justice system. After some other activities to distract them, they were tested again on their views on deference and compliance, and all had weakened.

Table 3.1 provides the results (Robinson et al., 2010, p. 2003). (The first column lists not the full text of the questions used but just a short-hand identification of the question.)

A follow-up study used a slightly different methodology (Robinson et al., 2010, pp. 2004–2008). Instead of the 'within-subjects design' used in the former study, it used a 'between-subjects design'. That is, instead of asking the same subjects their views before and after being 'disillusioned' about the criminal justice system, the study used separate groups. Some were

Table 3.1. Pre- and Post-Stimulation Averages

Question	Baseline average	Post-stimulation avg.	Significance (*p*-value)
1. Life sentence means offence conduct must be heinous	6.46	5.14	<.001
2. Law prohibition means posting false comments must be condemnable	6.14	5.76	<.07
3. High sentence for financial manoeuvre means condemnable	5.25	4.63	<.02
4. Report removal of arrowhead	5.93	5.14	<.01
5. Give found handgun to police	6.66	5.56	<.001
6. Report dog violation to authorities	5.15	4.59	<.01
7. Go back and report your mistake to gas station	7.05	5.69	<.001
8. Go back and report your mistake to restaurant	7.15	5.71	<.001

Table 3.2.

Question	Baseline: No disillusionment	Low disillusionment	High disillusionment
1. Life sentence means heinous	6.46[a]	6.59[a]	5.35[b]
2. Posting condemnable	6.14[a]	5.38[b]	5.59[a,b]
3. Financial move condemnable	5.25[a]	5.16[a]	4.34[b]
4. Report arrowhead	5.93[a]	5.65[a]	4.95[b]
5. Turn in hand gun	6.66[a]	5.40[b]	4.32[c]
6. Report dogs violation	5.15[a]	4.75[a,b]	4.43[b]
7. Return to gas station	7.05[a]	6.63[a]	5.63[b]
8. Return to restaurant	7.15[a]	6.47[b]	5.84[c]

Note: Where two cells on a row *do not* share the same letter, they are statistically significantly different.

seriously disillusioned, some only mildly disillusioned, and some were not disillusioned at all. Then all subjects were asked the same deference and compliance questions. As Table 3.2 reflects, the study found that the extent of the disillusionment determined the extent to which the subjects would defer to the criminal justice system (Robinson et al., 2010, p. 2007).

These are actually a quite surprising result, if you think about it. When adult subjects are being tested in a study like this, they come to the study with an already-formed opinion about the moral credibility of the criminal justice system. There is a limited amount that a researcher can do to shift this pre-existing view. But despite the fact that we can only slightly shift subjects' views, we nonetheless see a corresponding shift in the willingness of subjects to defer to and comply with the criminal justice system.

Another study did not collect new data but sought to determine whether the same dynamic was present in some of the very large data sets of previously collected survey data (Robinson et al., 2010, pp. 2016–2023). A regression analysis gave the results shown in Table 3.3 (Robinson et al., 2010, p. 2022). The moral credibility measure in the study explains more of the variance in the 'willingness to defer' measure than any of the other measures. In fact, it is the only predictor that is statistically significant.

One could summarise the conclusions of the empirical studies this way: Criminal law rules that deviate from the community's notions of justice are not cost-free, as has generally been assumed in the past. Rather, when the criminal law adopts rules or practices that produce criminal liability or punishment that is seen as unjust or as a failure of justice, the system suffers a loss in effectiveness. To be most effective, the criminal justice system should try to distribute liability and punishment in accord with the shared judgements of justice of the community that it governs. In that way, it can build moral credibility and, in turn, gain effectiveness by harnessing the power of social and normative influence.

I have detailed elsewhere the kinds of instances in which I believe a society ought to deviate from the community's views to promote a societal good by seeking to change community views. But a criminal law can help change community views only if it has previously earned a reputation as a credible moral authority whose views should be given weight (see Robinson, 2011, pp. 186–202).

Table 3.3.

Variable	Willingness to Defer to the Criminal Justice System in the Future	
	Standardised Regression Coefficient	Significance Level
Moral Credibility	.265	.002
Male	−.072	.395
Age	−.128	.148
White	.062	.476
Education	−.134	.144
Household Income	.017	.859
Married	.167	.069

2. IS IT POSSIBLE TO HAVE THE CRIMINAL LAW TRACK COMMUNITY VIEWS?

Section 2 suggests that there is practical value in having criminal law track the justice judgements of those it governs, but one can imagine, and some have expressly made, a variety of arguments for why this, even if it were theoretically true, simply is not practically possible: People's notions of justice are simply too vague to be the basis for creating criminal law rules, and, even if they were not, people simply disagree about notions of justice so it is not possible to determine a single community view. Indeed, some have argued that people's views about criminal liability and punishment are not based on desert (moral blameworthiness) in any case but rather upon principles of deterrence and incapacitation of the dangerous.

Notions of Desert as Hopelessly Vague

A common objection to empirical desert as a distributive principle is its supposed vagueness (for a more detailed discussion, see Robinson & Darley, 2007, pp. 32–35). Other critics may be willing to concede that moral blameworthiness is not a hopelessly vague concept, that it has some meaning, but would make a related but slightly different criticism: Desert cannot specify a *particular amount* of punishment that *should* be imposed; it can only identify a *range* of punishments that *should not* be imposed because such punishment would be seriously disproportionate.

These complaints are based in part on a failure to appreciate the specific demands of desert and of people's intuitions about it. The confusion arises in part from the failure to distinguish two distinct judgements: setting the endpoint of the punishment continuum and, once that endpoint has been set, ordinally ranking cases along that continuum. Every society must decide what punishment it will allow for its most egregious case, be it the death penalty or life imprisonment or fifteen years. Once that endpoint is set, the distributive challenge that desert must guide is to determine the relative blameworthiness of different offenders—an ordinal ranking of offenders according to their relative blameworthiness.

Because people make very nuanced judgements about the relative blameworthiness of different cases and because there is a limited punishment continuum (as punishment amount increases, the size of meaningfully different punishment units also increases), the result is a specific amount of punishment for each particular offence. That amount of punishment is not the product of some magical connection between that violator's offence and the corresponding amount of punishment. Rather, it is the specific amount of punishment needed to *set the offender's violation at its appropriate ordinal rank* according to blameworthiness, relative to all other offences. If the endpoint of the punishment continuum were changed, the appropriate punishment for each offender would change accordingly.

Those who complain that empirical desert is vague seem to assume (incorrectly) that it must provide a universal, absolute amount of punishment as deserved for a given offence no matter the time or the jurisdiction. But the real demand of empirical desert, at least as laypersons see it, is to ensure that offenders of different blameworthiness are given appropriately different amounts of punishment, each to receive an amount that reflects his or her blameworthiness relative to that of others. What critics see as vagueness or uncertainty about deserved punishment arises not from any vagueness in the ordinal ranking of offences according to offender blameworthiness but rather arises from differences in the punishment-continuum endpoint that different societies adopt or that different people would want their society to adopt. However, once that endpoint is set, the distribution of punishment to offenders according to empirical desert suffers no vagueness or uncertainty.

But this does not fully settle the vagueness complaints. Some writers argue that even ordinal ranking is something that can be done only in the vaguest terms; establishing specific rankings is impossible. The claim is that ranking offences according to blameworthiness is beyond the ability of people's intuitions of justice. People can roughly distinguish between 'serious' and 'not serious' cases but cannot provide the nuance needed to do more.

That claim is empirical, and empirically it is false. The evidence from a wide variety of studies is quite clear: Subjects display a great deal of nuance in their judgements of blameworthiness. Small changes in facts produce large and predictable changes in punishment. The empirical evidence suggests that people take account of a wide variety of factors and often give them quite different effect in different situations. Alexis Durham offers this summary: 'Virtually without exception, citizens seem able to assign highly specific sentences for highly specific events' (Durham, 1993). People's intuitions of justice are not vague or simplistic but rather sophisticated and complex.

Past research on lay intuitions of justice has included a wide range of topics, including such areas as the objective requirements of offences, complicity, attempt, and causation; the culpability requirements of offences, liability doctrines including mistake, accident, voluntary intoxication, and partial individualisation of reasonable person standard for negligence; the justification doctrines of defensive force; law enforcement use of force; the excuse doctrines of insanity, immaturity, involuntary intoxication, and duress and other general defences such as entrapment; grading doctrines, such as those relating to sexual offences and homicide offences; and extra-legal punishment factors such as remorse, forgiveness, hardship, and good-deeds. Research of lay judgements of justice has also been undertaken to test empirical claims of criminal law theoretical literature, testing competing scholarly theories, such as those relating to justification defences and to offence of blackmail and testing claims about the nature of the shift from common law to modern American criminal codes.

Hopeless Disagreement as to Notions of Desert

In response to the suggestion that the criminal law should look to the community view, one might challenge: what community? Different communities may have different views. Which community view should the law look to? The short answer is this: Look to the community that will be governed by the law at issue. If the question is the formulation of a provision of the state's criminal code, look to the state as the relevant community. If the question is the sentencing practice in a particular city, look to that city's residents.

A related objection to using empirical desert as a distributive principle is that, even if individuals may have a clear and specific notion of what desert demands, people disagree amongst themselves. But, as with the claim that judgements of justice are hopelessly vague, this common wisdom simply does not match the empirical reality (for a more detailed discussion, see Robinson & Darley, 2007, pp. 36–38). The studies show that there can be widely shared intuitions about the relative blameworthiness of different cases, at least with regard to a 'core' of wrongdoing: physical aggression, taking property without consent, and deceit in exchanges.

One recent study illustrates the striking extent of the agreement (Robinson & Kurzban, 2007, pp. 1866–1880). Subjects were asked to rank order twenty-four crime scenario descriptions according to the amount of punishment deserved. Despite the apparently complex and subjective nature of such desert judgements, the researchers found that the subjects had little difficulty performing the task and displayed an astounding level of agreement in their ordinal ranking.

A statistical measure of concordance is found in Kendall's W coefficient of concordance, in which 1.0 indicates perfect agreement and 0.0 indicates no agreement. In the study, the Kendall's W was 0.95, an astounding result. (One might expect to get a Kendall's W of this magnitude if subjects were asked to judge an easy and objective task, such as judging the relative brightness of different groupings of spots. When asked to perform more subjective or complex comparisons, such as asking travel magazine readers to rank eight different travel destinations according to their level of safety, one gets a Kendall's W of 0.52. When asking economists to rank the top twenty economics journals according to quality, one gets a Kendall's W of 0.095.)

Even more compelling, the astounding level of agreement cuts across all demographics. People from very different backgrounds, situations, and perspectives all agreed upon the relative blameworthiness of the twenty-four offenders. Similar conclusions are found in cross-cultural studies. The level of agreement is strongest for those core wrongs with which criminal law primarily concerns itself—physical aggression, taking property, and deception in exchanges—and becomes less pronounced as the nature of the offence moves farther from the core of wrongdoing. However, the data overwhelmingly refute the common perception that there is never agreement as to judgements of justice.

Disagreements amongst people's judgements of justice do exist. People obviously disagree about many things relating to crime and punishment, as the endless public debates make clear. But some appearances of disagreement are simply misleading. Poor testing methods will predictably underestimate the extent of agreement. When a test scenario is written ambiguously so that different test participants perceive the facts differently, the existence of shared nuanced intuitions of justice itself will predict different judgements amongst the participants. So too, when a case in the headlines has social or political implications, its relevant facts commonly will be perceived differently by different people. If people have different perceptions of the facts of a case, they are likely to have different views on the relative liability and punishment deserved.

One might wonder why core judgements of justice are so widely shared. Whether due to some evolutionarily developed mechanism or to shared social learning, or some combination of the two, it is clear that the source of these intuitions is beyond even the powerful influences of culture or demographics. Because one does not see those differences in life experiences reflected in core intuitions, it follows that they must be somehow fixed and therefore will be resistant to attempts by social engineers to manipulate them, at least using the kinds of intrusions on personal autonomy that modern societies would permit.

The point here is not to say that our existing intuitions of justice are good or bad. Rather, they are the reality, and effective social engineers must deal with the world as it exists, not as they wish it was. The criminal justice system must take account of these existing shared intuitions when in formulates its criminal law rules.

People's Natural Judgements about Punishment Are Based on Deterrence or Incapacitation, Not Desert

A third kind of criticism levelled against using empirical desert as the basis for distributing criminal liability and punishment is that people's punishment judgements are not really based on desert but rather on factors relating to effective deterrence or incapacitation. That is, when people ostensibly decide what punishment an offender should get, they are really deciding how much punishment is needed to deter or incapacitate. Having criminal law track people's judgements would not produce a desert distribution based on moral blameworthiness but a utilitarian crime-control distribution based on deterrence and dangerousness. Again, however, the view does not match the available data (for a more detailed discussion and for documentation, see Robinson & Darley, 2007, pp. 38–41). Studies examining the criteria on which people rely on when making punishment judgements have found it to be desert—the offender's perceived moral blameworthiness. People's punishment judgements typically ignore deterrence or incapacitation concerns.

For example, one such study exploring whether desert or incapacitation are the driving force in laypersons' judging criminal liability and punishment gave participants ten short descriptions of criminal cases, which were generated by combining five levels of case seriousness (theft of a CD, theft of a valuable object, assault, homicide, and assassination) with two levels of criminal history (no prior history and a history of actions consistent with the crime committed). Participants were asked to assign a proper punishment to each case without any indication as to what that decision should be based upon, using a 7-point scale of punishment severity and a 13-point scale of criminal liability grades. Participants were thereafter asked to reconsider the scenarios and assign punishments from a just deserts perspective and from a incapacitation perspective (Darley, Carlsmith, & Robinson, 2000).

Punishment assignments based on just deserts were closely aligned with the original intuitive decisions, while punishments assigned using the incapacitation criteria were not. The study's authors conclude, 'What this suggests is that the default perspective of sentencing is indistinguishable from the just deserts perspective, [and both the default and explicit desert perspectives] are significantly different from the incapacitation perspective' (Darley et al., 2000, p. 667). Other studies, which pitted justice against deterrence, reinforce this conclusion. People's intuitive default for assigning criminal liability and punishment is just deserts. While participants explicitly endorse deterrence justifications for punishment, they actually meted out sentences 'from a strictly deservingness-based stance' (Carlsmith, Darley & Robinson, 2002, p. 284).

3. RECONCEIVING THE CLASSIC RETRIBUTIVIST–UTILITARIAN DEBATE

The research findings suggest an important twist in the classic punishment-theory debate. That debate has always seen two opposing camps: On one side are the retributivists, who urge distributing punishment according to desert because they see doing justice as a value in itself, and therefore needing no practical justification. On the other side are the crime-control utilitarians, who would distribute punishment so as to avoid future crime. They believe that punishment can be justified only by the benefits, specifically future crime reduction, that it can provide. Traditionally, this meant distribute punishment to optimise the deterrence of future crime or the rehabilitation or incapacitation of dangerous offenders (see, generally, Robinson, 2008, chapters 4–6).

The two opposing camps would propose punishment of different people and different amounts, because they look to different criteria: The retributivists, wanting to do justice, would look to an offender's moral blameworthiness, as defined by moral philosophers. The utilitarians, who want to reduce crime, would look to what would most effectively deter, rehabilitate, or incapacitate potential offenders. Historically, these two camps have been seen as diametrically opposed and unavoidably in conflict. The two goals—doing justice or fighting crime—commonly conflict, and, when they do, one must choose between them. But the recent empirical studies suggest that the picture is actually quite different. These two positions—the retributivists versus the utilitarians—may not be so entirely incompatible.

As the recent studies suggest, the best way to fight crime may be to do justice. Thus, the utilitarians ought to be interested in 'empirical desert' (shared community judgements of justice). And the retributivists ought also to be interested in it. Empirical desert is not the transcendent deontological desert of moral philosophers but, given the obvious difficulties of operationalising the latter (moral philosophers seem to disagree on many if not most issues), empirical desert may be the best feasible approximation of deontological desert that one can hope for in the real world.

4. THE AMERICAN DEBATE: THE DISUTILITY OF INJUSTICE

This perspective is consistent with recent developments in the United States. The American Law Institute, which is something like the national academy for law in the United States, promulgated the Model Penal Code in 1962. In the several decades following, about three-fourths of the states have since codified their criminal law in ways modelled after that code. The Model Code was amended a few years ago for the first time in the nearly half century since its promulgation. The amendment revised the statutory section setting out the purposes of the code and how its provisions are to be interpreted. The new model provision sets doing justice—looking to the moral blameworthiness of the offender—as the primary and inviolable principle for determining who should be punished by how much.[1]

While this dramatic reform is consistent with the recent studies discussed above, some American scholars had reservations about the shift to moral blameworthiness. The concerns are of two sorts. One group was concerned that the shift to focusing on desert was giving in to the 'retributivists' and was a defeat for those concerned about effective crime control (see Bottoms, 1995, pp. 39–41; Garland, 2001, pp. 13–14). But the empirical studies discussed above can help allay those concerns, because they show that doing justice in the community's view can actually improve the criminal law's crime-control effectiveness. By building the criminal law's moral credibility with the community, it can better harness the powerful forces of social and normative influence. (As I develop in my book, *Distributive Principles of Criminal Law*, crime-control utilitarians should be comfortable with empirical desert as a distributive principle not only because of its crime-control benefits but also because of the comparative weakness of the crime-control benefits of the traditional principles of deterrence and incapacitation; see generally Robinson, 2008, chapters 4, 6).

But another group of American scholars had a very different concern. They feared that deference to community views of justice would make the criminal justice system extremely punitive, which they would very much disapprove. They noted, for example, that democratic action had brought about a series of modern crime-control programs that seemed, in their view, to impose harsh and unjust sentences. They feared that giving a greater deference to community views would make the criminal law even more draconian than it already was (see Kaplow & Shavell, 2001; Luna, 2003, pp. 223–237).

I understand and sympathise with this view, but let me explain why I think it is seriously misguided. These scholars are correct in pointing out a variety of modern criminal law rules that do in fact generate serious injustice, but they are wrong to think that these rules reflect shared community notions of justice. On the contrary, these modern rules were designed not to do justice but rather were efforts to increase crime-control without regard to whether they did injustice. That is, when legislatures adopted these kinds of programs, they did so not because the community saw these rules as just but rather because crime-control experts had told legislators that these programs would reduce crime.

Let me give six examples of the kinds of modern programs that are at issue here—each adopted because it was thought to improve the control of crime (for a more detailed discussion and for documentation, see Robinson et al., 2010, pp. 1949–1961). The 'three strikes' doctrine provides for long-prison terms for an offender who has two previous criminal convictions. High penalties for low-level drug offences are thought to be useful in providing an added deterrence. Many jurisdictions have adopted rules that reduce the age at which an offender is prosecuted as an adult and thus is subjected to the full force of criminal penalties. Many jurisdictions have narrowed or eliminated the insanity defence, as a way of taking better control over people whose mental illness can cause harm. Some jurisdictions use what are called 'strict liability' offences, which do not require that the offender had a culpable state of mind towards the offence—that is, they do not require a showing that the offender committed the offence purposely, knowingly, or recklessly. Finally, the 'felony murder rule' provides that anyone causing a death even entirely accidentally during the commission of a felony is liable for murder, the most serious form of homicide, which normally requires that the offender intentionally caused the death. Not every application of these doctrines produces injustice, but the doctrines are formulated such that unjust sentences—punishment more than an offender deserves—are not uncommon.

Recent empirical studies show that the criminal liability and punishment generated by these doctrines generate results that seriously conflict with peoples' shared intuitions of justice. In one recent study, subjects were asked to rate the relative blameworthiness of a variety of cases, each of which dealt with one of the six crime-control doctrines just listed (Robinson et al., 2010, pp. 1961–1979). (Each of the cases used was a real case, in which the doctrine was applied as it was designed to be.) The subjects' views were then compared to the punishment judgements reflected in the legal rules. Figure 3.2 shows the results (Robinson et al., 2010, p. 1973).

The twelve cases listed on the left in Figure 3.2 are what might be called 'milestone cases'. They provide a range of cases that mark out points of comparison along the full length of the continuum of offence seriousness and punishment. The solid lines from the cases to the centre line show how the subjects 'sentenced' each of these cases. Note that punishment scale provided is exponential rather than linear. Moving from ❶ to ❷ triples the punishment (from two months to six months); just as moving from ❸ to ❹ triples the punishment (from one year to three years). (This reflects both the approach of criminal code offence grading schemes and the way that laypersons think about punishment differences: The more serious the punishment, the larger the noticeably different unit of punishment.)

The cases on the right are the 'test offences', each relying upon one of the modern crime-control doctrines noted above. The subjects 'sentenced' the

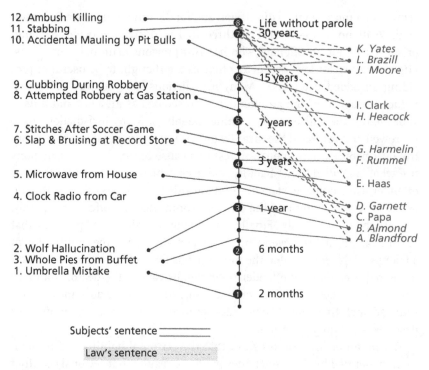

12. Ambush Killing
11. Stabbing
10. Accidental Mauling by Pit Bulls

Life without parole
30 years

K. Yates
L. Brazill
J. Moore

9. Clubbing During Robbery
8. Attempted Robbery at Gas Station

15 years

I. Clark
H. Heacock

7. Stitches After Soccer Game
6. Slap & Bruising at Record Store

7 years

G. Harmelin
F. Rummel

5. Microwave from House

3 years

E. Haas

4. Clock Radio from Car

1 year

D. Garnett
C. Papa
B. Almond
A. Blandford

2. Wolf Hallucination
3. Whole Pies from Buffet
1. Umbrella Mistake

6 months

2 months

Subjects' sentence ═══════

Law's sentence ·············

Figure 3.2

offender in these cases to sentences at various points along that punishment continuum—scattered amongst the various 'milestone cases'. For example, the subjects saw the Haas case (a strict liability case) as more serious than the theft of a radio from a car but less serious than the theft of the microwave from a house. The solid lines on the right (from each case to the punishment scale) show the amount of punishment that the subjects would impose in each of the test cases.

The important point here is to look at the dotted lines on the right. The dotted lines show the punishment that the law would and did actually impose in these cases. Compare each dotted line with the solid line associated with the same case. As you see, the law's punishment is dramatically higher than that imposed by the study's subjects. The difference is even more striking when you take into account that the punishment continuum used here is exponential. The large difference in slope between the solid line and the dotted line for each test case shows that the punishment that the law imposes is commonly many times higher than what study's subjects would impose.

How could such a discrepancy occur in a democracy, where the laws are enacted by elected representatives of the people? This conflict of criminal law with community judgements of justice arises for two reasons (for a more detailed discussion and for documentation, see Robinson et al., 2010, pp. 1979–1995). First, as noted above, the doctrines that generate these results have been adopted because they were thought to reduce crime. That is, the lawmakers were intentionally sacrificing justice because they were told it that would reduce crime. Second, there is an unfortunate distortion effect in American politics when it comes to legislation relating to crime. Politicians have a tendency to exaggerate the seriousness of the crime problem and to be overly optimistic that legislation will have an effect in reducing crime. It is also common that legislators use crime-related legislation as a vehicle to make a reputation with the voters to get elected, even if the legislation really will not reduce crime.

Another misleading source of community views are so-called public opinion surveys, which purport to show public support for some political initiative. But these surveys are more often a test of subjects' politics than of their judgements of justice. When asked questions about abstract policies, the surveys get the test subjects' allegiance or rejection of the politics behind the policy. If you ask people whether they support 'three strikes' legislation, for example, those who count themselves as conservative will support the issue because they know it to be part of the conservative political view. But we know from more responsible testing than 'public opinion' polls, as with the laboratory experiment reported above, that conservatives and liberals will in fact see real 'three strikes' cases as dramatically less serious than the law treats them, contradicting the premise of the three-strikes policy.

The original point of the discussion here was some scholars' fear that shifting the criminal law to track community views would create draconian rules. In truth, however, the modern programs producing the unjust sentences to which these people object—three strikes, felony murder, and so on—do not reflect community views of justice but rather conflict with them. Relying upon community views of justice would not encourage draconian punishments but rather would lead criminal law to discard rules, like these six, that produce what the community sees as unjust punishment. To worry that community views are draconian is to confuse people's judgements of justice with politicians' rhetoric. The empirical studies on empirical desert could in fact serve as an important antidote to false political claims about what the community thinks is just.

Moreover, because people do not have fixed intuitions about the general severity of punishment—different societies can and do have noticeably different severity levels—reformers could over time shift a society's expectations towards lower severity. It would be a mistake to try to do so abruptly, for it might undercut moral credibility, but one could regularly reduce punishment levels across the board by an amount that would seem trivial in itself. For example, as an effort to reduce the overall cost of imprisonment on strained state budgets, one could reduce all sentences by 5 per cent, and could do so repeatedly over many years.

5. THE CHINESE DEBATE: THE DANGERS OF CONSIDERING COMMUNITY VIEWS IN THE DISPOSITION OF INDIVIDUAL CASES

I recently had occasion to give a series of lectures in China about these issues, including the idea of having criminal law track community views. There is serious debate in China about these issues, but, interestingly, it is along quite different lines than those of the American debate. One group of Chinese academics very much welcomes the notion of having criminal law based upon 'empirical desert'—that is, derived from social science studies of shared lay judgements of justice. Chinese culture has had a long tradition of seeing wisdom in the people. It is said to be a classic Confucian theme. But that tradition has been used, these academics worry, to justify the increasingly common practice by newspapers or Internet bloggers or others to undertake a public campaign for or against a particular defendant in a current case.

When a case attracts the attention of a newspaper or Internet blogger, who presses a public campaign of hostility or of favouritism, one might conclude that 'the people's view' is important to follow, that prosecutors and judges ought to defer to the expressions of views in such public campaigns. But if building the moral credibility of the criminal law is the goal, giving influence to these kinds of public campaigns is dangerous because it invites a result that—longer term, after passions cool—may be seen as unjust and thus serve to undermine the system's long-term reputation with the community.

In one case, for example, the defendant, Fu Zhongtao, struck and killed a ten-year-old girl (Zhiguang & Guangyu, 2005). He was driving a Lincoln sedan, which showed him to be a rich person. The media played on the people's anti-rich bias and gave great attention to the case, fanning a public outrage over the offence. Fu was sentenced to death and executed. (It was only later revealed that Fu bought the car second hand and that it was about to be scrapped, a fact omitted from the media coverage before the execution.)

In another case, the Police Commissioner Zhang Jinzhu at a police station in Zhengzhou, Henan Province, was driving drunk and hit a person on a bicycle. He drove away from the scene, intending not to report it. Unknown to him, the cyclist was stuck under his car and his driving away caused the cyclist's death. Because of a standing concern about official misconduct, the media continuously featured the case in its headlines, whipping up anger in the community and demanding that Zhang be given the death penalty. There was no indication that Zhang knew the cyclist was under his car and normally would be sentenced to no more than seven years for negligent homicide, but the courts bowed to public pressure and sentenced him to death (Zhiguang & Guangyu, 2005).

Let me suggest a variety of ways in which public campaigns about a particular case can promote results that later, upon closer examination and more thoughtful reflection, may be seen as unjust. First, the public reaction to a case may depend upon false or incomplete reporting of the true facts. The account of a case given in a newspaper article or an Internet blog is necessarily only a partial presentation of the facts presented at a fair trial, where both prosecution and defence have an opportunity to tell their full story. And when newspapers or bloggers give their shortened version of the facts, it is common for them to select those facts consistent with their point of view and to omit facts that are inconsistent with it. A distorted presentation of the case facts can produce only a distorted view of the liability and punishment that is deserved.[2]

Public influence in deciding individual cases also is a problem because some people may be biased in their judgements because of a defendant's ethnicity, religion, age, gender, political views, family affiliations, race, social background, sexual orientation, or, as in the Fu case, apparent economic status. Further, we know from social science research that even if one tries to be unbiased in one's judgements, it is sometimes difficult to do so. People tend to be more sympathetic to defendants who are like themselves, for example, and are less sympathetic to defendants who are different from themselves. The beauty of relying upon empirical research to determine community judgements of justice is that we can determine those judgements independent of potential biases by using testing methods that exclude the personal characteristics of a defendant that might bias people's judgement. We can get the true principles of justice that guide people's assessment of blameworthiness, insulated from the unfortunate biases that may exist with regard to a particular defendant.

An even greater problem in having public views influence individual cases is the extent to which this has a defendant's liability and punishment depend upon his or her good or bad luck—in avoiding or in attracting newspaper or blogger attention. A defendant's criminal liability and punishment ought to depend upon what he or she has done and his or her blameworthiness for doing it. It ought not to depend upon whether the case happens to attract or escape media attention, especially if the media attention is the result of political or social influence by a victim's family or friends or is prompted by the political or social views or characteristics of a defendant.

A final difficulty with giving influence to public campaigns for or against a particular defendant is that they tend to focus on the defendant at hand in isolation and fail to put the case in the broader perspective of other similar cases. We know from social science research that people have very nuanced and sophisticated judgements about the relative blameworthiness of different cases and feel strongly that greater punishment ought to be imposed where there is greater blameworthiness and that less punishment ought to be imposed where there is less blameworthiness. Indeed, it is this *relative blameworthiness* judgment that is at the core of a criminal justice system's reputation for doing justice.

It is getting these judgements of relative blameworthiness correct that is essential to the criminal justice system earning long-term moral credibility with the community it governs. Yet it is just that judgment—of relative blameworthiness—that is most commonly distorted when there is a public campaign about a particular case. A common effect of such a campaign is to exaggerate the seriousness of the case as against other cases, producing a punishment that later, after passions have cooled, will stand out as excessive.

Many Chinese academics welcome the notion of empirical desert as the basis for criminal law rules because they see it as a way to give deference to the traditional 'wisdom of the people' while avoiding the dangers that they see in the ad hoc public campaigns like those above—a view that seems to make good sense.

The practical value of following people's views of justice, described in Section 2, exists only if those views accurately reflect the judgements of the community upon thoughtful reflection. The point, recall, is to build the reputation of the criminal justice system as being an institution that the community can rely upon to do justice and avoid injustice. This means that there is danger in following the views of an unrepresentative minority of the community or in following views formed in passion and emotion that will later be seen as unjust after the heat of the moment passes. To build a reputation for being just, the criminal justice system must not simply do what it thinks is popular in the case at hand but must also aim to be proud of what it has done in all its past cases.

To summarise, community views ought to be influential in *setting the rules* for criminal liability and punishment but not in deciding individual cases. Once community views have been used to set the criminal law's rules, those rules ought to be applied the same to all offenders in all cases.

However, there are academics in China who have an important alternative view of the situation. They would support giving deference to community views in individual cases, even given its dangers. They argue that, given how corrupt and discredited the criminal justice system is, some-times the only way of getting justice or of avoiding injustice is to look to public campaigns that rally public support against the normal workings of the official system. Left to its own devices, they argue, the official criminal justice system commonly will look not to what is just but rather to what the political or otherwise well-connected powers find to be expedient. The public voice is the only available means of keeping those corrupting forces in check.

In one recent case, for example, a young man, Xu Ting, found that an ATM machine from which he withdrew a thousand yuan only reduced his bank balance by one yuan. He then took advantage of the malfunction and withdrew a total of 175 thousand yuan (US$27,750). He was convicted and sentenced to life in prison, but after a public outcry, his sentence was changed to five years in prison.[3] In another case, a local official, Deng Guida, and his deputy were drunk at the Dream Fantasy City bath centre. He demanded sex from a local worker who was washing clothes in a room. When she explained that she was not a sex worker, he became angry, chased her, and verbally and physically assaulted her. The victim finally stabbed him with a fruit knife to stop his aggression, killing him, and was charged with murder. The local authority tried to censor many of the details of the case because of its embarrassment over the official being very drunk in a place selling sex. When the facts did come out, the public was highly suspi-cious of the case and argued strongly that the victim acted in self-defence. While initially charged with murder, the woman was ultimately convicted of intentionally inflicting injury but exempt from punishment (Baoxin, 2009).

Clearly, there are special difficulties with a criminal justice system that, due to corruption or illicit political influence, will regularly do injustice and fail to do justice. At some point do the normal dangers of direct community influence in individual cases become the lesser of the two evils? One would hope that a society could find a way to move towards a more just system rather than having to suffer the dangers of ad hoc public influence in indi-vidual cases.

6. CONCLUSION

Community views of justice have an important role to play in assessing criminal liability and punishment. Normally, that important role is not in pressuring prosecutors or judges to influence the adjudication of an indi-vidual case. Rather, the community's views, as established through empiri-cal research, ought to be to set the basic criminal law rules for liability and punishment, and those rules ought to be applied the same to all defendants. A defendant should be judged by what he or she has done and with what culpability and capacity. The defendant's liability and punishment ought not to depend on his or her good or bad luck in avoiding or attracting publicity by newspapers, bloggers, or others.

If the criminal justice system can earn a reputation for trying to be just in all its cases, its greater moral credibility with the community will increase its power to gain deference, co-operation, and acquiescence, which will increase its crime-control effectiveness. That is, the best way of fighting crime is by being devoted to doing justice.

REFERENCES

Baoxin, C. 2009. 'The Characteristics of Current China Justice Practice Exposed by Deng Yujiao Case.' *Law and Society* 20: 96.

Bottoms, A. 1995. 'The Philosophy and Politics of Punishment and Sentencing.' In C. M. V. Clarkson and R. Morgan (eds.), *The Politics of Sentencing Reform*. New York: Oxford University Press.

Carlsmith, K. M., John M. Darley, and Paul H. Robinson. 2002. 'Why Do We Punish? Deterrence and Just Deserts as Motives for Punishment.' *Journal of Personality & Social Psychology* 83: 284–299.

Darley, J. M., K. M. Carlsmith, and P. H. Robinson. 2000. 'Incapacitation and Just Deserts as Motives for Punishment.' *Law and Human Behavior* 24: 659–683.

Durham, A. M., III. 1993. 'Public Opinion Regarding Sentences for Crime: Does it Exist?' *Journal of Criminal Justice* 1(2): 1–12.

Garland, D. 2001. 'The Culture of Control.' *Crime and Social Order in Contemporary Society*. Oxford: Oxford University Press.

Kaplow, L., and S. Shavell. 2001. 'Fairness Versus Welfare.' *Harvard Law Review* 114: 961–1388.

Kennedy, J. E. 2009. 'Empirical Desert and the Endpoints of Punishment.' In Paul H. Robinson, Stephen P. Garvey, and Kimberly Ferzan (eds.), *Criminal Law Conversations*. New York: Oxford University Press.

Luna, E. 2003. 'Punishment Theory, Holism, and the Procedural Conception of Restorative Justice.' *Utah Law Review* 2003: 205–301.

Robinson, P. H. 2008. *Distributive Principles of Criminal Law: Who Should Be Punished and How Much?* New York: Oxford University Press.

Robinson, P. H., G. P. Goodwin, and M. D. Reisig. 2010. 'The Disutility of Injustice.' *New York University Law Review* 85(6): 1940–2011.

Robinson, P. H. 2011. 'Criminalization Tensions: Empirical Desert, Changing Norms, and Rape Reform.' In Antony Duff, Lindsay Farmer, S. E. Marshall, Massimo Renzo, and Victor Tadros (eds.), *The Structure of Criminal Law*. Oxford: Oxford University Press.

Robinson, P. H., and J. M. Darley. 2007. 'Intuitions of Justice: Implications for Criminal Law and Justice Policy.' *Southern California Law Review* 81(1): 1–68.

Robinson, P. H., and R. Kurzban. 2007. 'Concordance and Conflict in Intuitions of Justice.' *Minnesota Law Review* 9(6): 1829–1907.

Zhiguang, W., and C. Guangyu. 2005. 'The Case in Which Ten-Years-Old Little Girl Killed by Lincoln Sedan Will Be Tried Today.' *East Asia Economic and Trade News*, 3 March.

Zhiguang, W., and C. Guangyu. 2005. 'The Offender Who Killed a Ten-Years-Old Little Girl by Lincoln Sedan Was Sentenced to Death, and Will Be Executed Today,' *East Asia Economic and Trade News*, 6 April.

NOTES

1. Model Penal Code §1.02 (Tentative Draft No. 1, 2007) (emphasis added):

    (2) The general purposes of the provisions governing sentencing and corrections, to be discharged by the many official actors within the sentencing and corrections system, are:

    (a) in decisions affecting the sentencing and correction of individual offenders:

    (i) to *render punishment within a range of severity proportionate to the gravity of offences, the harms done to crime victims, and the blameworthiness of offenders;*

    (ii) when possible with realistic prospect of success, to serve goals of offender rehabilitation, general deterrence, incapacitation of dangerous offenders, and restoration of crime victims and communities, *provided that these goals are pursued within the boundaries of sentence severity permitted in subsection (a)(i)*; and

    (iii) to render sentences no more severe than necessary to achieve the applicable purposes from subsections (a)(i) and (ii); . . .

2. For example, note that the factual error in representing Fu as a rich person or, in note 28 infra, the attempt of authorities to hide the location of the killing in the stabbing case.

3. The First Instance Written Judgment of Xuting Case, http://wenku.baidu.com/view/b155a9d484254b35eefd3464.html.2012-10-11; The Final Instance Written Judgment of Xuting Case, http://www.ycxy.com/cn/lw/2010/26247.html,2012-10-11.

4

Proportionality in Sentencing: The Need to Factor in Community Experience, Not Public Opinion

Mirko Bagaric

Sentencing is the sharp end of the criminal law; it is the process through which the state acts in its most coercive manner against individuals. The crimes underlying sentencing determinations often relate to the most extreme forms of human depravity; hence, they generate strong emotions in the community, including in those not directly affected by the events. It seems to be an ingrained aspect of the human condition that people are interested in events that relate to extreme forms of conduct. Individuals often are shocked, appalled, stunned, annoyed, or disappointed at criminal acts. Feelings of this nature translate into an 'interest' in many criminal proceedings. Thus, it is the innate nature of crime itself that attracts public interest in the sentencing. This engagement almost invariably invokes views and opinions about sentencing outcomes.

Given that crime nearly always invokes negative emotions, when the public express a shared opinion about a sentencing disposition, it is normally a call for a harsh sanction (e.g. Ryberg, 2010). In democracies, this often understandably leads to penalty escalation. While it might 'feel' right and cohere with the democratic ethos to allow public opinion to shape sentencing law and practice, there are possible normative obstacles or limits to the association between sentencing and community attitudes.

This chapter examines one such limit: the principle of proportionality. In its simplest, and arguably most persuasive, form it is the view that the punishment should equal the crime. The principle has received widespread endorsement by philosophers and lawyers. It acts as a restraint on excessive (and lenient) sanctions. Accordingly, it has the potential to dilute (and even negate) the role of public opinion in sentencing.

The capacity for proportionalism to override shared community sentiment is contingent on the principle being coherent and justifiable. Examining the content and the normative underpinning of the proportionality
principle is a key focus of this paper.

In the next part of the chapter, I provide an overview of the current role
of proportionality in sentencing. Section 2 examines the justification for
the principle. This is followed by a discussion of the content of the proportionalism. I suggest that in its current form it is too obscure to provide
meaningful guidance to sentencers; however, it is tenable to give content to
the principle if victim and offender 'well-being' are adopted as the criteria
for measuring both limbs and more empirical data are obtained regarding
the matters that influence human well-being.

I conclude that public opinion should have no role in proportionalism.
This is the conventional philosophical view. However, it would be premature for the discussion to end there. The reality is that there is often a dis-
connect between the considerations that do influence and those which
should influence government decision making. The difficult part of the
analysis is suggesting how governments can effectively remove public opinion from key sentencing considerations (such as proportionalism) without
damaging their reelection chances.

A possible solution is advanced in the last part of the paper. I argue that
while reflexive public views on sentencing should not be endorsed, shared
community experience regarding the impact of crime should inform the
proportionality thesis. Scientific data regarding the punitive impulses of
people and the circumstances in which they can be abated support the view
that this is a position that an informed public will accept.

1. THE CURRENT ROLE OF PROPORTIONALITY

Recognition of the Principle

The legal approach to proportionality has been set out in numerous legal
judgments and is typically stated with elegant simplicity. For example, the
High Court of Australia in *Hoare v R* stated: 'A basic principle of sentencing
law is that a sentence of imprisonment imposed by a court should never
exceed that which can be justified as appropriate or *proportionate to the gravity of the crime considered in light of its objective circumstances*' (emphasis
added).[1]

The key aspect of the principle is that it has two limbs. The first is the
seriousness of the crime; the second is the harshness of the sanction. Further, the principle has a quantitative component—the two limbs must be

matched. For the principle to be satisfied, the seriousness of the crime must be equal to the harshness of the penalty.

Proportionality is one of the main objectives of sentencing in many jurisdictions. The White Paper forming the basis of the Criminal Justice Act 1991 (United Kingdom) declared that the aim of the reforms was to introduce a 'legislative framework for sentencing, based on the seriousness of the offence and just deserts'.[2] In Finland, proportionality was adopted as the main sentencing determinant in 1976, and approximately a decade later in Sweden (Ryberg, 2004). It has a constitutional foundation in Germany (von Hirsch & Ashworth, 2005).

Proportionality is also a requirement of the sentencing regimes of ten states in the United States (Schneider, 2012). The precise considerations which inform the proportionality principle vary in those jurisdictions, but generally there are six relevant criteria:

1. whether the penalty shocks a reasonable sense of decency;
2. the gravity of the crime;
3. the prior criminal history of the offender;
4. the legislative objective relating to the sanction;
5. a comparison of the sanction imposed on the accused with the penalty that would be imposed in other jurisdictions; and
6. a comparison of the sanction with other penalties for similar and related offences in the same jurisdiction (Schneider, 2012).

It has also been argued that the cruel and unusual punishment clause in the US Constitution also prohibits disproportionate punishment (Stinefford, 2011).

In *Veen (No1) v R*[3] and *Veen (No 2) v R*[4] the High Court of Australia stated that proportionality is the primary aim of sentencing. It is considered so important that it cannot be trumped even by the goal of community protection, which at various times has also been declared as the most important aim of sentencing.

Departures from the Principle

It is not obvious to what extent the proportionality principle is trumped by other considerations. As discussed below, the key reason is that it is not clear what factors are included within the scope of the proportionality principle. In particular, the relevance of prior convictions to proportionality remains unsettled. However, departures from the proportionality principle are evident in circumstances where the legislature expresses a preference for sentencing objectives without regard to proportionalism and are clearer still where there is an express requirement to disregard proportionality in the imposition of a sentence.

The most obvious incursion into the proportionality principle stems from the increasing emphasis on community protection as an objective of sentencing. Imprisonment is the most effective means of preventing reoffending, and, in this context, community protection comes within the narrower aim of incapacitation (Bagaric & Alexander, 2012).

In the United Kingdom, incapacitation is one of the rationales most evident on the face of the Criminal Justice Act 2003. Most Australian jurisdictions expressly permit violation of the proportionality principle in relation to offenders who commit 'serious offences', even to the point of permitting indefinite jail terms where the court is satisfied that the offender is a serious danger to the community.[5] In the United States, while incapacitation is generally not expressly invoked as a discrete sentencing objective, it is nonetheless the primary rationale (Henham, 1997; Stolzenberg & D'Alessio,1997) underlying the increasingly harsh sentencing regimes that have resulted in a significant increase in the number of United States inmates (Zimring & Hawkins,1995). For the first three-quarters of the last century, the United States imprisoned about 110 persons per 100,000 of the adult population (Blumstein, 1998); the rate is now nearly 750 per 100,000 of the adult population (the highest in the world).[6] Thus, proportionality plays an important part in sentencing, but it is sometimes trumped by other sentencing considerations and, in particular, community protection.

2. THE JUSTIFICATION FOR PROPORTIONALITY

The justification for proportionalism appears to be more assumed than proven. The main focus of punishment theory which has been considered by philosophers is the justification for the practice. Less attention has been directed to the issue of how much to punish (Ryberg, 2004). However, the extent to which a person should be punished is itself an ethical question. Given the near universal agreement that offenders should be punished (but see Christie 1981; Maithesen 1990), the issue of how much offenders should be punished is arguably the more pragmatically relevant inquiry.

As discussed in Section 4, it emerges that the main elements of proportionalism are so indeterminate that they are incapable of providing meaningful guidance to sentencing courts. There are no established criteria by which the severity of an offence is evaluated. It is accepted that the pain suffered by the victim of the crime is an important consideration. However, there is no existing methodology for measuring victim suffering. Proportionalism is further clouded by the uncertainty regarding whether other variables, such as the offender's prior criminal history, should be incorporated into the principle. The uncertainty of the principle is also compounded by the fact that there is no common standard which can be used to match sanction hardship with offence gravity. If proportionalism is devoid of content, the central issue being considered by this paper loses significance. The next part of the paper focuses on injecting content into proportionalism.

3. MAIN THEORIES OF PUNISHMENT

To thoroughly explore the content of proportionalism, a logical starting point is the normative justification for the principle. While proportionality is an intuitively appealing concept, it is not sound to rely on self-evident appeal as a justification, especially given that the unchecked application of the principle can result in undesirable outcomes. Followed to its logical conclusion, proportionalism requires punishment even when no good would stem from it. Arguably, it is wrong to impose a harsher punishment if an offender could be reformed by a lesser sanction: 'retributive [i.e. proportionate] justice may be a very good thing, but the saving of souls is a much better thing' (Ewing, 1929, p. 18).

The principle of proportionality is not a stand-alone construct. It purports to define how much to punish but does not justify the practice of state-imposed punishment. The justification for the institutionalisation of criminal punishment must derive from an overarching theory, and proportionality is only itself justified if it comes with the framework of a theory of punishment. Moreover, proportionalism is only justified to the extent that the overarching punishment theory is valid.

It is not feasible in a paper this size to consider in detail the merits of the respective theories of punishment. However, it is important to note that the prevailing orthodoxy is that proportionalism is the defining aspect of many retributive theories. A unifying aspect of most retributive theories is the claim that punishment must be equivalent to the level of wrongdoing. Thus, proportionalism is an in-built definitional aspect of many retributive theories. This view, however, is not settled. Jesper Ryberg argues that on closer examination the leading retributive theories do not justify proportionalism. I have argued elsewhere that retributivism cannot justify proportionalism or, indeed, any other ideal because the retributive account of punishment is itself flawed, essentially because ultimately it relies for its coherence on consequentialist considerations (Bagaric, 2001). Even if retributive theories can support proportionalism, they cannot provide clarity regarding the criteria that are relevant to a measurement of its respective limbs.

To illustrate this, I now discuss two retributive theories: the one which most expressly encapsulates proportionalism and the theory often regarded as the most influential contemporary retributive theory.

LexTalionis and Proportionality

The retributive account that most clearly endorses the proportionality thesis is the *lextalionis* or the 'eye for an eye, a tooth for a tooth' approach to punishment. This theory, however, provides little guidance regarding the proper workings of proportionalism. The *lextalionis* has no clear application in relation to most offences: 'What penalty would you inflict on a rapist, a blackmailer, a forger, a dope peddler, a multiple murderer, a smuggler, or a toothless fiend who has knocked somebody else's teeth out?' (Kleinig, 1973, p. 120).

It has been suggested that a more plausible interpretation of the *lextalionis* is that the punishment and the crime should be equal or equivalent (Ten, 1987). While this expands its potential scope of application, the *lextalionis* is normally advanced as a stand-alone theory, devoid of a further rationale and, hence, is not capable of providing insight regarding the content of the proportionality limbs. What 'equivalent' pain can be inflicted on an impecunious and homeless burglar?

Nevertheless, as discussed below, the *lextalionis* does provide some direction regarding the development of proportionalism. For the theory to gain traction and content, it is desirable to commence with an evaluation of offence severity in relation to offences where there is an identifiable victim who suffers tangible harm and then move to other offence categories.

Censure and Proportionality

Perhaps the leading retributive theory is that advanced by Andrew von Hirsch. He contends that the principal justification of punishment is censure: that is, to convey blame or reprobation to those who have committed a wrongful act (von Hirsch, 1993). Von Hirsch (1993) believes that censuring holds offenders responsible and accountable for their actions and that, by giving them an opportunity to respond to their misdeeds through acknowledging their wrongdoing in some form, it recognises their moral agency.

For von Hirsch, punishment has a dual objective. The other justification is to prevent crime. He believes that human nature is such that the normative reason for compliance must be complemented with a prudential one, otherwise 'victimising conduct would become so prevalent as to make life nasty and brutish' (von Hirsch 1985, p. 48), and that 'it is the threatened penal deprivation that expresses the censure as well as serving as the prudential disincentive' (von Hirsch, 1994, p. 127). Although he believes that deterrence is not a sufficient reason for punishment, he claims it is a necessary one: 'If punishment has no usefulness in preventing crime, there should . . . not be a criminal sanction' (von Hirsch, 1985, p. 53).

Von Hirsch believes that the following three steps justify the proportionality principle within his theory of punishment:

1. The State's sanctions against proscribed conduct should take a punitive form; that is, visit deprivations in a manner that expresses censure or blame.
2. The severity of a sanction expresses the stringency of the blame.
3. Hence, punitive sanctions should be arrayed according to the degree of blameworthiness (i.e. seriousness) of the conduct (von Hirsch, 1985, p. 15).

Thus, according to von Hirsch, punishment has in fact two purposes: '(1) to *discourage* [criminal] conduct . . . and (2) to express disapproval of the [criminal] conduct and its perpetrators' (von Hirsch, 1985, p. 52; emphasis added).

If deterring criminals is a central plank of von Hirsch's theory, it may be necessary to impose sanctions that are significantly more severe than is required to match the blameworthiness of criminal conduct. Von Hirsch responds to this criticism by stating that prevention cannot be invoked in deciding how much to punish, because proportionality would then be undermined (von Hirsch, 1985, p. 16). However, this is unpersuasive because proportionality is not a justification for punishment, merely a restraint on it, derived from the rationale for punishment. Further, even if it is conceded that offence seriousness is gauged by the level of 'blameworthiness', it does not advance his justification for proportionality. Blameworthiness is a nebulous concept which has no fixed meaning and one which is incapable of accurate precision. Accordingly, it cannot shed meaningful light on offence severity. This is a point which seems to have been, at least tacitly, accepted by von Hirsch. As discussed below, in developing a hierarchy of offence severity he ultimately relies solely on consequentialist considerations.

I now discuss whether a utilitarian theory of punishment is capable of providing firmer guidance regarding the content of the proportionality limbs.

Proportionality and Utilitarianism

Proportionality has traditionally been thought to have no role in a utilitarian theory of punishment. Rather than focusing on retrospective considerations to do with the nature of an offence to determine how much to punish, utilitarians place emphasis on prospective matters, such as the need for deterrence and rehabilitation. Given this, criticisms of utilitarianism have been made to the effect that it justifies substantial punishment for minor offences, where this is necessary to reform or deter the offender (Armstrong, 1971).

However, proportionalism and the utilitarian theory of punishment are not necessarily incompatible. Jeremy Bentham (1970) argued in favour of the proportionality principle on the basis that if crimes are to be committed, it is preferable that offenders commit less serious rather than more serious ones. In his view, sanctions should be graduated commensurate with the seriousness of the offence so that those disposed to crime will opt for less serious offences. In the absence of proportionality, potential offenders would not be deterred from committing serious offences any more than minor ones and hence would just as readily commit them. This argument, however, has been persuasively criticised by von Hirsch, who points out that there is no evidence that offenders make comparisons regarding the level of punishment for various offences (1985, p. 32). Further, the weight of empirical evidence suggests that higher penalties do not result in less crime (Bagaric and Alexander, 2011).

However, there is yet another basis upon which proportionality may have a role in utilitarian punishment. It has been suggested that disproportionate sentences risk placing the criminal justice system into disrepute because such sentences would offend the principle that privileges and hardships ought to be distributed roughly in accordance with the degree of merit or blame attributable to each individual. Violations of this principle lead to antipathy towards institutions or practices which condone such outcomes. Harding and Ireland believe that 'proportion in punishment is a widely found and deeply-rooted principle in many penal contexts. It is . . . integral to many conceptions of justice and, as such, the principle of proportion in punishment generally acts to annul, rather than to exacerbate, social dysfunction' (1989, p. 205).

A similar point is made in the Canadian decision of *Reference re s 94(2) Motor Vehicle Act*[7] where the court stated that the principle of proportionality is important because 'only if this is so [i.e. the principle is satisfied] can the public be satisfied that the offender "deserved" the punishment he received and feel a confidence in the fairness and rationality of the system'.[8]

Accordingly, there is a utilitarian foundation for proportionalism *if* the proportionalist ideal is so inherently ingrained in the human psyche that nonobservance of the doctrine will disincline individuals from complying with legal norms. In theory, this argument is tenable. Empirically, it has not been substantiated. Anecdotal evidence exists in the fact the Scandinavian nations, which ostensibly place most weight on the proportionality principle, also have amongst the lowest crime rates in the world. However, it is notoriously difficult to identify conclusively the cause and effect systems in operation regarding societal practices. The main reason for this is the number of other variables that contribute to individual and collective behaviour (see e.g. Levitt, 2004). The reason for the lower crime rate in

Scandinavia could be unrelated to proportionalism and could, for example, relate to the wide social welfare net in those countries which reduces the incidence of poverty—which is known to increase criminal behaviour (Bagaric, 2011).

Nevertheless, at this point of human learning, enough has been said to suggest that proportionalism has a tenable foundation in the context of a utilitarian theory of punishment. This is important because, as discussed below, a consequentialist approach to proportionalism is the most promising way forward to provide clear and stable criteria that inform both proportionality limbs. Thus, it emerges that while proportionalism is, on face-value, an ingrained part of most retributive theories, such theories provide little guidance regarding the content of the proportionality limbs. Greater guidance emerges against a utilitarian backdrop of punishment, although the empirical validity of a proportionalist principle in this context remains to be proven.

4. FACTORS RELEVANT TO THE SERIOUSNESS OF THE OFFENCE

Agreement Does Not Provide a Justification for Offence Severity

As noted by Jesper Ryberg (2004), to give content to proportionalism it is necessary to rank crimes, rank punishments, and anchor the scales. However, one of the key criticisms of the theory is that it 'presupposes something which is not there, namely some objective measure of appropriateness between crime and punishment' (Ryberg, 2004, p. 185). The absence of stable and clear criteria for measuring offence severity is one of the main difficulties associated with the proportionality principle.

This is a challenge noted by numerous scholars. However, from the pragmatic perspective, this problem has not proved to be insurmountable. Legislatures routinely set maximum penalties for offences, which is a crude method for ranking offence seriousness. While the maximum penalty is not a defining criterion regarding the sanction in any particular case, even when it comes to precisely prescribing a predetermined sanction for an offence type, this has often been undertaken with little difficulty. This is an observation made by von Hirsch and Ashworth in relation to guideline penalty grids, which exist in some parts of the United States:

The rulemaking bodies that have tried to rank crimes in gravity have not run into insuperable practical difficulties, moreover. Several US state sentencing commissions (including those of Minnesota, Washington, and Oregon) were able to rank the seriousness of offences for use in their numerical guidelines. While the grading task proved time-consuming, it did not generate much dissension within these rule-making bodies (von Hirsch & Ashworth, 2005, p. 144).

The methodology used to set such penalties is not clearly set out. However, a crude measure that seems to give at least ball park figures is public opinion. To this end, von Hirsch and Ashworth state: 'How is crime-seriousness to be assessed? Ordinary people, various opinion surveys have suggested, seem capable of reaching a degree of agreement on the comparative seriousness of criminal offences' (2005, p. 143).

While, in practice, public opinion can and often does inform the offence severity limb of the proportionality principle,[9] this approach is doctrinally flawed.

Sentencing is a purposive social endeavour, and, accordingly, it should be guided by a process of inductive and deductive logic and analyses of empirical evidence to determine what objectives are and are not achievable through a system of state-imposed punishment. It is a complex subject matter with its own area of discrete knowledge and information. If it is driven by the whims of lay members of the community, it is almost certain that errors will occur.

Allowing public opinion to shape important aspects of sentencing (such as proportionalism) is no different from formulating medical protocols, hospital priority lists, environmental strategies, road and bridge construction techniques, and the starting age at which children should commence school. It is not in accordance with scientific knowledge but on the basis of what lay members of the community believe is appropriate. Decisions which effect human flourishing in other domains are made strategically on the basis of empirically validated information. Likewise, sentencing practices should be informed by the views of criminologists, penologists, sociologists, moral philosophers, and econometricians, whose collective wisdom should inform the public—not the other way around.

Ryberg observes:

> Even if it is correct that there is general agreement between people as to how the seriousness of different crimes should be rated, this does not of itself show that the rating should be morally accepted. This would require an independent argument. Moreover, it is generally agreed that there might be a divergence between popular judgements and what is morally well-grounded. The need for a theoretical enquiry clarifying what is morally relevant in the comparison of crimes is, therefore, generally acknowledged among proportionalists. (2004, p. 60)

Some theorists have contended that public opinion should have a cardinal sentencing role.[10] The satisfaction theory of retributivism provides that punishing wrongdoers satisfies 'the feeling of hatred—call it revenge, resentment, or what you will—which the contemplation of such conduct excites in healthy constituted minds' (Stephen, 1873, pp. 161–162) and thereby diminishes the prospect of harmful vendettas by victims and their associates, who may be tempted to exact their own revenge. On occasions it has received judicial support:

> One of the objects of punishment, and by no means the least important object of punishment, is to prevent, so far as possible, the victims of crime from taking matters into their own hands. It is no great step from private vengeance to vendetta, and there is no knowing where the vendetta will stop.[11]

However, at its highest, it merely justifies *some* punishment for offenders but says nothing about how much punishment is appropriate or necessary. Accordingly, it does not provide a foundation for public opinion to have a significant role in setting offence severity.

A closely associated view to the satisfaction theory is that public opinion must be factored into the sentencing regime; otherwise, a lack of confidence in the courts will result and, ultimately, less respect for and compliance with the law. Certainly, numerous surveys across a number of different jurisdictions, including Scotland, the United States, Germany, and England, have shown that most members of the community believe sentences are too lenient (Roberts, 2011). Despite this, there are no empirical data indicating that this has resulted in diminished legal compliance (Ryberg, 2010).[12]

A more sophisticated justification for incorporating public opinion into sentencing is that the seriousness of a crime is, at least to some degree, determined by the extent to which it 'offends community mores' (Roberts, 2011, p. 116). To this end, Roberts provides examples of flag burning and hate crime offences and concludes that the social nature of sentencing and the cultural relativity associated with crime severity provide a basis for public opinion to some degree informing offence severity (Ryberg, 2010).

It is clear that cultural considerations inform not only sentencing but also criminality. However, it is not desirable that this practice should continue. Criminal sanctions involve the direct infliction of pain on individuals and, hence, require a moral justification. This cannot be achieved through norms based on regional and transient customs. We should be aspiring to an objective value system which is not dependent on historical and cultural customs and rituals (for the capacity to achieve this, see Bagaric, 2005). Allowing community mores to inform crime and sentencing has the capacity to entrench and promulgate existing practices which by any measure are inhumane and even savage. It is for this reason that women accused of adultery are still executed by stoning in some parts of the world; homosexual sex is an imprisonable offence in many countries, and the death penalty remains a sanction in over seventy countries even for even nonheinous crimes such as drug trafficking.

Thus, public opinion does not seem to be relevant to proportionalism. This conclusion, however, can only firmly be established if the criteria that actually inform penalty and sanction severity can be identified—and to the exclusion of public opinion. It is to this that I now turn.

Living Standard Approach to Offence Seriousness: Promising But Flawed

One of the most comprehensive examinations of the factors relevant to proportionality has been undertaken in the context of the 'living standard' approach to proportionality. This was first advanced by Andrew von Hirsch and Nils Jareborg and refined more than a decade later by von Hirsch and Andrew Ashworth. Von Hirsch and Jareborg start with the assumption that the seriousness of a crime has two dimensions: *harm and culpability*. Harm refers to the injury done or risked by the act; culpability to the factors of intent, motive and circumstances that determine the extent to which the offender should be held accountable for the act (1991, p. 1; emphasis added).

In relation to the culpability component, von Hirsch and Jareborg import substantive criminal law doctrines of culpability such as intention, recklessness, and negligence and excuses such as provocation into the sentencing stage. But they contend that such an approach is not possible with respect to harm, where they claim that 'virtually no legal doctrines have been developed on how the gravity of harms can be compared' (von Hirsch & Jareborg, 1991, p. 3). Thus, the focus of their inquiry is giving content to the harm component.

Von Hirsch and Jareborg approach this task by considering the seriousness of an offence against a background of important human concerns, and confine their analysis to conduct that is (already) criminal and injures or threatens identifiable victims. Aggravating or mitigating considerations are not addressed due to the complexity that this would import. In a bid to gauge the level of harm caused by an offence, the starting point for von Hirsch and Jareborg is to use a broad-based 'living standard' criterion where the gravity of criminal harm is determined 'by the importance that the relevant interests have for a person's standard of living' (1991, p. 12). The living standard focuses on the means or capabilities for achieving a certain quality of life, rather than actual life quality or goal achievement, and is adapted from the criteria set out by Amartya Sen, which encompasses noneconomic and economic interests (von Hirsch & Ashworth, 2005, p. 144).

They formulate four living standard levels, which are used to determine the degree to which a particular crime affects a person's living standard.

The most important is subsistence, which equates to survival with no more than basic capacities to function and then follow minimal well-being and adequate well-being, which mean maintenance of a minimum and adequate level of comfort and dignity, respectively. Finally, there is enhanced well-being, which is defined as significant enhancement of quality of life. The most grievous harms are those which most drastically diminish one's standard of well-being. Thus, a crime which violates the first level (subsistence) is the most serious, whereas one which infringes only enhanced well-being is the least serious.

Next, they determine the type of interests which are violated or threatened by the paradigm instances of particular offences. They identify four basic types of interests. In descending order, they are physical integrity, material support and amenity (ranging from nutrition and shelter to various luxuries), freedom from humiliating or degrading treatment, and privacy and autonomy. Some interest dimensions such as physical integrity are applicable to all of the grades on the living-standard scale, depending on the level of intrusion, whereas other interests such as privacy and autonomy are confined to levels including and below minimum well-being. After the interest violated by the typical instance of a particular offence is ascertained, the effect on the living standard is then determined.

A deficiency with their ranking system is that despite conceding that their analysis is normative, since it is a theory on how harms ought to be rated (von Hirsch & Jareborg, 1991, p. 5), it is devoid of an underlying rationale or an empirical or scientific foundation—it is built on armchair speculation. Von Hirsch and Jareborg accept the need for a moral theory; however, they are content to rest their case on the basis that an 'articulated moral theory' underpinning the living standard is beyond the scope of their discussion (ibid., p. 15). They go on to state that they are 'not trying to develop an invariant harm-analysis but, instead, to derive ratings applicable *here,* given certain prevailing social practices and also certain *ethical traditions'* (ibid.; emphasis added). Some of the social practices they assume are spelled out, such as the social convention that home is important for a comfortable existence. However, the detail not provided is which 'ethical traditions' have been assumed.

Von Hirsch and Jareborg state that the living standard for gauging harm is used because 'it appears to fit the way one ordinarily judges harms' (1991, p. 11). Further, the 'living standard provides not a generalised ethical norm, but a *useful* standard which the law can use in gauging the harmfulness of criminal acts' (ibid., pp. 11–12; emphasis added). This, however, raises the questions: useful in what sense? And, how useful?

The selection and adoption of certain harms in preference to others can only be justified by reference to an underlying moral and social theory, which is informed by empirical data. To this end, an obvious candidate is utilitarianism, which offers a simple method for determining the types of interests that are relevant to harm seriousness: The reason that some interests are important and worthy of protection by the criminal law is because they are integral to the attainment of happiness. In fact, the approach adopted (and conclusions reached) by von Hirsch and Jareborg have much in common with a transparently utilitarian evaluation of harm analysis.

Studies Measuring the Variables Relevant to Happiness and Moving from 'Happiness' to 'Well-Being' as a Standard Measure

A more doctrinally consistent manner to gauge the seriousness of harm is to adopt a utilitarian primary rationale and then to prescribe weight to defined interests in accordance with empirical observations regarding their importance. The potential disadvantage of this approach is that the notion of happiness is inherently vague. However, over the past few decades there has been an increase in the number of studies conducted into human happiness and well-being. Happiness has become a scientific rather than a purely theoretical concept. The overriding pursuit of happiness is now increasingly a psychological truism rather than an obscure aspirational objective. There is now a dedicated international journal (the *Journal of Happiness Studies*) which is devoted to research in what makes people happy (or indeed unhappy). Over the last few years there has been a number of important works looking at what makes people happy and, in particular, looking at whether there is a positive or negative correlation between happiness and wealth creation.

While noting the diversity in the range of activities through which people choose to express themselves, the studies show that basically we are not that different after all. At the core, humans are wired pretty much the same. While some people prefer singing in a choir as opposed to boxing in a ring and others prefer repairing motor vehicles to writing poetry, we should not allow these superficial differences to divert us from the fact that we have the same basal needs and our well-being is promoted by the same type of things (Bagaric, 2006).

The studies indicate that we can now, with a growing degree of confidence, identify the things that make people happy. People have the same basic wants and needs. In a nutshell, the things that are conducive to happiness are fit and healthy bodies, realistic goals, self-esteem, optimism, an outgoing personality, a sense of control, close relationships, challenging work, and active leisure, punctuated by adequate rest and a faith that entails communal support, purpose, and acceptance. Myths about happiness include that it is bought by money and that religious faith suppresses happiness (Bagaric, 2006).

However, the relevant studies have not been conducted with a view to providing insight into calculations of offence seriousness or sanction severity. Nevertheless, a number of tentative conclusions can be made regarding the relevance of the studies to proportionalism.

First, property offences are probably overrated in terms of their seriousness. Wealth has little effect on personal happiness; hence, the criminal justice system should view these offences less seriously. The only occasions where property offences make a significant adverse impact on victims is where they result in the victim living in a state of poverty. Second, offences which imperil a person's sense of security or otherwise negatively affect a person's health and capacity to lead a free and autonomous life should be punished severely.

These implications are of limited value for informing the proportionality principle because, as noted above, they do not directly examine the effects of crime. Further, the studies are not conclusive regarding the criteria that are relevant to happiness.

However, the concept of developing an index of the variables that affect human prosperity is becoming increasingly mainstream. The indexes, however, generally use different nomenclature from that conventionally adopted by utilitarians. The key concept is normally defined as 'well-being' as opposed to 'happiness'. It is not clear whether this is a difference in substance. However, in principle, it is preferable because the notion of well-being appears, at least intuitively, to relate to enduring (as opposed to transient) traits and hence is likely to have wider appeal.

The concept of well-being is becoming so mainstream that in some contexts it is replacing or complementing conventional and widely accepted economic indicia for evaluating human progress and achievement. The Organisation for Economic Cooperation and Development has developed a 'Better Life Index', which attempts to set out and prioritise the matters that are most essential for human well-being. The index lists eleven criteria for measuring life quality that allows nations to develop their priorities and distinguishes between responses from men and women. It transpires that men and women have near identical priorities.[13] The order from most to least important is life satisfaction, health, education, work–life balance, environment, jobs, safety, housing, community, income, and civic engagement.[14]

Studies that Directly Measure the Impact of Crime

Even more relevant to an assessment of the severity of crime are studies that measure the impact of certain crime offence categories on victims. The best information available suggests that, typically, victims of violent and sexual crime suffer considerably and, in fact, more than is manifest from the obvious and direct effects of crime.

Rochelle Hanson, Genelle Sawyer, Angela Begle, and Grace Hubel (2010) reviewed the existing literature regarding the effects of violent and sexual crimes on key quality of life indices. The crimes examined included rape, sexual assault, aggravated assault, survivors of homicide (i.e. relatives of those killed), and intimate partner violence. The key quality of life indicia examined were role function (i.e. capacity to perform in the roles of parenting and intimate relationships and to function in the social and occupational domains), reported levels of life satisfaction, and, well-being and social–material conditions (i.e. physical and mental health conditions). The report demonstrated that many victims suffered considerably across a range of well-being indicia, well after the physical signs had passed. The report concluded:

> In sum, findings from the well-established literature on general trauma and the emerging research on crime victimization indicate significant functional impact on the quality of life for victims. However, more research is necessary to understand the mechanisms of these relationships and differences amongst types of crime victimization, gender, and racial/ethnic groups. (Hanson et al., 2010, pp. 191–192)

Findings showed that victims of violent crime and sexual crime in particular have:

- Difficulty in being involved in intimate relationship and far higher divorce rates;
- Diminished parenting skills (although this finding was not universal);
- Lower levels of success in the employment setting (especially in relation to victims who had been abused by their partners) and much higher levels of unemployment;
- Considerable impairment and dysfunction in social and leisure activities, with many victims retreating from conventional social supports; and
- High levels of direct medical costs associated with violent crime (over $US24,353 for an assault requiring hospitalisation).

A study published in 2006 (Dixon, ReedRogers, & Stone, 2006), focusing on victims in the United Kingdom, found that:

- Victims of violent crime were 2.6 times as likely as nonvictims to suffer from depression and 1.8 times as likely to exhibit hostile behaviour five years after the original offence; and,
- For 52 per cent of women who had been seriously sexually assaulted in their lives, their experience led to either depression or other emotional problems, and for one in twenty it led to attempted suicide (64,000 women living in England and Wales today have tried to kill themselves following a serious sexual assault).

The (Ir)relevance of Other Factors to Crime Severity

The ranking of crime is made complicated by the fact that, typically, it is thought to involve consideration of both the harm caused by the offence and the culpability of the offender and, according to some theorists, certain aggravating and mitigating considerations (and, in particular, the prior criminality of the offender; Ryberg, 2004). There is, however, no principled reason for infusing either of these considerations into an assessment of offence severity.

The variable-rich approach to offence severity is consistent with the manner in which courts have often interpreted the proportionality principle. However, it is flawed. There are several problems with allowing factors not directly related to the offence to have a role in evaluating offence seriousness.

First, it is contradictory to claim that the principle of proportionality means the punishment should be commensurate with the *objective* seriousness of *the offence* and then allow considerations external to the offence to have a role in determining how much punishment is appropriate. Once the inquiry extends to matters not even remotely connected with the crime, such as the offender's upbringing or previous convictions, the parameters of *the offence* have been exhausted.

Second, by importing other considerations (especially aggravating and mitigating factors) into proportionalism, much of the splendour of the principle of proportionality is dissipated. The principle then cannot be claimed as being indicative of anything: To ascertain how much to punish, the appealing idea of looking only at the objective seriousness of the offence is abandoned and the inquiry must move elsewhere—and, indeed, everywhere. Giving content to the principle of proportionality would become unworkable—as is currently the case. In each particular sentencing inquiry the principle would need to be flexible enough to accommodate not only the objective circumstances of the offence but also the mitigating circumstances. Given the uniqueness of each offender's personal circumstances and the vast number of variables which are supposedly relevant to such an inquiry[15] and the fact that mitigating factors often pull in a diametrically opposite direction to the objective factors relevant to the offence, any attempt to provide a workable principle of proportionality must fail. It is for this reason that von Hirsch and Jareborg, when elaborating on the matters that are relevant to gauging the seriousness of the offence, declined to consider aggravating and mitigating circumstances.

While von Hirsch and Jareborg believe that culpability has a role in the proportionality principle (1991, p. 60), the better position is that it stands outside the doctrine. Culpability is a broad concept and involves varying degrees of blameworthiness. The broadest demarcation normally focuses on whether the offence was committed intentionally, recklessly or, in some cases, negligently. However, within these categories are numerous subcategories. Hence, intentional offences which are planned are normally regarded as more blameworthy than those committed on the spur of the moment. Incorporating this range of considerations into the principle would considerably negate the capacity for measurability and is not doctrinally coherent because it relates to a subjective consideration of the offenders' mental state and does not relate to the harm experienced by the victim. A person who is crippled by a crime suffers no less depending on whether the act is negligent or intentional.

This is not to deny that culpability is relevant to sentencing. It is relevant to overall offence seriousness but not to the objective seriousness of the offence. Once the harm stemming from the offence is quantified, a premium can be added to incorporate different levels of offence blameworthiness. The culpability adjustment should not be too great given that, from the victim's perspective, pain is pain, and it is not clear that the motivation behind the act changes the intensity or duration of the pain. Similar considerations apply regarding the role that aggravating and mitigating factors have in the sentencing calculus. There may still be a role for circumstances which are not relevant to the objective seriousness of the offence in the determination of the appropriate penalty. However, the basis for their relevance must stem from other considerations which are thought to be integral to the sentencing calculus, such as rehabilitation and community protection.

The above analysis provides some guidance regarding measuring offence seriousness. Further clarity will emerge if the focus on graduating offences commences with offences that have identifiable victims. Once a degree of consensus is obtained in that context, assessments should then be made in relation to offences that have less identifiable and more remote forms of harm, such as drug and motor traffic offences.[16]

5. EVALUATING THE HARDSHIP OF SANCTIONS

While there has been some consideration of measuring crime severity, there has been less attention given to the other side of the proportionality equation: measuring punishment severity. Ryberg contends this is because of the underlying belief that the 'answer is pretty straightforward' (2004, p. 102)—with imprisonment being clearly the harshest disposition. As Ryberg notes, the answer would seem to rest on 'negative impact on the well-being of the offender' (ibid., pp. 102–103).Von Hirsch and Ashworth (2005) also believe that it is less complex to rank punishments because the appropriate reference point seems to be the degree of suffering or inconvenience caused to the offender.

Other criteria have been invoked, including community views about the hardship of a penalty. To this end, a number of opinion surveys have been undertaken. These are noted by Ashworth and von Hirsch, who have also highlighted the inadequacy of this approach.

A number of studies have attempted to measure sanction severity through opinion surveys. A selected group of respondents is shown a list of penalties of various sorts and asked to rate their severity on a numerical rating scale. The surveys tend to show a degree of consensus (see e.g. Sebba and Nathan, 1984). This research, however, generally does not attempt to elucidate what is meant by severity, to elicit respondents' reasons for their rankings, or to assess the plausibility of those reasons. It is necessary to consider what *should* be the basis of comparing penalties—that is, to develop a theory of severity. A possible account of severity would be that it depends upon how disagreeable the sanction is typically experienced as being. On this view, opinion surveys would be a useful way of assessing penalties, as they would reflect how unpleasant various penalties are perceived as being. Unpleasantness or discomfort is, ultimately, subjective: a matter of how deprivations typically are experienced. If penalty x is experienced as being more onerous than penalty y, that simply would make it so (using this approach, an issue might be whether the persons surveyed have actually experienced the penalties involved; this might call for a survey of punished offenders as a way of checking the findings of wider opinion surveys; von Hirsch & Ashworth, 2005).

Thus, while community attitudes are a tool that can be used to assess penalty severity, they are an inadequate measure because of the lack of practical knowledge of the survey participants. To this end, the relevant insight can only come from those who have experienced the relevant sanction.

The starting point is to evaluate the adverse impact of imprisonment, given that it is the harshest sanction and the one which probably has the least amount of diversity in its application. In all societies it minimally involves physical confinement. It is surprising how little research has been conducted into the extent to which this sanction actually sets back well-being.

The direct adverse impact of prison conditions has been well documented. And it has been known for several decades that the 'pains' of imprisonment extend far beyond the deprivation of liberty. Other negative consequences of imprisonment are:

- The deprivation of goods and services;
- The deprivation of heterosexual relationships;
- The deprivation of autonomy; and
- The deprivation of security (Sykes, 1958).

What is less well understood is how these deprivations affect the life trajectories of prisoners. The evidence available indicates that it has a considerable negative impact which transcends the actual term of imprisonment. Imprisonment seems to have an adverse effect on well-being measures after the conclusion of the sentence, even to the point of significantly reducing life expectancy.

A study (Spaulding et al., 2011) which examined the 15.5-year survival rate of 23,510 ex-prisoners in the US state of Georgia, found much higher mortality rates for ex-prisoners than for the rest of the population. There were 2,650 deaths in total, which was a 43 per cent higher mortality rate than normally expected (799 more ex-prisoners died than expected). The main causes for the increased mortality rates were homicide, transportation accidents, accidental poisoning (which included drug overdoses), and suicide.

The data, although only cursory, suggest that imprisonment is a more painful disposition than it appears at face value. It is even more complex to make an assessment of the severity of other sanctions such as probation, community work orders, and fines because of their variability. But at least, in theory, the problem is not insurmountable. The severity of sanctions would be evaluated by reference to their level of 'onerousness' (von Hirsch & Ashworth, 2005). Ryberg uses similar terminology in suggesting that the answer would seem to rest on 'negative impact on the well-being of the offender' (Ryberg, 2004, p. 103). This requires the same types of considerations as those involved in the assessment of the other limb of the proportionality thesis. This closely resembles the approach endorsed by Ashworth and von Hirsch in the following passage:

> A fine of how many days' earnings, for example, is 'worth', say, a day under home detention? Severity . . . is a matter of how much a sanction intrudes upon the interests a person typically needs to live a good life. Gauging comparative severity thus would involve assessing how much the various sanctions typically would intrude on persons' living standards, in the sense discussed. (2005, p. 156)

It has been suggested that one cannot grade the severity of penalties because painfulness is a subjective concept (Walker, 1991). A taxidriver who is deprived of his or her licence feels the pain more severely than a person who works from home. This is no doubt true, but the same applies regarding the harm caused by criminal offences. Pickpocketing US$5 from Bill Gates is hardly likely to cause him even the slightest angst, whereas stealing the last US$5 from a hungry, homeless person may have a devastating effect upon him or her. Despite the enormous difference in the impact of these offences, the law has no difficulty in making theft an offence, and it has not resiled from evaluating the general seriousness of such conduct. This is because in relation to any branch of law, generalisations must be made about the things that people value and the typical effect of certain behaviour on those interests.

6. MATCHING THE PUNISHMENT TO THE OFFENCE: WORST CRIMES TO THE WORST FORMS OF PUNISHMENTS

The final problem regarding proportionality is how to match the severity of the punishment with the seriousness of the offence. The relative brevity of this discussion is not a reflection of the importance or the level of controversy in this area. Rather, given the discussion above, the answer is straightforward. The type and degree of punishment imposed on offenders should cause them to have their well-being set back to an amount equal to that which the crime sets back the well-being of the victim.

The approach in Sections 4 and 5 of this article assesses both the hardship of punishment and the severity of crime from the perspective of the extent to which they set back typical human well-being. This enables a theoretical matching at least to be made. There are insufficient data currently to allow a precise ranking.

However, some tentative conclusions can be drawn. The above data indicate that the effects of being either a victim of a serious sexual or violent crime or an inmate of a prison may both have been underestimated. These experiences all seem to have profoundly negative effects on life trajectories, which continue well after the immediate event has ceased. On this crude measure they are matched in terms of the relative negative impacts; hence, imprisonment is an appropriate disposition for serious sexual and violent offences. Of course, this says nothing about the length of imprisonment that is appropriate for certain categories of sexual and violent offences. Yet, this crude empirically based technique is preferable to the randomness that currently exists in relation to offence and sanction matching.

This approach suggests that, as a general principle, imprisonment should be reserved for serious and violent offenders. This would constitute a profound change to prison demographics and result in a large reduction in prison numbers.[17]

7. CONCLUSION

Public opinion should not drive sentencing because sentencing is an important social institution, which has established objectives and normative dimensions. They are not established by consensus or emotion. They are determined by empirical and normative inquiry.

The principle of proportionalism is the bedrock against which appropriate sanctions are determined. However, in its current form it is incapable of providing concrete guidance to sentencing courts and legislatures because both of its limbs are devoid of content. This can be remedied if human well-being is invoked as the common variable by which offence severity and sanction severity can be matched. This provides at least a theoretical basis for matching the limbs. The theoretical alignment can only be transformed into a practical reality if more research is undertaken into the extent to which human well-being is set back by typical criminal offences and common sanctions.

Public opinion has no direct role in shoring up the principle of proportionality. However, this conceptually sound view should not be a basis for lawmakers to ignore community views about sentencing. This could be counterproductive, by leading to louder calls for harsher sentences and, hence, an inevitable shift to harsher sentences through the democratic process.

The public interest in sentencing should be acknowledged not by taking on their opinions regarding appropriate sanctions but by exploring their experiences about the effects of crime and allowing them to inform the offence severity side of the proportionality principle. Promulgation to the community that this is occurring will provide a sure sign to the community it is being heeded in relation to sentencing matters and, hence, dilute reflex calls for tougher sentences.

This approach is tenable. As a species, it is true that humans actually enjoy punishing wrongdoers. A study published in *Science* shows that the part of the brain associated with enjoyment (the dorsal striatum) is activated when we impose a penalty on a wrongdoer, even where there are no benefits stemming from the punishment (Dominique de Quevain et al., 2004).

However, the study also revealed that we are not slaves to our dorsal striatum. The study showed that another part of the brain, the prefrontal cortex, is activated when subjects need to weigh the satisfaction derived from punishment against the cost of punishing. The results show that if we are informed that the price of punishment is too high, our brain 'kicks in' to save us from our unrestrained emotion.

This means the community will be attracted to the prospect of lowering prison numbers if it views an unremitting tough-on-crime policy as being self-defeating, in that it inhibits expansion of important services such as health and education. Reducing prison numbers will be even more palatable if the community is guaranteed that under the reformed sentencing system, all serious offenders will go to jail. Thus, ignoring public opinion in relation to proportionalism is not only doctrinally necessary but politically achievable as long as governments make clear to the community that the fiscal savings and wider social benefits that arise from less money being spent on crime can equate to more revenue being devoted to goals such as health and education.

REFERENCES

Armstrong, K. G. 1971. 'The Retributivist Hits Back.' In S. E. Grupp (ed.), *Theories of Punishment*. Bloomington: Indiana University Press.

Bagaric, M. 2001. *Punishment and Sentencing: A Rational Approach*. Cavendish: London.

Bagaric, M. 2005. 'Scientific Proof that Humans Enjoy Punishing Wrongdoers: The Implications for Punishment and Sentencing.' *International Journal of Punishment and Sentencing* 1: 98–110.

Bagaric, M. 2006. *How to Live: Being Happy and Dealing with Moral Dilemmas*. University Press of America: Maryland. i

Bagaric, M., and T. Alexander. 'The Fallacy that Is Incapacitation: An Argument for Limiting Imprisonment Only to Sex and Violent Offenders.' *Journal of Commonwealth Criminal Law* 2012: 95–124.

Bagaric, M., and Alexander T. 2011. '(Marginal) General Deterrence Doesn't Work – and What It Means for Sentencing.' *Criminal Law Journal* 234: 69.

Bentham, J. 1970. *An Introduction to the Principles of Morals and Legislation*. Edited by J. Burns and H. L. A. Hart. London: Athlone.

Bianchi, H. 1981. 'Abolition: Assenus and Sanctuary'. In H. Bianchi and R. Van Swaaningen (eds.), *Abolitionism: Towards a Non-Regressive Approach to Crime* (Amsterdam) 113.

Blumstein, A. 1998. 'U.S. Criminal Justice Conundrum: Rising Prison Populations and Stable Crime Rates.' *Crime and Delinquency* 44: 127–135.

Britt, C. L. 2001. 'Health Consequences of Criminal Victimization.' *International Review of Victimology* 8: 63–73.

Christie, N. 1981. *Limits of Pain*. London: Martin Robertson.

Dominique de Quevain, J. F., U. Fischbacher, V. Treyer, et al. 2004. 'The Neural Basis of Altruistic Punishment.' *Science* 305: 1254–1258.

Dixon, M., H. Reed, B. Rogers, and L. Stone. 2006. *The Unequal Impact of Crime*. London: Institute for Public Policy Research.

Ewing, A. C. 1929. *The Morality of Punishment and Some Suggestions for a General Theory of Ethics*. London: Paul, Trench, and Trubner.

Fletcher, G. 1993. *Loyalty: An Essay on the Morality of Relationships*. New York : Oxford University Press.

Hanson, R., G. Sawyer, A. Begle, and G. Hubel. 2010. 'The Impact of Crime Victimization on Quality of Life'. *Journal of Trauma Stress* 23: 189–197.

Harding, C., and R. W. Ireland. 1989. *Punishment: Rule, Rhetoric and Practice*. London: Routledge.

Henham, R. 1997. 'Anglo-American Approaches to Cumulative Sentencing and Implications for UK Sentencing Policy.' *Howard Law Journal* 44: 263–283.

Kleinig, J. 1973. *Punishment and Desert*. The Hague: Martinus Nijhoff.

Levitt, S. 2004. 'Understanding Why Crime Fell in the1990s: Four Factors that Explain the Decline and Six that Do Not.' *Journal of Economic Perspectives* 18: 163–190.

Roberts, J. V. 2011. 'The Future of State Punishment: The Role of Public Opinion in Sentencing.' In M. Tonry (ed.), *Retributivism Has a Past: Has It a Future?* Oxford: Oxford University Press.

Ryberg, J. 2004. *The Ethics of Proportionate Punishment.* Dordrecht, The Netherlands: Kluwer Academic.

Ryberg, J. 2010. 'Punishment and Public Opinion.' In J. Ryberg and A. Corlett (eds.), *Punishment and Ethics: New Perspectives.* New York: Palgrave Macmillan.

Schneider, G. S. 2012. 'Sentencing Proportionality in the States.' *Arizona Law Review* 54: 241–275.

Sebba, L., and Nathan, G. 1984, 'Further Explorations in the Scaling of Penalties.' *British Journal of Criminology* 24: 221.

Spaulding, A. C., R. M., Seals, V. A. McCallum, S. D. Perez, A. K. Brzozowski, and N. K. Steenland. 2011. 'Prisoner Survival Inside and Outside of the Institution: Implications for Health-Care Planning.' *American Journal of Epidemiology* 173: 479–487.

Stephen, J. F. 1873. *Liberty, Equality, Fraternity.* London: Smith and Elder.

Stinefford, F. F. 2011. 'Rethinking Proportionality under the Cruel and Unusual Punishments Clause.' *Virginia Law Review* 97: 899–978.

Stolzenberg, L., and S. J. D'Alessio. 1997. 'Three Strikes and You're Out: The Impact of California's New Mandatory Sentencing Law on Serious Crime Rates.' *Crime and Delinquency* 43: 457–469.

Sykes, G. 1958. 'The Pain of Imprisonment.' In *The Society of Captives: A Study of a Maximum Security Prison.* By G. Sykes. Princeton, NJ: Princeton University Press.

Ten, C. L. 1987. *Crime, Guilt and Punishment.* Oxford: Clarendon.

von Hirsch, A. *Past or Future Crimes: Deservedness and Dangerousness in the Sentencing of Criminals.* New Brunswick, NJ: Rutgers University Press, 1985.

von Hirsch, A. 1993. *Censure and Sanctions.* Oxford: Clarendon.

von Hirsch, A. 1994. 'Censure and Proportionality.' In R. A. Duff and D. Garland (eds.), *A Reader on Punishment.* Oxford: Oxford University Press.

von Hirsch, A., and A. Ashworth. 2005. *Proportionate Sentencing: Exploring the Principles.* Oxford: Oxford University Press.

von Hirsch, A., and N. Jareborg. 1991. 'Gauging Criminal Harm: A Living-Standard Analysis.' *Oxford Journal of Legal Studies* 11: 1–38.

Walker, N. 1991. *Why Punish?* Oxford: Oxford University Press.

Zimring, F. E., and G. Hawkins. 1995. *Incapacitation: Penal Confinement and the Restraint of Crime.* New York: Oxford University Press.

NOTES

1. (1989) 167 CLR 348, 354.
2. Great Britain, Home Office, 1990. White Paper, *Crime, Justice and Protecting the Public.* London.
3. (1979) 143 CLR 458, 467.
4. (1988) 164 CLR 465, 472.
5. See, for example, the *Dangerous Prisoners (Sexual Offenders) Act 2003* (Qld); *Crimes (Sentences) Act 1999* (SA), s 23; *Sentencing Act 1991* (Vic), s 18B(1). *Penalties and*

Sentences Act 1992 (Qld) s 163; *Sentencing Act* (NT) s 65; *Criminal Law (Sentencing) Act 1988* (SA) s 23; *Sentencing Act 1997* (Tas) s 19; *Sentencing Act 1995* (WA) s 98.

6. This reflects a near doubling in the past 20 years; see Bureau of Justice Statistics, *Correctional Population* <http://bjs.ojp.usdoj.gov/content/glance/tables/corr2tab.cfm> accessed 1 May 2012.

7. (1985), 23 CCC (3d) 289.

8. Ibid., p. 325.

9. Courts sometimes factor community sentiment into an assessment of offence severity. For example, see *WCB v R* [2010] VSCA 230; *Stalio v The Queen* [2012] VSCA 120, at [72].

10. See, for example, the contribution of Chris Bennet (this volume), 'Public Opinion and Democratic Control of Sentencing Policy', who argues that juries should determine sentences if a retributive theory of punishment is endorsed.

11. See *Darby* (1986) 8 Cr App R (S) 487, 490.

12. But see the contribution of Paul H. Robinson (this volume), 'The Proper Role of the Community in Determining Criminal Liability and Punishment', who notes that studies have shown when a legal system deliberately implements rules that cause injustice, subjects are less likely to defer to and comply with the law. As noted by Jan W. de Keijser (this volume) in, 'Penal Theory and Popular Opinion: The Deficiencies of Direct Engagement', however, the punitiveness (or lack of it) of a sentence is not a characteristic that undermines the legitimacy of the legal system.

13. Although women rank income less highly and health more highly than men.

14. http://www.oecdbetterlifeindex.org/wpsystem/wp-content/uploads/2012/06/WMA.jpg. These measures are designed to be more informative than economic statistics, especially in the form of gross domestic product: http://www.oecdbetterlifeindex.org.

15. The principle would need to be very extensive to include all of the three hundred or so factors that the courts have recognised as being relevant sentencing considerations (Bagaric, 2001).

16. Fletcher notes the lesser evident role of proportionality in relation to such offences: 'Just punishment requires a sense of proportion, which in turn requires sensitivity to the injury inflicted. . . . The more the victim suffers, the more pain should be inflicted on the criminal. In the context of betrayal, the gears of this basic principle of justice, the lextalionis, fail to engage the problem. The theory of punishment does not mesh with the crime when there is no tangible harm, no friction against the physical welfare of the victim' (1993, p. 43). However, more accurately, it is not that proportionality has no role in relation to such offences, rather, in such cases it must focus on generalising the harm involved in that *type* of behaviour and is hence more difficult to apply.

17. This is not the case. For example, in Australia in 2010, only 50 per cent of people in prison were there for committing a serious violent offence (defined as homicide, a sexual offence, or robbery). In another 16 per cent of cases, the most serious offence was a property offence. In the remaining 34 per cent of cases, imprisonment was the result of some other offence type (defined as either fraud offences, justice offences, offences against government, driving offences, or drug offences). See the Australian Institute of Criminology: http://www.aic.gov.au/en/publications/current%20series/facts/1-20/2011/6_corrections.aspx.

5

Penal Theory and Popular Opinion: The Deficiencies of Direct Engagement[1]

Jan W. de Keijser

With reference to notions of public confidence and legitimacy, it is an attractive idea and common intuition that there should be a role of significance for public opinion at sentencing (cf. Roberts, 2008). More generally, as Robinson and Darley note: 'When a criminal law offends the moral intuitions of the governed community, the power of the entire criminal code to gain compliance from the community is risked' (1997, p. 485). The exploitation of this intuition by populist politicians has been well documented over the past two decades, resulting in ever increasing punitive policies (cf. Bottoms, 1995; Pratt, 2007; Roberts, Stalans, Indermaur, & Hough, 2003). Apart from this political exploitation, the fundamental question is whether public views can be fit within a coherent penal theory. After all, the function of penal theory is to place any relevant variable within a coherent and logical framework of justifications and goals. If penal theory does not succeed in connecting public views to punishment within such a coherent framework, this casts doubts on the common intuition about the connection between public views and sentencing.

But there is more to this than a mere exercise in penal theory. As Roberts (2011) has argued, the realms of penal theory and empirical research should be connected more closely. Indeed, we cannot discuss popular opinion within a theoretical framework without connecting to empirical evidence of public views. Moreover, if public opinion is to have an established place within penal theory, the more existential question: 'What form of public opinion?' or rather 'Opinion of what public?' cannot be ignored. These are not primarily theoretical deliberations; they are empirical questions that need to be addressed to have a meaningful theoretical debate on the issue. Answers to these questions inevitably refer to discussions of research approaches and methodologies. The answers may also lead, I will argue, to empirically based doubts about the necessity and desirability of directly incorporating public opinion in penal theory and practice. Moreover, some of the matters that I will address indicate that pursuing the goal of explicit integration of public views in penal theory and subsequent sentencing practice may be self-defeating. Especially from the perspective of promoting criminal justice legitimacy, public opinion may well prove to be a wolf in sheep's clothing. I will return to this shortly.

From the idea that sentencing practice and popular opinion should not drift too far apart, the well-documented gap between public opinion about levels of sentencing and actual sentencing practices in Western jurisdictions has drawn a lot of attention from academics and politicians alike. Ryberg (2010) identifies two strategies to reduce this gap and its supposed detrimental effects on the legitimacy of criminal justice. The first involves adjusting sentencing to public opinion (generally the preferred option by populist politicians), whereas the second involves aligning public opinion with current levels of sentencing (Ryberg, 2010, p. 158). But this two-track scheme gets more complicated when we ask the question: *What public opinion?* Answers to this question will be the main concern of my contribution to this volume.

There is a well-documented *information effect* on public attitudes towards sentencing and more specifically on punitiveness. Survey methodologies that allow for more information and more time to deliberate generally lead to more nuanced and less punitive public opinion than traditional survey techniques using global questions and nondeliberative responses. To uncover the 'true nature of public opinion'(as Roberts [2001, p. 106] describes it), more refined techniques, such as deliberative polling would be called for (cf. Green, 2006; Hutton, 2005; Park & Hough, 2002). Today, in the criminological literature, the preferred position appears to be that public views should only be given serious attention if they are the views of a public that has been given sufficient information and opportunity to deliberate (Green, 2006; Roberts, 2011; Stalans, 2002).

As a result of the frequently demonstrated and indisputable information effect on public opinion about sentencing, the argument for an exclusive focus on informed and deliberated public opinion appears to be a strong one. However, in discussing the question whether there is a principled role for public opinion in penal theory, a fixation on this 'true public opinion' may have consequences that are detrimental to such a principled role. Labelling the informed and deliberated opinion of a sample of the public as the true nature of public opinion which should (or could) be given a principled role is in fact dismissive of general public opinion which is global, uninformed and 'top of the head'. Uninformed and 'top of the head' opinion is real and is, perhaps, from a principled perspective the only true public opinion.

The arguments advanced below will show that regardless of the theoretical perspective, dismissing the general public and focusing on the true nature of public opinion from an informed sample leads to fundamental problems for which a principled solution is far from obvious. In what follows I first discuss the main theoretical perspectives on a principled role for public opinion and then elaborate on the information effect and subsequently dwell on the connected question 'What public opinion?' or rather 'What public?' The argument will then be advanced that in discussions of a principled role for public views in penal theory and practice, replacing the views of the general public with attitudes measured from a well-informed and deliberated sample will be self-defeating. I will argue this both for a desert-related perspective on proportionality and for the instrumental argument focusing on legitimacy and compliance.

It should be borne in mind that this essay examines the deficiencies of connecting penal policy and practice to public opinion from the idea of a direct importation model. This direct importation model assumes an immediate link between public views and practice and thereby best exposes any critical questions. This direct importation model may be considered a caricature as most of the prevailing models or ideas about the link between penal practice and community views can be characterised as indirect or limiting models. In such models public views are taken as starting points, or as one amongst many other factors that may be considered at some stage in deliberations of sentencing policy. Moreover, in indirect or limiting models the public views that are considered may not even be grounded in explicit measurement of public opinion. Nevertheless, I argue that with a direct importation model in mind the issues exposed bear relevance to any model that considers the connection between public views and penal policy and theory, albeit in a more diluted manner.

I will make frequent reference to empirical research findings drawing on my own research in the Netherlands, recognising that this contextual or cultural focus may well be a limitation for the external validity of my statements.[2]

1. PUBLIC OPINION IN PENAL THEORY

Most principled arguments for public opinion are, or turn out to be, consequentialist. Strict deontological arguments for considering public views are rare. Most directly, the utilitarian argument is that without considering public views, the criminal justice system becomes disconnected from society and loses its moral credibility. This will undermine public confidence in the system and reduce the system's ability to elicit compliance (cf. Tyler,

1990). From this perspective the engagement between public opinion and penal theory and practice is imperative.

Roberts (2011) discusses three justificatory models for considering public views. The first model involves the straightforward instrumental issue that legitimacy of sentencing will be lost if it is disconnected from public views. In this consequentialist perspective, citizens' compliance with the law will decline. The second model, closely related to the first, addresses effective censuring. If the system of punishments is devised to express censure, the moral disapprobative message communicated through punishment is not effectively communicated if it does not reflect community sentiments. In other words, if censure expressed by punishment does not reflect community disapprobation of the crimes that are punished, the message cannot effectively get across and social norms will not be reaffirmed. This is detrimental for the (individual and general) preventive function of punishment. The third model argues that the penal value of crimes has an inherent element of social consensus (Roberts, 2011, p. 110). While the first two approaches are essentially consequentialist, the third one is not. In this third model public opinion may be considered a tool for answering proportionality questions in desert-based rationales for punishment.

Desert-based approaches to the role of public views are predominantly focused on the issue of proportionality. It will suffice here to touch upon the case for ordinal proportionality. The argument for referring to public opinion is that the seriousness ranking of crimes that underlies sentencing decisions should reflect public notions of seriousness and severity. But why should it? Not necessarily for instrumental reasons as Roberts argues, but simply for the reason that 'community views constitute an inherent element of crime seriousness' (2011, p. 114). In other words, crime seriousness is to a certain and fundamental degree defined by a public element. There is indeed nothing utilitarian about this line of reasoning. Public views in this desert model are relevant for just distribution of punishment.

Robinson (2006; also see Robinson & Darley, 1997) argues that desert-based accounts should eventually draw upon the consequentialist notion of moral credibility and its benefits for the functioning (compliance and obedience) of the criminal justice system. 'Criminal laws based on community standards of deserved punishment enhance this obedience' (Robinson & Darley, 1997, p. 498). As a result, Robinson and Darley argue, through the linkage with shared community intuitions, both retributivists and consequentialists will agree on the distribution of punishment. In their just deserts model the essence of what constitutes a just desert is not based on deontological arguments, nor on underlying moral principles, but on community views on blameworthiness (ibid.).

2. PUBLIC OPINION, INFORMATION, AND DELIBERATION:
THE INFORMATION EFFECT

Research has demonstrated the limitations of a global survey measurement of public opinion. The punitive public opinion resulting from surveys is said to be an artefact of the methodology applied (Hough & Roberts, 1999; Hutton, 2005) because public views are particularly sensitive to questioning technique, information, and context (cf. Green, 2006; Hutton, 2005; Roberts & Hough, 2005; Roberts et al., 2003; Stalans, 2002). The research methodology, the information provided to respondents and the opportunity for deliberation all determine the measurement outcome. Providing people with concrete cases results in less punitive responses than global survey questions (Cullen, Fisher, & Applegate, 2000; Hutton, 2005; Kuhn, 2002). Moreover, focus groups and deliberative polling techniques in particular have produced public views that conform to actual sentences by judges (Green, 2006; Hutton, 2005; Roberts et al., 2003).

In a Dutch study (De Keijser, Van Koppen, & Elffers, 2007), I demonstrated a direct effect of information on peoples' punitive attitudes where a controlled (i.e. experimentally manipulated) increase in detailed case and offender information produced more lenient sentences by the public for specific cases. Nevertheless, the effect was insufficient to bridge the gap with real judges who had been handed the same cases. Taking the provision of information and opportunity to deliberate a step further, Wagenaar (2008) demonstrated a completely vanishing gap between judges and the public in another recent Dutch study. Before making sentencing decisions, his participants first studied complete case files, attended the real court hearings, and deliberated amongst each other. The study, albeit on a small and predominantly qualitative scale, found no difference in sentencing preference between the informed and deliberated panels of laypersons and actual judges' sentencing decisions. These Dutch studies and research in other jurisdictions have demonstrated that within the framework of concrete cases, and provided with specific information, members of the general public prefer sentences that approximate sentencing by real judges (for reviews, see also Roberts et al., 2003; Roberts & Stalans, 1997).

However, with such research approaches, the concept of 'public opinion' or 'community views' is stretched well beyond what may be considered representative of the general public. It has, in fact become something else, that is, what the public *would* think if it only had the relevant information and opportunity to consider the issues at hand. It is referred to as a hypothetical public (Green, 2006). It is, thus, crystal clear that the views of a well-informed sample and the opinion of the ill-informed general public are two very different things. Figure 5.1 further visualises this. In the top left corner of the

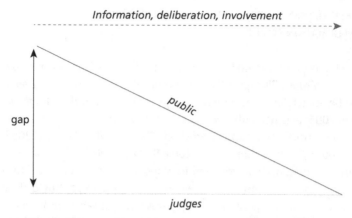

Figure 5.1. The Vanishing Punitiveness Gap between Judges and the Public

figure we find the general and ill-informed public whose punitive views are remote from judges' sentencing. This gap gets smaller with the provision of more information, opportunity for deliberation and (some degree) of involvement in the judicial process. At the bottom right corner of Figure 5.1, we find the hypothetical public that is highly informed, involved, and had ample opportunity to deliberate. The views of this hypothetical public are equal to judges' views: the gap is gone. But the gap is only gone for a tiny and highly specific sample of the public that has been transformed more or less into judges, whereas the uniformed public is still out there and remains real, massive and tangible.

Deliberative polling on a large and repetitive scale is impractical (Hough & Park, 2002). Moreover, and apart from the question what or who exactly such samples represent, there is the question whether the changes as a result of deliberation and information are durable and reliable (Chapman, Mirrlees-Black, & Brawn, 2002; Indermaur, Roberts, Spiranovic, Mackenzie, & Gelb, 2012; Mirrlees-Black, 2002). Due to a number of methodological shortcomings, findings from studies that address the durability of attitude change are inconclusive (Indermaur et al., 2012). For instance, while Hough and Park (2002) reported durable attitude change as a result of a British deliberative poll, their study did not make use of a control group, nor could they rule out a substantive effect of participants merely being engaged in such a venture.

Focusing specifically on the question of durability, and remedying methodological shortcomings of earlier studies, Indermaur et al. (2012) recently executed a carefully designed experiment with members of the Australian public. While they observed immediate changes in respondents as a result of being involved in such a study, there were no differences between intervention group and control group. Moreover, the observed attitude changes disappeared within the follow up period of nine months. This is an important finding: public attitudes have a tendency to revert back to their original position. This is in line with the idea that punitive public attitudes are not simply something instrumental. Rather, symbolic motivations underlie such positions. These are symbolic orientations that reflect people's broader moral and social values (Tyler & Boeckmann, 1997).

To sum up, deliberative polling techniques measure attitudes of a hypothetical public, a nonexistent public. These deliberated views are not representative for the views of the ill-informed general public; moreover, they are the views of a tiny transformed sample of the public which are temporary and which revert to general public opinion after some time has passed. We must now realise that any findings from more informed and deliberated samples are generalisable only to a hypothetical population of similar samples whose views have only a limited life span.

3. CONNECTING TO INFORMED PUBLIC OPINION MUST BE SELF-DEFEATING

Opinion of a Hypothetical Public Cannot Serve the Acclaimed Purpose

The exclusive focus on the views of an informed sample of the public (cf. Roberts, 2011) is extremely important when considering the viability of public opinion as a principled factor in penal theory. Connecting to general uninformed public views is considered inappropriate by most. The uninformed public makes mistakes, is volatile, and does not take into account all relevant facts and aspects. Therefore, in current writings of penal theory, reference to public opinion entails reference to either deliberated opinion of a well-informed sample of the public (cf. Roberts, 2008, 2011) or to the presupposition of a fully informed public on the relevant aspects (cf. Roberts, 2011; Ryberg, 2010).

The fact is that public views are not fully informed and informing the populace at large is not feasible (Ryberg, 2010). So from a realistic point of view, the well-informed *sample* of the public is all that remains. And herein lies the fundamental problem with consequentialist rationales for incorporating public views in penal theory and sentencing practice. They must be self-defeating because the legitimacy argument refers to the *general* public or to common moral intuitions, while the views of the informed sample are certainly not representative of the prevailing moral intuitions of the governed community. Hough and Park already pointed to a similar criticism that has been uttered against the political usage of deliberative polling results: 'Deliberative polls are irrelevant as politicians need to take account of the reality of public opinion as it emerges from "snapshot" public opinion polls, in which the respondent has neither sufficient information nor the opportunity to reflect on the issue' (2002, p. 166). Moreover, while Roberts justifiably argues that findings from a simple question posed to a representative sample of the public are not representative of an informed public, the fact remains that an informed public does not exist or is, at best, a temporal glitch created by social scientists (2011, p. 106).

How then can penal policy based on the temporary views of an unrepresentative sample of the public command legitimacy and compliance of the general public? It cannot. Moreover, the argument that this is what the general public would believe if they only had the opportunity to be informed and had the time to deliberate will not likely come across as a very convincing nor sympathetic argument towards the general public. Such penal policy, albeit connected to the temporary views of a small and well-informed sample, is certainly not connected to general public views. Therefore, and apart from any questions about cost effectiveness (which I will touch upon below), the consequentialist compliance argument for a principled role for informed public opinion cannot stand its ground.

But what about the proportionality argument, namely that seriousness rankings of crimes have an inherent element of public disapprobation of those behaviours? Using *uninformed* public opinion as a basis for determining ordinal proportionality, the argument goes, may very well result in distorted and even unjust rankings. Reference to informed public opinion is supposed to solve that problem (cf. Roberts, 2011, 116). But the idea that community views are inherent to crime seriousness is not served, rather harmed, by focusing on the views of a select informed sample of the public. The inherent element of crime seriousness is then that of a hypothetical public, not of the real public. As a result deliberated seriousness rankings by a well-informed public sample may become much disconnected from and even conflict with those of the uninformed wider public. Dismissing or ignoring the wider public risks rendering proportionate sentencing *unjust* in the public eye. Obviously this harms the criminal justice system's ability to promote legitimacy and compliance.

In summary, while there are some attractive rationales for taking public opinion into account, the choice for restricting public opinion to the deliberated views of a well-informed sample is detrimental from a consequentialist point of view. If only the deliberated views are included of a well-informed sample, the consequentialist rationale cannot serve its instrumental goal because this particular sample of the public is not the public that lives under the law. Furthermore, proportionate sentences based on informed public opinion may be considered just from a metaphysical point of view but may very well be considered unjust and in violation of ordinal proportionality intuitions that are commonly shared by the general public.

Robinson and Darley (1997) discuss an alternative approach. They robustly advocate connecting criminal justice to public views. However, they appear to escape the pitfall of putting an exclusive focus on the opinion of an informed sample of the public. Rather, within the framework of code drafting, they stick to shared moral intuitions as a *starting point* for specialists such as lawyers, criminal law experts, and social scientists (Robinson & Darley, 1997, p. 488). 'We stress the importance of the moral intuitions of the community as a valued beginning for code drafting done in public with an eye to educating and involving the public' (ibid., p. 489). However, while Robinson and Darley escape the pitfall, it is questionable if their model gives public opinion a truly principled role in penal theory.

In his chapter in this volume, Robinson nevertheless takes a much more robust approach to the connection to public opinion. Arguing against the validity of community views contained in newspapers or other media, he states that true community notions of justice (i.e. empirical desert) can be measured by social scientists. Criminal law is to be connected closely to these community notions of desert. The lack of such a close connection would imply a loss in effectiveness. Responding to critics who claim that ordinal rankings of crimes according to blameworthiness can only be accomplished in vaguest terms, Robinson argues that this claim is empirically false. Using the right social scientific techniques, subjects display much nuance, sophistication, and complexity in blameworthiness judgments. Poor testing methods, however, will underestimate the extent of public agreement on issues of crime and punishment. Still, the core question remains: what exactly are the right measurement approaches, and of what particular public the opinion is actually measured? As such my objections to direct engagement between public views and penal policy are immediately relevant for Robinson's empirical desert.

Let's Give the Public What It Really Wants

The legitimacy argument is attractive for seeking a connection between public opinion and the practice of sentencing. It presupposes that dissatisfied public opinion is detrimental to the legitimacy of the system. It also presupposes that these detrimental effects are of such magnitude that we must resolve the problem. As discussed above we need to know how ill connected from public views current practice is and what public we want to connect to. Many studies in Western jurisdictions have shown that more information (and more deliberation) reduces the gap between judges and the public. But this is a very specific gap that we tend to discuss against the backdrop of legitimacy questions. However, even if there is a considerable punitiveness gap, we need not immediately fear for the legitimacy of the courts. Is punitiveness or, rather, a close connection between sentencing levels preferred by the general public and sentences delivered by the courts that high on the public's wish list?

I agree with Bagaric and Edney (2004) who argue that such a legitimacy claim tends to be overstated. Some research findings from Dutch studies are in place here. As in so many other countries general uninformed public opinion in the Netherlands is that sentences are too lenient. Typically, more than 75 per cent of the Dutch agree with a statement of such content (cf. Dekker, Den Ridder, & Schnabel, 2012; Sociaal en Culureel Planbureau, 2002, 2005; De Keijser & Elffers, 2009a). This finding has remained quite stable over the past decades. However during the same time, public confidence in the courts has also remained quite stable around 60 per cent expressing confidence (Dekker & van der Meer, 2007). Also overall evaluations of the courts have remained consistent and mostly positive (De Keijser et al., 2007; Elffers, de Keijser, Van Koppen& Van Haeringen, 2007). Again, in recently collected data (May 2012) amongst a sample of 714 Dutch train passengers, I observed that overall satisfaction with judges was seven on a ten-point scale.[3]

The implications are clear: The courts' lack of punitiveness, as perceived by the general public, is not detrimental to the legitimacy of the system. One straightforward explanation for this would be that punitiveness is not a highly valued priority for the public when considering the work of the courts. If punitiveness is not considered that important, the legitimacy argument is much less potent than at first glance.

An important question in this context is what constitutes a good judge in the eyes of the general public. Elffers and De Keijser (2007) had members of the public rank order ten typical traits that a criminal judge may be supposed to have. Results showed that punitiveness was ranked on average as ninth in the list of ten. Only 3 per cent of respondents ranked punitiveness as the most important characteristic. In contrast, the three most favoured characteristics by the public were: *just, impartial,* and *independent.* Moreover, in response to other topics in the same questionnaire, 71 per cent of that sample also indicated that judges should focus on characteristics of the case itself, rather than on public opinion. Based on these and other statistics, we concluded that the Dutch general public appears to have no difficulty in accepting the fact that a punitiveness gap exists (see also De Keijser & Elffers, 2009b). One of the methodological objections may be that we asked respondents to rank order *given* characteristics, amongst which some very fundamental ones, which were indeed top ranked.

To further examine this, in the May 2012 sample referred to above, we established an experimental manipulation by a (random) split half of the sample. One half received a closed question with the given list of character-istics to rank order. The other half was handed an open ended question simply requesting participants to name three characteristics that a good judge must have and to rank order these. The version with the given list yielded 32 per cent ranking *impartial* as most important; 19 per cent, *independent*; 21 per cent, *just*; 10 per cent, *careful*; and only 1 per cent, *punitive*. As a result of the open-ended question (with no given characteristics), the good judge must have the following characteristics: *impartial*, 15 per cent; *independent*, 12 per cent; *objective*, 16 per cent; *just*, 11 per cent; and *honest*, 10 per cent. Punitive was *not* mentioned spontaneously by our sample as an important characteristic for a judge.

Three things are striking about these findings. First, as already stressed, public dissatisfaction with levels of sentencing is not necessarily a threat to the legitimacy of the courts. Not even in the longer run (decades). Second, punitiveness is not a characteristic that comes to mind when the public contemplate the attributes of a good judge. Moreover, if it is preferred at all, it is only by negligible minority of the public. Third, the most favoured char-acteristics by our Dutch uninformed public are far removed from, if not in contrast to, being responsive to public opinion. Rather, the public mostly wants their professional judges to be independent, impartial, and just.

To summarise, despite the existence of a punitiveness gap, the Dutch public does not appear to crave for punitive judges, nor for judges with a keen eye for public views. The effect of a punitiveness gap on declining confidence, legitimacy, and compliance may therefore be expected to be quite limited. This is especially interesting with respect to the utilitarian rationale for considering public views. Obviously, if the benefits of resolving the mismatch between public opinion and sentencing practice are not that large, the costs of such a resolution must be quite restricted. As Ryberg (2010) points out, the costs of resolving the mismatch between popular opinion and sentencing practice through an increase in punitiveness are likely to be large. It will be a great challenge to show that these costs are outweighed by the benefits. Ryberg's argument gains further strength in the Dutch context as these benefits can be expected to quite be limited to begin with. It is also likely that similar public preferences can be observed in other jurisdictions.

4. INFORMED PUBLIC OPINION ON A LEASH: THE ACHILLES HEEL

Let's suppose that there is a way out of the difficulties discussed above. If, still arguing with a direct importation model in mind, there is a principled place for informed public opinion in penal theory and as a result in sentencing practice, it is worth exploring some potential consequences. First, suppose that well-informed and deliberated public judgment remains highly punitive or is even strengthened in its initial punitiveness (cf. Rowan, 2012). Then what should be done? From the point of view of legitimation of state punishment and its subsequent ability to gain compliance, the obvious answer to this question should be to follow-up on those public views and adapt the penal system accordingly. The only escape from that would be to build in thresholds or clearly defined limits for when and how the role of public judgment is to be curtailed. This implies devising specific rules for the conditions when to ignore public opinion, or when to stop following-up on it because its consequence would be immoral or undesirable.[4]

But any explicit determination of such thresholds or rules negates the whole exercise that we began with. After all, who will define these rules, how and on what grounds or principles? Or to connect it more directly to the issue at hand, what role is there for (informed) public views in establishing this particular set of exclusionary rules? If the answer to this question is that there is *no role for public views*, it remains unclear why there should be a *principled* role for public opinion in sentencing at all. Thus, sooner or later, proponents of engaging penal theory with public opinion categorically dismiss not only *uninformed* public opinion, but *informed* public opinion as well. For instance, Roberts argues that the threat to principled sentencing posed by short-term waves of public emotion can be contained by placing limits on the use of research into public views (2011, p. 110). But who determines these limits, on what grounds, and would such determinations be devoid of public considerations? We now either categorically dismiss public opinion or start over with the exercise because we are back at square one.

Perhaps the above is a caricature. After all, as of yet, there is evidence supporting the idea that public views become less punitive with more information and with more deliberation (as has been illustrated earlier in this chapter). Nevertheless, this does not preclude the occurrence of circumstances or places where this well-documented pattern is arrested or even reversed. The issue is certainly not unimaginable. For instance, in the earlier mentioned study on attitude change as a result of the British 1994 deliberative poll on crime, it was demonstrated that a minority of respondents *hardened* their attitudes as a result of information and deliberation (Hough & Park, 2002).

Public Opinion on the Standard of Evidence

That the issue is not entirely theoretical can be further illustrated by taking one step away from the topic of sentencing severity and punitiveness. There is also a public opinion on the related matter of the standard of evidence that judges maintain for deciding on the issue of guilt. This is directly tied to the volume of people who become available for punishment through criminal procedure. And, as an aspect of punitiveness it is directly connected to people's willingness to dismiss or abandon procedural protections that are designed to safeguard the rights of suspects (Tyler & Boeckmann, 1997). In all Western jurisdictions the strong sentiment is that before convicting an accused, the judge or jury should be convinced of guilt 'beyond reasonable doubt'. Well known expressions of this fundamental principle are variations of the so called Blackstone ratio, that is, 'it is better to acquit ten guilty persons than to convict a single innocent person'.[5] The principle cannot be quantified for deciding upon guilt in individual criminal cases. Such individual decisions remain to be based on a subjective conviction, which is commonly labelled *beyond a reasonable doubt*, or, in continental Europe, the French phrase *conviction intime* is frequently used. Nevertheless, we can deliberate whether judges should maintain higher or lower standards of proof depending on the type of criminal case to be decided upon. This topic is in fact highly salient in public opinion as evidenced by widespread indignation and media attention both to publicised cases of wrongful convictions and to acquittals of persons accused of serious cases for lack of evidence.

Peter van Koppen and I tested the so-called conviction paradox (De Keijser & Van Koppen, 2007) with a large sample of professional judges in Dutch criminal courts. Using an experimental design with detailed and realistic case files, we examined whether judges are inclined to lower their standard of proof if the allegation is a very serious one as opposed to a less serious case containing the same type and amount of evidence. After all, the consequences for society of a false negative decision of guilt may be much larger for very serious cases than for less serious cases.

The judiciary has always maintained that the decision criterion for the issue of guilt is and should be a static one. Indeed, the experiment confirmed that judges maintain a static decision criterion for guilt, independent of the seriousness of the criminal case and possible consequences of wrong decisions. But is this in line with public views on the matter? In a recent study (De Keijser, De Lange, & Van Wilsem, 2014) we provided a sample of over five hundred members of the Dutch public with brief descriptions of a shoplifting case, a residential burglary case, and a case of rape. Respondents were asked to determine for each case the number of guilty persons that they were willing to acquit to protect one innocent person from being wrongfully convicted.

Findings showed a clear and strong effect of the seriousness of the case: with increasing seriousness, the public unequivocally lowered their standard of proof. People are more willing to convict in serious cases as compared to

less serious cases. In our experiment we had added an experimental information factor: balanced or single sided information about the consequences
of false positive and false negative decisions of guilt for society and for the
accused. It turned out that presence and type of information offered to the
public had no effect on their preference for a dynamic standard of proof.

Contrary to the well-documented research on punitiveness, this study on
determination of guilt showed no information effect at all on public views.
Now, if this lack of information effect were to be replicated using a more deliberative methodology, what should the implications be for the standard of proof
maintained by judges? Should it become dynamic depending on the case at
hand? If so, this would undermine some fundamental principles upon which
our criminal justice system is founded and would render criminal justice illegitimate, paradoxically so also in the eyes of the general public as wrongful
convictions will become (much) more frequent. Consultation of informed
public views on judicial decisions of guilt thus produces the same fundamental problems, which again lead to dismissal of (informed) public opinion.

5. CONCLUSION

I have argued that an informed sample of the public does not represent
'real' public opinion. Moreover, there is evidence that the views of such a
transformed sample of the public are only temporary views that tend to
revert to mainstream ill-informed opinion. Penal policy directly tailored to
a hypothetical public, that is, to the deliberative opinion of an informed
sample, will necessarily be remote from prevailing public opinion. In fact,
it may even be more mismatched with general public opinion than it is
without the connection to views of such an informed sample. As a result
legitimacy will not be promoted, rather harmed.

Gauging informed public disapprobation of various types of misconduct
to promote the proportional expression of censure suffers from a similar
pitfall. Such proportionality is informed by a nonexistent public and may
well result in distribution of punishment that is experienced by the general
public as disproportionate and unjust. The inherent *public* element in crime
seriousness may not be the informed public element.

Proponents of a link between informed public opinion and penal policy
recognise the risk of unjust and unprincipled outcomes. The connection to
informed opinion must therefore be curtailed. However, if public opinion
is to be given a principled role in penal theory and sentencing practice, the
rules and thresholds for such curtailment need to be specified on principled
grounds. If this is done without public input at that stage, the principled
argument for connecting to public opinion is invalidated.

POPULAR PUNISHMENT: ON THE NORMATIVE SIGNIFICANCE
OF PUBLIC OPINION; ED. BY JESPER RYBERG.

Cloth   262 P.

NEW YORK: OXFORD UNIVERSITY PRESS, 2014
SER: STUDIES IN PENAL THEORY AND PHILOSOPHY.

ED: ROSKILDE U. COLL. OF NEW ESSAYS ON HOW MUCH
PUBLIC OPINION SHOULD INFLUENCE SENTENCING, ETC.
LCCN 2013038974
  ISBN 0199941378   **Library PO#** FIRM ORDERS

		List	55.00	USD
8395 NATIONAL UNIVERSITY LIBRAR	**Disc**	14.0%	
App. Date 12/17/14 SOPS 8214-08	**Net**	47.30	USD

SUBJ: 1. PUNISHMENT--PUBLIC OPINION. 2. CRIMINAL
LIABILITY--PUBLIC OPINION.

CLASS K5101   DEWEY# 364.6   LEVEL ADV-AC

YBP Library Services

POPULAR PUNISHMENT: ON THE NORMATIVE SIGNIFICANCE
OF PUBLIC OPINION; ED. BY JESPER RYBERG.

Cloth   262 P.

NEW YORK: OXFORD UNIVERSITY PRESS, 2014
SER: STUDIES IN PENAL THEORY AND PHILOSOPHY.

ED: ROSKILDE U. COLL. OF NEW ESSAYS ON HOW MUCH
PUBLIC OPINION SHOULD INFLUENCE SENTENCING, ETC.
LCCN 2013038974
  ISBN 0199941378   **Library PO#** FIRM ORDERS

		List	55.00	USD
8395 NATIONAL UNIVERSITY LIBRAR	**Disc**	14.0%	
App. Date 12/17/14 SOPS 8214-08	**Net**	47.30	USD

SUBJ: 1. PUNISHMENT--PUBLIC OPINION. 2. CRIMINAL
LIABILITY--PUBLIC OPINION.

CLASS K5101   DEWEY# 364.6   LEVEL ADV-AC

I have also argued that a mismatch between public opinion and sentencing practice does not necessarily affect legitimacy in a substantive way. In fact, other and more fundamental issues are valued more by the general public. The alleged costs of a gap between uninformed public opinion and sentencing are not as significant as those proclaiming the legitimacy argument would have us believe.

I have argued that giving public opinion a direct and principled role in penal theory and practice of sentencing is self-defeating. Moreover, dismissing uninformed public views by referring to findings from more deliberative techniques could be considered offensive to the general public. It boils down to a simple message that is conveyed to the larger public: 'We are not following-up on your opinion and feelings because they constitute general and uninformed sentiments. If you were completely informed and would have had the capacity and opportunity to develop deliberated views, you would think differently'. And this is taken a step further when informed public opinion turns out to be undesirable from yet some other external perspective (such as morality or expert views). In such instances it is to be curtailed, even if it concerns issues of heated public debate. Connecting to public opinion then appears to be desirable and admissible only if that public opinion conforms to the opinion of elite expert groups.

Against the backdrop of a direct importation model, there is no sound, principled reason for connecting sentencing policy and practice to popular opinion. Criminal justice should be left to the experts, to the criminal justice policy elite, and to professional judges. While at first glance this point of view may appear elitist, in fact this is what the general public desires, at least in the Netherlands. Bagaric and Edney, who take an exclusionary stance towards public opinion, state that sentencing matters should be left to the experts; public opinion should be ignored (2004, p. 129). Their argument is a meritocratic one. Bagaric and Edney exclude public opinion because they argue that the public is ill-equipped to deal with intricate sentencing principles. They do not, however, address the possibility of connecting to an informed sample of the public, nor do they seem to recognise the argument that the expression of censure through sentencing carries with it an inherent element of public disapprobation (cf. Roberts, 2008).

If we relax the direct importation model, more indirect or diffuse connections between informed public opinion and penal theory and practice come to mind, some of which are discussed in detail by other contributors to this volume. Nevertheless, the issues that I have discussed above are relevant, albeit in a more diluted way, for any connection between penal practice and popular views, specifically when these views are the product of measurement. For instance, in his exposé on empirical desert, Paul Robinson (this volume) states that shared community values that result from empirical research should play an important role in assessing criminal liability and punishment. The question remains if such study results represent truly shared community views or rather the shared views of a selected few who were exposed to sophisticated measurement methods.

There remains of course one very straightforward connection between sentencing and public opinion—one unprincipled in terms of penal theory. In a representative democracy judges apply laws and impose sentence within a system that is subject to change as a result of the constitutional democratic process. These dynamics can hardly be qualified as being disconnected from or devoid of a collective nature. Moreover, in a Western democracy such as the Netherlands there is an implicit link between community views and the judiciary because judges, much more so than a few decades ago, see themselves as members of the larger community, rather than as decision makers completely insulated from society. As such judges see it as their task to be, to a certain extent, responsive to the community which they are a part of (De Keijser, Elffers, & Van de Bunt, 2008). Instead of direct importation of measured public opinion, this may be considered to be within the realm of indirect or rather diffuse importation of community views in the judiciary.

REFERENCES

Bagaric, M., and Edney, R. 2004. 'The Sentencing Advisory Commission and the Hope of Smarter Sentencing.' *Current Issues in Criminal Justice* 16(2): 125–139.

Bottoms, A. E. 1995. 'The Philosophy and Politics of Punishment and Sentencing.' In C. M. V. Clarkson and R. Morgan (eds.), *The Politics of Sentencing Reform.* Oxford: Clarendon, 17–50.

Chapman, B., C. Mirrlees-Black, and C. Brawn. 2002. *Home Office Research Study 245: Improving Public Attitudes to the Criminal Justice System. The Impact of Information.* London: Research Development and Statistics Directorate.

Cullen, F. T., B. S. Fisher, and B. K. Applegate. 2000. 'Public Opinion about Punishment and Corrections.' *Crime and Justice: A Review of Research* 27: 1–79.

De Keijser, J. W., E. De Lange, and J. A. Van Wilsem. 2014. Wrongful convictions and the Blackstone ratio: An empirical analysis of public attitudes. *Punishment & Society* 16: 32–49.

De Keijser, J. W., and H. Elffers. 2009a. 'Cross Jurisdictional Differences in Punitive Public Attitudes?' *European Journal on Criminal Policy and Research* 6: 47–62.

De Keijser, J. W., and H. Elffers. 2009b. 'Public Punitive Attitudes: A Threat to the Legitimacy of the Criminal Justice System?' In M. E. Oswald, S. Bieneck, and J. Hupfeld (eds.), *Social Psychology of Punishment of Crime.* Chichester, UK: Wiley.

De Keijser, J. W., H. Elffers, and H. G. van de Bunt. 2008. Responsive but Misunderstood: Dutch Judges on their Relation to Society. In H. Kury (ed.), *Fear of Crime—Punitivity: New Developments in Theory and Research.* Bochum, Germany: Universitätsverlag Brockmeyer, 471–488.

De Keijser, J. W., and P. J. Van Koppen. 2007. 'Paradoxes of Proof and Punishment: Psychological Pitfalls in Judicial Decision Making.' *Legal and Criminological Psychology* 12: 189–2005.

De Keijser, J. W., P. J. Van Koppen, and H. Elffers. 2007. 'Bridging the Gap between Judges and the Public? A Multi-Method Study.' *Journal of Experimental Criminology* 3(2): 131–161.

Dekker, P., J. Den Ridder, and P. Schnabel. 2012. *Burgerperspectieven* 2012-1. Den Haag, The Netherlands: Sociaal en Cultureel Planbureau.

Dekker, P., and T. V. D. Meer. 2007. *Vertrouwen in de rechtspraak nader onderzocht.* Den Haag, The Netherlands: Sociaal en Cultureel Planbureau.

Elffers, H., and J. W. De Keijser. 2007. 'Different Perspectives, Different Gaps: Does the General Public demand a More Responsive Judge. In H. Kury (ed.), *Fear of Crime—Punitivity: New Developments in Theory and Research.* Bochum, Germany: Universitätsverlag Brockmeyer, 447–470.

Elffers, H., J. W. De Keijser, P. J. Van Koppen, and V. Haeringen. 2007. 'Newspaper Juries: A Field Experiment Concerning the Effect of Information on Attitudes towards the Criminal Justice System.' *Journal of Experimental Criminology* 3(2): 163–182.

Green, D. A. 2006. 'Public Opinion Versus Public Judgment about Crime: Correcting the "Comedy of Errors."' *British Journal of Criminology* 46: 131–154.

Hough, M., and A. Park. 2002. 'How Malleable Are Attitudes to Crime and Punishment? Findings from a British Deliberative Poll.' In J.V. Roberts and M. Hough (eds.). *Changing Attitudes to Punishment: Public Opinion, Crime and Justice.* Cullompton, UK: Willan, 163–183.

Hough, M., and J. V. Roberts. 1999. 'Sentencing Trends in Britain.' *Punishment and Society* 1(1): 11–26.

Hutton, N. 2005. 'Beyond Populist Punitiveness.' *Punishment & Society* 7(3): 243–258.

Indermaur, D., L. Roberts, C. Spiranovic, G. Mackenzie, and K. Gelb. 2012. 'A Matter of Judgment: The Effect of Information and Deliberation on Public Attitudes to Punishment.' *Punishment & Society* 14(2): 147–165.

Kuhn, A. 2002. 'Public and Judicial Attitudes to Punishment in Switzerland.' In J. V. Roberts and M. Hough (eds.), Changing Attitudes to Punishment: Public Opinion, Crime and Justice. Cullompton, UK: Willan, 115–127.

Mirrlees-Black, C. 2002. Improving Public Knowledge about Crime and Punishment. In J. V. Roberts and M. Hough (eds.), *Changing Attitudes to punishment: Public Opinion, Crime and Justice.* Cullompton, UK: Willan, 184–197.

Park, A., and M. Hough. 2002. *Public Attitudes towards Crime and Punishment.* London: National Centre for Social Research.

Pratt, J. 2007. *Penal Populism.* London: Taylor and Francis.

Roberts, J. V. 2008. 'Sentencing Policy and Practices: The Evolving Role of Public Opinion.' In A. Freiberg and K. Gelb (eds.). *Penal Populism, Sentencing Councils and Sentencing Policy.* Cullompton, UK: Willan, 15–30.

Roberts, J. V. 2008. *Punishing Persistent Offenders.* Oxford: Oxford University Press.

Roberts, J. V. 2011. 'The Future of State Punishment: The Role of Public Opinion in Sentencing.' In M. Tonry (ed.), *Retributivism Has a Past. Has It a Future?* Oxford: Oxford University Press, 101–129.

Roberts, J. V., and M. Hough. 2005. *Understanding Public Attitudes to Criminal Justice.* Berkshire, UK: Open University Press.

Roberts, J. V., and L. J. Stalans. 1997. *Public Opinion, Crime and Criminal Justice.* Boulder, CO: Westview.

Roberts, J. V., L. J. Stalans, D. Indermaur, and M. Hough. 2003. *Penal Populism and Public Opinion: Lessons from Five Countries.* New York: Oxford University Press.

Robinson, P. H. 2006. 'How Psychology Is Changing the Punishment Theory Debate.' In Belinda Brooks-Gordon and Michael Freeman (eds.), *Law and Psychology: Current Legal Issues 2006.* Oxford: Oxford University Press, 94–104.

Robinson, P. H., and J. M. Darley. 1997. 'The Utility of Desert.' *Northwestern University Law Review* 91(2): 453–499.

Rowan, M. 2012. 'Democracy and Punishment: A Radical View.' *Theoretical Criminology* 16(1): 43–62.

Ryberg, J. 2010. 'Punishment and Public Opinion.' In J. Ryberg and J.A. Corlett (eds.), *Punishment and Ethics: New Perspectives.* New York: Palgrave Macmillan, 149–168.

Sociaal en Cultureel Planbureau. 2002. *Sociaal en cultureel rapport 2002: De kwaliteit van de quartaire sector.* Den Haag, The Netherlands: Sociaal en Cultureel Planbureau.

Sociaal en Cultureel Planbureau. 2005. *De sociale staat van Nederland 2005.* Den Haag, The Netherlands: Sociaal en Cultureel Planbureau.

Stalans, L. J. 2002. 'Measuring Attitudes to Sentencing.' In J.V. Roberts and M. Hough (eds.), *Changing Attitudes to Punishment: Public Opinion, Crime and Justice.* Cullompton, UK: Willan, 15–32.

Tyler, T. R. 1990. *Why People Obey the Law.* New Haven, CT: Yale University Press.

Tyler, T. R., and R. J. Boeckmann. 1997. Three Strikes and You're Out, But Why? The Psychology of Public Support for Punishing Rule Breakers. *Law & Society Review* 31(2): 237–265.

Volokh, A. 1997. 'N Guilty Men.' *University of Pennsylvania Law Review* 146(1): 173–211.

Wagenaar, W. A. 2008. *Strafrechtelijke oordelen van rechters en leken. Bewijsbeslissingen, straffen en hun argumentatie.* Research memorandum 4/2. Den Haag, The Netherlands: Raad voor de rechtspraak.

NOTES

1. I am grateful to Julian Roberts, Jesper Ryberg, and Thomas Søbirk Petersen for their comments and suggestions on an earlier version of this chapter. I am also grateful to all participants at the Copenhagen meeting in October 2012 for their views during the discussion of this manuscript.
2. However, with my colleague Elffers (De Keijser & Elffers, 2009a) I have shown that many differences in empirical research findings between the Netherlands and other jurisdictions are the result of variations in research methodology. Nevertheless, some findings do appear typically Dutch because they persisted even after replicating research approaches in studies outside the Netherlands.
3. Previously unpublished data. I collected these data with students at Leiden University. I am grateful to Esmee Geisink, Kristel Jansen, Sam Pauwels, Vivianne Poortinga, Bauke van der Sande, and Lianne de Vries.
4. Rowan, in a critical discussion of deliberative democracy, mentioned that deliberative methods risk legitimating the illegitimate (2012, p. 52).
5. See Volokh (1997) for a historical analysis of the Blackstone ratio and its variants.

6

Why Should We Care What the Public Thinks? A Critical Assessment of the Claims of Popular Punishment[1]

Frej K. Thomsen

Sometimes the public gets it wrong, even on relatively simple questions of fact. For example, recent polls indicate that a majority of the US adult population continue to believe that a deity created humans in their present form (46 per cent), while a large minority recognise that humans have evolved, but maintain that a deity 'guided the process' (32 per cent). Only 15 per cent hold that humans evolved in a process devoid of supernatural interference (Gallup Politics, 2012).

Presumably, few would dispute that public opinion can be and sometimes is mistaken, in the manner indicated by such examples. After all, the difficulty of forming an accurate opinion under the constraints that we all face as epistemic agents is one of the reasons why most countries capable of doing so educate and employ highly specialised experts to research and assess complex issues. And yet, in public and political debates on punishment one is likely—sooner or later—to run into statements along the lines of: 'The leniency with which the courts treat serious criminals offends the public's sense of justice'. When such statements are made, it is typically either implied or concluded that the discrepancy between popular sentiments and the sentences meted out by courts can justify revising penal codes to remove or diminish the discrepancy. Proponents of this view, penal populists, affirm what I shall call the claim of popular punishment:

> *The basic claim of popular punishment*: We ought to punish in accord with popular sentiments about punishment.

When it comes to punishment, at least, public opinion is considered by penal populists to give us reason *in and of itself* to adjust policy. What are we to make of this? Is it a sensible view?

Despite its prevalence, the claim for popular punishment is a curiously underexplored topic. And to the extent that it has received attention from academics, the approach has often been the mirror opposite of the proponents': since penal populism is (obviously!) evil and counterproductive what we need to do is explain why it is that it occurs and find a way to stop its spread of contagion to justice (e.g. Lacey, 2008; Pettit, 2002; Pratt, 2007; for opposed arguments cf. Dzur, 2012; Roberts, 2011). Perhaps there is no great mystery here, and the normative issues are as clear-cut as assumed by (some) proponents and critics, but I suspect that this is not the case and that it may be worth therefore to explore the normative claim for popular punishment in greater depth. My main purpose in this article is to investigate the ways in which such a claim can be supported by a rational argument.

I proceed as follows: I first explore and attempt to clarify the claim of popular punishment, that is, the idea that we ought to punish in accord with how popular sentiments hold that we ought to punish. I then illustrate the general structure that an argument to support the claim must have and distinguish between three ways of fulfilling the critical second premise. Finally, I investigate each of these three attempts to complete the argument in turn and demonstrate the difficulty of making the argument at once plausible and potent. I conclude that only one version of the argument can be successful and that the limited circumstances under which it applies, as well as the demanding background conditions for its plausibility, makes it far less interesting than proponents tend to assume. Thus, I shall reveal myself as a moderate critic of the claim rather than a proponent, but I believe that all parties can benefit from the increased clarity about the terms of the debate.

1. STAKING THE CLAIM

In thinking about the claim of popular punishment we need to separate two issues: the question of whether and if so how to involve the public in the institutions that shape penal policy (e.g. Dzur, 2012; Dzur & Mirchandani, 2007; Lacey, 2008; Lovegrove, 1998; Morgan, 2002; Pettit, 2002; Pratt, 2007) and the question of what a good reason for shaping penal policy one way or the other would be (e.g. Bagaric & Edney, 2004; Golash & Lynch, 1995; Roberts, 2011; Robinson & Darley, 2007; Ryberg, 2010). We might call them the participatory and the justificatory issues of the relation between popular opinion and punishment, respectively. The two issues are at risk of being conflated because they both involve taking public opinion into consideration, but deciding whether and if so how to do so in the first manner—by allowing the public to participate in or influence the decision-making procedure—does not exhaust the scope of the issue.

Of the two issues, I shall be concerned only with the second, and I intend to bracket the question of what the best arrangement for the relevant institutions would be; whatever your preferred model, feel free to assume that we are dealing with it. My concern is not who should deliberate, but which reasons should carry weight in the deliberations of those that do. Having determined the scope of the discussion, it may be worth exploring the components of the claim itself in slightly greater detail. I suggested above that the fundamental idea of penal populism could be boiled down to the basic claim that 'we ought to punish in accord with popular sentiments about punishment'. I shall discuss three points in turn regarding sentiments, information, and conflicts.

First, it is worth asking what exactly we are to understand by 'popular sentiments'. I mean for the term to capture the foundation of this specific type of argument, which could be referred to also as, for example, 'the public's sense of justice', 'our common-sense feeling of right and wrong', and so on, and I suggest the following working definition:

> *Popular sentiments*: A popular sentiment is a widely shared (within the society at stake) belief with normative content, e.g. 'we ought to punish offence O with punishment P'.

Furthermore, I employ the term 'sentiment' to stress the particular character of the beliefs at stake in this discussion. These are, as I think penal populists will admit, arrived at through largely unconscious judgments, intuitive and normally strongly emotionally laden. For comparison, we could imagine that public opinion held that crime O ought to be punished with P because the members had all individually applied a particular theory of criminal justice, such as communicative retributivism qua Antony Duff (2001) or utilitarian deterrence-theory qua Jeremy Bentham ([1789] 1996), carefully and consciously calculated the weight of the moral factors emphasised by the theory given the relevant empirical conditions and concluded that P was the correct response to what justice required. However, not only is it obviously not the case that the public sentiments which penal populists demand that we show consideration are derived in this manner, but it also seems to me that if public sentiments *were* derived in this manner they would not be the type of beliefs that the argument is supposed to capture (cf. Robinson & Darley, 2007, pp. 4–8).[2]

Second, a traditional distinction with regards to popular sentiments on punishment separates sentiments that are and are not informed. By uninformed sentiments we are to understand something like the average layperson's sentiment, based as this typically is on a limited and superficial knowledge of criminology, the law, the penal system, crimes, offenders and victims. By informed sentiments, we are to understand the sentiment that the same person has once in possession of a reasonable amount of relevant information about these topics.[3] Clearly, if interpreted as a binary concept this would be too crude, but however we qualify the concept it raises an important problem: given that there will in at least some cases be a difference between a person's lesser and more informed sentiments, which of the two sentiments are we to take as the basis of the claim for popular punishment?[4]

In the following I shall assume that we can give lexical priority to more informed sentiments in intrapersonal comparisons, that is, we can assume that whenever a person's lesser and more informed sentiments diverge we can ignore the less informed and give full credit to the more informed sentiments.[5] For simplicity's sake, I shall mostly refer to these simply as sentiments.

Third, the requirement that the sentiment be widely shared is slightly inaccurate. In practice it seems to me that any version of the argument will have to understand popular sentiments in a way that meets the following condition: The strength of the claim must correlate with both the strength of the sentiment and its prevalence. We have more reason to punish in accordance with the sentiment, the more widely shared the sentiment or the stronger the sentiment is. An implication of this condition is that to the extent that intractable disagreements exist in the relevant population, that is, when popular sentiments are genuinely divided, there will be conflicting reasons. The proponent of popular punishment can accept this implication, I believe, without undue concern. After all, there is no reason why the claim would have to be that there is an exclusive reason, and it seems perfectly legitimate to let the claim cash out in practice, for example, as one reason outweighing the others (because it is more strongly held or more prevalent), its resulting strength being weakened by contrary sentiments but, so long as it outweighs them, still counting as a reason in favour of adjusting penal practices in the appropriate direction.[6] Given these clarifications, we might restate the claim of the argument to be:

> The revised claim of popular punishment: We ought to punish in accord with informed popular sentiments about punishment, the strength of this claim varying in direct proportion to both the strength and the prevalence of the sentiment.

This is a workable definition, but I will suggest that we make two further small qualifications to the revised version of the claim. First, I have already discussed the claim by referring to competing 'reasons', and I believe that we can achieve greater clarity by rephrasing the normative claim in terms of a reason rather than the less precise 'ought'. But the reason at stake is clearly a *pro tanto* reason, not a decisive ('all things considered') reason. I believe proponents of popular punishment ought to accept that there can be other reasons for or against a particular punishment than those based on popular sentiments and even that these other reasons can potentially outweigh the reason supplied by the claim of popular punishment.[7] Even if some might wish to challenge this, I will stick to this assumption since it extends maximal charity to the proponent: the moderate claim of a *pro tanto* reason is less demanding, while conversely if the case for a *pro tanto* reason fails, the case for a decisive reason cannot succeed.

Second, we need to limit the acceptable type of reason. To illustrate why, consider the fact that there may be persons who hold what is intuitively the wrong kind of reason for adjusting penal practices to fit popular punishment. At the risk of being cynical, it seems that this is true of some politicians who are proponents of popular punishment, for example, because they believe this will aid in their reelection. Clearly, they have a reason for adjusting penal practices, but their self-interested reason for the advancement of a political career is not the kind of reason that will satisfactorily support the claim of popular punishment. There may be different suggestions for how to properly constrain the range of appropriate reasons, but I believe that impartiality will do the trick. By an impartial reason I understand a reason that applies independently of the situation of the individual agent.[8] This condition rules out the kind of reason available to the self-serving populist politician since that reason only applies given his or her individual situation as a politician seeking reelection.

We can introduce these two qualifications explicitly to more accurately specify the claim:

> *The minimal claim of popular punishment*: There is at least one impartial *pro tanto* reason to punish in accord with informed popular sentiments about punishment, the strength of this reason varying in direct proportion to both the strength and the prevalence of the sentiment.

This is the claim that I shall take popular punishment to hold, and the minimal conclusion that an argument capable of supporting popular punishment must achieve. Let us turn therefore to how such an argument might look.

2. THE ARGUMENT(S)

The minimal claim of popular punishment is not self-evidently true, so we will want an argument to support it. Let me start by saying a little about how I think we should understand an argument like this to work. In practice, the basic structure of the argument is frequently something like the following:

(i) Popular sentiments about punishment hold that offence O ought to receive punishment P.

QED: Hence we ought to punish O with P.

As is apparent, the argument contains (or at least, must contain, to be valid) an implicit premise, connecting the first premise with the conclusion; something along the lines of:

(ii) If popular sentiments hold that O ought to be punished with P, then we ought to punish O with P.

But although logically sufficient, as banal a premise as this would be unsatisfactory, because it is not apparent why or that we ought to accept it. Proponents of popular punishment must come up with a more plausible version of the second premise.

The argument for popular punishment, then, taking into account the minimal version of the claim I developed in the preceding section and the necessary elaboration mentioned above must look something like the following:

(i) Popular sentiments about punishment hold that offence O ought to receive punishment P.

(ii) If popular sentiments hold that O ought to be punished with P, then there is at least one impartial *pro tanto* reason to punish O with P, the strength of this reason varying in direct proportion to both the strength and the prevalence of the sentiment, because [. . .].

QED: There is at least one impartial *pro tanto* reason to punish to punish O with P, the strength of this reason varying in direct proportion to both the strength and the prevalence of the sentiment.

In addition, whatever elaboration of the second premise the proponent offers, it must be capable of meeting what seems to me the most obvious challenge to the claim of popular punishment: the argument that popular sentiments should reflect, not constitute reasons for punishment. That is, if there is a right answer to the question of how to punish, it will be determined by reasons for and against punishing, and if popular opinion is to be interesting or relevant, it must be based on and subject to revision by these reasons, not the other way around. In Bagaric and Edney's much cited illustration: 'Seeking public views on sentencing is analogous to doctors basing treatment decisions on what the community thinks is appropriate or engineers building cars, not in accordance with the rules of physics, but on the basis of what lay members of the community "reckon" seems about right' (2004, p. 129; cf. Golash & Lynch, 1995, p. 719). So while popular sentiments can be based on or even express the reasons that we have for punishing (although, as Bagaric and Edney's examples suggest, we often suspect that they are not), they are at best superfluous and at worst mistaken. In a slightly more formal way, we may express this as *the dilemma of reasonableness*:

1. A belief about whether to φ is either reasonable or unreasonable. It is unreasonable if there is no reason for or against φ'ing; it is reasonable if there is at least one reason for or against φ'ing.[9]

2. In forming a belief about whether to φ, we should not let unreasonable beliefs affect our belief.[10]

3. In forming a belief about whether to φ, we should let the reasons for and against φ'ing affect our belief.

4. We should not double count reasons.

5. In forming a belief about whether to φ, we should let the reasons that support a reasonable belief about whether to φ affect our belief (from 1 and 3).

6. In forming a belief about whether to φ, letting a reasonable belief about whether to φ affect our beliefs is double-counting reasons, if we have already let the reasons that support this belief affect our belief.

7. In forming a belief about whether to φ, we should not let a reasonable belief about whether to φ affect our belief (from 4 and 6).

   QED: Whether a belief is reasonable or unreasonable, we should not let it affect our belief about whether to φ (from 2 and 7).

To my mind, the dilemma is fatal to the vast majority of arguments for the claim of popular punishment encountered in public debates. And it serves the purpose of immediately refocusing the debate where many scholars probably feel it belongs: on the traditional issues of whether punishment should be based on just deserts, deterrence, some third factor or some mixture of factors, and how to determine the specific policies that would follow from whatever factor(s) we pick. Whether they are or are not based on reasons, it seems that we can skip sentiments entirely and just get to grips with the traditional debate about the problem of punishment. The result is a further condition on the type of argument available to the proponent. The argument must show both that popular sentiments do provide us with reasons and that these reasons are different from and cannot be reduced to the traditional concerns of criminal justice ethics, such as just deserts, deterrence, reconciliation, and so on.

What could such an argument look like? Overall, it seems to me that an argument for popular punishment must fall into one of three categories, the proper elaboration and individual appeal of which will be determined by background assumptions in ethical theory:

1. There can be an epistemic argument that popular sentiments are truth-tracking and that we have a reason for bringing penal practice into alignment with them since they provide some reason to think that this level corresponds to moral reality.
2. There can be an institutional argument that popular sentiments are reasons-creating and that we have a reason for bringing penal practice into alignment with them since they influence (or even determine) what moral reality is.
3. There can be an instrumental argument that popular sentiments create costs and benefits for a system of justice and that we have a reason of beneficence to bring penal practice into alignment with them since this will minimise the costs of divergence and maximise the benefits of correspondence.

Let me briefly flesh out each of them in turn before we examine them critically in detail in the second half of the paper.

The epistemic argument must involve something like the following version of the second premise:

(iia) Informed popular sentiments are fallibly indicative of how we have reason to act; and (iib) we have a reason to act in accordance with how we have reason to think we have reason to act.

The second half of the premise is uncontroversial enough, I believe, that I shall set it aside. The first half implies that if popular sentiments hold that we ought to φ, there is a reason to think that we ought *in fact* to φ. The premise supports the conclusion of the argument for popular punishment because, if true, it translates directly to the claim of popular punishment once we insert 'punish O with P' for φ. It tackles the dilemma of reasonableness by challenging the first horn of the dilemma: a reasonable belief is interesting in itself because of its evidentiary value, where it might be taken to constitute evidence directly for the belief or for the soundness or importance of the reasons consistent with it.

Note that to be charitable once more, I am assuming the claim to be only that popular sentiments are *fallibly* indicative, which is to say that they can be wrong but that they are not mistaken so often as to be useless or misleading. We can leave open the question of how strong an indication they provide—the range is everything between only minimally better than chance and up to near certainty—because while this will affect how strong the resulting reason is, the claim that we are examining is merely that such a reason exists, so any value in the range will do.

Similarly, the institutional argument will involve something like the following version of the second premise:

> (iia) Informed popular sentiments express the values of members of a community; and (iib) we have reason to treat members of a community in accordance with the values of members of the community.

Whereas the claim of the epistemic argument is that popular sentiments help us discover what we have reason to do, the claim here is that popular sentiments provide us with reasons for action that we would not otherwise have had. And such reasons emerge because those involved are part of a joint community wherein shared (but subjective) values can justifiably determine how persons ought to treat each other. It tackles the dilemma by insisting that normative beliefs are reasons-generating independently of their being based or not based on reasons but owes an account, of course, of why that is the case; the critical part of the premise is therefore likely to be the second half.

Note also that there is an important ambiguity concerning 'members'. Depending on how we ultimately defend the premise, we may want to hold one of two views. We might prefer to hold that there can be competing sentiments but, as I have previously suggested, the strongest can win out, with the force of the resulting reason being diminished proportionally to but not cancelled by disagreement. Or, we may wish to hold that only unanimously held sentiments can justify treating members of the community in accord with the values they express, since anything else will be the imposition of the values of some members of the community on others who do not share them. To have any practical importance the argument must hold the former, since unanimously held popular sentiments are unlikely to ever obtain in modern societies, and I shall assume that this is the version of the argument at stake.

And finally, the instrumental argument involves something like the following version of the second premise:

> (iia) When actual punishment P_a for O diverges from P, this imposes costs $C_{Pa\text{-}p}$; and (iib) we have reasons of beneficence to avoid imposing costs.

Whereas the institutional claim above is that popular sentiments create reasons directly by virtue of the normative force of the values they embody, the instrumental claim is that popular sentiments provide us with reasons we would not otherwise have had only because the sentiments impose costs and benefits on our actions in terms of whatever values we take to apply independently. It dodges the dilemma by pointing out that even if not directly reasons-generating, beliefs have implications for how other reasons cash out.

The key component in this argument is likely to be the first premise, given that the second premise is both widely accepted and strongly opposed by those who dissent, so that we are unlikely to be capable of changing anyone's mind about it. The central task of the argument, therefore, will be to make credible the idea that over- or underpunishment imposes, or at least is likely to impose, noteworthy costs.

3. ASSESSING THE EPISTEMIC ARGUMENT

I sketched out above how both the general argument and the specific premise of the epistemic version must fit together. Putting the two together we get *the epistemic argument for popular punishment*:

> (i) Informed popular sentiments about punishment hold that offence O ought to receive punishment P.
>
> (iia) Informed popular sentiments are fallibly indicative of how we have reason to act; and (iib) we have a reason to act in accord with how we have reason to think we have reason to act.
>
> *The minimal claim of popular punishment*: There is at least one impartial *pro tanto* reason to punish in accord with informed popular sentiments about punishment, the strength of this reason varying in direct proportion to both the strength and the prevalence of the sentiment.

As I noted above, the second half of the epistemic premise is less interesting because less controversial than the first. It is not, after all, apparent why or that we should accept that popular sentiments are indicative of moral truth, even fallibly so. Indeed, we might think it quite likely that the public could get it as wrong on normative questions as on factual ones, if not more so, for at least two reasons: First, the methods of establishing moral facts are indisputably both more controversial and less precise than those of establishing nonnormative facts of almost any kind. Second, almost everybody recognises that the general public has been gravely mistaken about important moral issues in the (relatively) recent past—slavery, racism, and sexism are widely accepted examples—and there is overwhelming reason to think that it remains mistaken about other crucial issues—the ethics of war, speciesism, and poverty aid are prime examples that have strong support in the literature. (McMahan, 2009; Regan, 2004; Singer, 1995; Unger, 1996) Given these concerns, is there any reason to think that public sentiments are 'truth tracking'?

One way of supporting the epistemic premise, which draws on lines of argument advanced in the so-called epistemic justification of democracy (Cohen, 1986; Estlund, 2009), would be to argue that the Condorcet jury theorem applies to sentiments about punishment. The Condorcet jury theorem as classically stated shows that in any group of people in which individuals are fallible but more likely to be right than wrong, the majority opinion in a binary choice situation is more likely to be true than false, the probability of its being true increasing with the size of the group (Condorcet, 1785). For populations as big as those involved in modern societies, the probability swiftly approaches certainty.

An obvious objection to the application of the classical theorem is that in situations where 'how we ought to punish?' means, for example, how long we ought to imprison the offender; we are not dealing with a binary choice situation but with a choice between a range of options. However, there are formal solutions for applying the theorem to nonbinary choice situations (List & Goodin, 2001), and it remains true that so long as the average person's choice is better than chance (i.e. the probability of selecting the right option is greater than $1/n$, where n is the number of options) *and* not less preferred than a false option (i.e. no wrong option has a greater probability of being selected than the right option), the majority have an increasing probability of being right the greater the number of participants in the decision. And this fits our common-sense views in at least some scenarios. It would not be unreasonable to suppose, for example, that if we were to ask people to guess how many beans are in a large jar the average guess would become increasingly accurate the more people we ask.

The important question, however, is whether it is reasonable to suppose that the sentiments of the average person about the type of issue at stake are reliable enough to be at once better than chance and better than all false alternatives. Such sentiments are, I have suggested, the results of a largely intuitive judgement that involves weighing reasons with or against each other to arrive at an opinion, such as 'offence O should be punished with P'. There are essentially two ways in which public sentiments (if reasonable beliefs of this type) could diverge from the correct conclusion: they could be based on a different set of reasons (fewer, more, or other, including supposed but invalid reasons), and they could be based on an incorrect weighing of the reasons.[11] We ought, I suspect, to be sceptical of the epistemic quality of public opinion on both counts.

Starting with the weighing, the worry one might raise concerns the susceptibility of the type of judgement at stake to cognitive biases. An intuitive normative judgement of the sort involved in the claim of popular punishment is clearly composite: it must take into account a number of often conflicting reasons. The trouble is that as the number of moral factors involved increases, so do both the complexity, the possibility of mistakes and the influence of the cognitive heuristics necessary to lighten the cognitive load and make an intuitive judgement possible.[12] However, cognitive heuristics, while undoubtedly helpful and perhaps even necessary, unavoidably lead to cognitive biases. As behavioural economics has shown in fascinating detail, there are predictable and serious mistakes that agents will perform when making intuitive judgements, which are best explained by the agents' employment of generally useful but predictably flawed cognitive heuristics (e.g. Kahneman & Tversky, 1979, 2009a, 2009b; Kahneman, Knetsch, & Thaler, 2009).

Anchoring Effects

Let me illustrate with just one bias that we can expect to be prominent in the type of judgements that we are discussing: anchoring effects. An anchoring effect occurs when a person adjusts subsequent estimates in the light of an initial factor, which either has no relevant relation to the issue or should not be given the influence it is granted.[13] In a classic decision theoretical experiment Amos Tversky and Daniel Kahneman made two experimental groups observe the results of a spinning roulette wheel, stopping in one case at the number 10 and in the other at the number 65. Immediately afterwards participants were asked to guess the percentage of African nations which had obtained membership of the United Nations, indicating first whether the percentage number was higher or lower than the number the roulette wheel had landed on and, second, what the percentage was. The group who had witnessed the wheel stopping at the number 10 estimated on average 25 per cent, while the group that had witnessed the wheel stopping at 65 estimated on average 45 per cent, a difference that appears both irrational and incredible given that it was apparent to both groups that the results of the roulette wheel had no relation to the question being asked (Kahneman & Tversky, 1974).[14]

Obviously, whether anchoring effects occur in the context of intuitions about punishment is an empirical question, but it seems likely that they might. A prime candidate would be the perceived current punishment. If in effect, it would exert an intuitive pull towards what the person believes the current punishment to be. But of course there can be no guarantee that an anchoring effect pulls intuitions in the right direction, nor any reason to believe that the perceived level of current punishment would do so. The result would be that we would get convergence around the wrong estimate. Whether intuitions in such a case happen to have evidentiary value will be an effect of how the convergent level of intuitions, the actual level of punishment, and the appropriate level of punishment happen to be related: if the convergent level is located between the actual and appropriate levels then intuitions will temporarily retain evidentiary value; although inaccurate, they will at least point us in what is initially the right direction (e.g. less severe or more severe punishment). If not, then they will be entirely misleading.[15]

The second and more fundamental problem for the epistemic argument is that there is good evidence that the intuitive judgements at stake fail to take into account the relevant reasons *and only* the relevant reasons. (Greene Sommerville, Nystrom, Darley, & Cohen, 2001; Singer, 2005) There is a blooming and extensive literature documenting the apparent influence of irrelevant factors on moral intuitions, but let me describe just one.

In 2008 Schnall, Haidt, Clore, and Jordan published the results of a series of experiments concerning the relation between the emotion of disgust and moral judgement. Briefly, one of their experiments involved asking participants to intuitively assess the degree of moral wrongness, if any, in the action of the protagonist in each of three different detailed scenarios. All participants were seated in an empty office environment during off-hours, but the test group had their environment manipulated in that the 'workspace was set up to look rather disgusting: An old chair with a torn and dirty cushion was placed in front of a desk that had various stains, and was sticky. On the desk there was a transparent plastic cup with the dried up remnants of a smoothie, and a pen that was chewed up. Next to the desk was a trash can overflowing with garbage including greasy pizza boxes and dirty-looking tissues.' (Schnall et al., 2008, p. 7).

The results were unequivocal: test group participants judged the behaviour of the protagonists in the scenarios much more harshly than the control group, that is, were more likely to judge the action wrong and judged it as more wrong on average, although they were unaware of the influence of provoked disgust on their judgements.[16] Admittedly there were variations within the test group correlating with self-reported susceptibility to disgust, but the results must be considered disconcerting by those who mean to give credit to intuitive judgements of moral scenarios nonetheless. If intuitions are to be considered evidence in favour of normative beliefs, they should not vary with such factors as the presence of greasy pizza boxes.

One final challenge is worth noting. In the preceding I have discussed the epistemic qualities of public opinion in isolation. But to support the second premise, popular sentiments must meet a more demanding standard than this, for they must be not merely fallibly indicative in the sense that they do better than chance but less fallible, that is, better than the alternative procedure which they are meant to correct. Recall that popular sentiments are meant to give us a reason to think that we have reason to φ. But while this *may* be true *in situations* with no contrary epistemic background— although the reservations that I have presented above suggest otherwise— clearly the claim of popular punishment is meant to apply even in the situation where, as today, there exist well-developed theories of criminal justice as competitors. And here it is no longer obvious that even popular sentiments that met the standard of better-than-chance could give us reasons to think that we have reason to φ.

Consider that given two different measuring instruments, one of which is both more accurate and precise than the other, adjusting our beliefs in the light of the results of the less accurate instrument is no longer desirable. Return for illustration to the bean-guessing example I mentioned earlier and suppose that we now allow a second group of people to measure the jar, look up the average size of a bean, and calculate an estimate on that basis. In effect this is to allow them to make a cumbersome, conscious, and calculated assessment of essentially the same factors as the members of the first group base their guess on. If we accept reasonable assumptions about the advantages of this procedure compared to guessing by sight alone, we would both expect the average of the estimates of this second group to be more accurate than the average of the first group, and we would expect including the guesses of members of the first group in an average of the estimates of the second group to *decrease* the accuracy. Here the power of the Condorcet jury theorem works in reverse: because the estimates of the first group are *less* accurate, as the number of misleading opinions included grows, so too does the probability of reaching the right answer rapidly deteriorate to zero. And the situation is analogous, because for all its defects and controversy, the characteristics of being a cumbersome, conscious, and calculated assessment of essentially the same factors as popular sentiments are (ideally) based on seems to me an accurate (if incomplete) depiction of the work of criminal justice thinkers. The possibility remains that popular sentiments are better at tracking moral truth than criminal justice ethics, either because it better weighs the reasons or takes into account reasons that philosophers have missed. But barring a successful argument to that effect, and in light of the concerns I have sketched above, I see no grounds for assuming this to be the case.

In conclusion, although there are perhaps situations in which the average person's intuitive judgement is more likely to be better than chance, the assessment of concrete moral scenarios is not necessarily amongst them. As has been pointed out, the problems raised by awkward influences on intuitions may be difficult to contain (Sandberg & Juth, 2010; Tersman, 2009). It may be hard to cordon off a set of intuitions that remain trustworthy, in which case the use of any intuitions is cast into doubt, and moral philosophy faces a severe methodological challenge. This remains a hotly contested subject in contemporary moral philosophy.[17] But even if true, this can hardly save the epistemic argument. It simply means that providing *any reason* for or against a particular type of punishment is going to be much more difficult than we have supposed, if not impossible.

4. ASSESSING THE INSTITUTIONAL ARGUMENT

Having assessed the possibilities of completing an epistemic argument for the claim, let us turn to the institutional version. Recall that the general premise I suggested was the following:

(iia) Informed popular sentiments express the values of members of a polity, and (iib) we have reason to treat members of a polity in accordance with the values of members of the polity.

And as I pointed out previously, the critical part is the account of why we have reason to treat members in accord with their values.

One version of the argument might be based on the duties of democratic representatives and allow for the intersection of the participatory and justificatory issues that I initially separated. Suppose that there are reasons to have a representative democratic institution which makes the decisions regarding punishment (e.g. a parliament which legislates for a criminal code containing sentencing guidelines) and furthermore that the representatives have reason (perhaps in the strong sense of having a moral duty) to represent the *Demos*, that is, to take decisions in accord with the values of the public that they represent. This, it seems, could provide the required reason.

There might be good grounds for objecting to the assumptions of the argument, such as whether representatives genuinely have a reason to represent the current values of the demos in the direct way necessary, but let us grant the argument these assumptions. Even if we do so, this version of the institutional argument fails to provide the impartial reason required by the claim. To see this, consider that it cannot provide a reason for those *represented*, only for those representing them. The situation is parallel to the situation in which an agent has made a promise to punish in accord with popular sentiments. Now, moral philosophers disagree on whether and if so why and how making promises creates reasons for action, but let us suppose for a second that it does. Then, surely, the promiser now has a *pro tanto* reason to punish in accord with popular sentiments. 'Certainly', he or she might say, 'I know that popular sentiments are misguided and unjust. Impartially, they give us no reason to do anything. But it just so happens that I have promised to act in accordance with them. Hence, I have a reason to do as they suggest.' Nobody, I suspect, would take this to be the kind of reason at stake in the claim of popular punishment, nor are we likely soon to encounter proponents of the claim lamenting the fact that they happen to be in a situation where they have reason to act in accord with popular sentiments that are otherwise unsupported.

A different variation might start with the widely accepted premise that there is reason to let the sentence vary with the seriousness of the crime, argue that the seriousness of the crime varies with cultural norms, that popular sentiments are, or at least can be, an expression of such cultural norms, and that therefore the sentence should vary with popular sentiments. Roberts sketches the contours of such an argument when he suggests that 'the seriousness of any particular act is determined, to some degree, by the extent to which it offends community mores' (2011, pp. 115–116).[18]

Now, there are two ways in which community views might affect the seriousness of offences. We can imagine that they directly determine, or at least affect, the seriousness, that is, 'serious is as the public says'. Alternately, we can imagine that sentiments indirectly affect the seriousness, for example, because the factors that determine seriousness, such as the amount of harm caused, are influenced by community views. The trouble is that neither is plausibly capable of completing the institutional argument. The first reading of the argument implausibly holds that mere belief can affect seriousness independent of other factors (such as harm). This runs straight into the dilemma of reasonableness, and while it may be possible to extend the argument so as to avoid this objection, I cannot see how (cf. Golash & Lynch, 1995, p. 714; Ryberg, 2010, pp. 161–165). Meanwhile, the latter is really a variant of the instrumental argument. Thus, while it is undoubtedly true that sentiments can have this effect, for example, because harm is at least partially a psychological phenomenon and as such is subject to the influence of cultural norms (and, we might add, individual psychological idiosyncracies), popular sentiments only enter the picture as part of the background conditions which together determine how much harm the action causes and, as a result thereof, how serious it is. The seriousness remains a function of the harm, not the sentiment (for a related point, cf. Golash & Lynch, 1995, pp. 711–712).

Finally, an argument might be made on the basis of the voluntary relinquishing of individual rights. Thus, if individuals possess moral rights, for example, a right to liberty based on autonomy, and if subjecting them to punishment will constitute *prima facie* violations of these rights, it seems that a system of justice must require individuals to conditionally relinquish those rights. And it is arguable that at least citizens in a democratic society do so but on the condition that they are capable of collectively deciding the system of justice which they are potentially subject to punishment by. Hence, the argument would run, if the system is not one that is endorsed (or, endorsable) by the persons subject to it, for example, because actual punishment is disanalogous to the punishment that would be meted out by a system consented to, the conditional relinquishment of rights has not been triggered and punishment is unjustified.[19] An argument along these lines will mesh well with libertarian intuitions, which some may consider an advantage. As Dzur puts it, there is a 'concern' 'prominent in Anglo-American political thought' that 'citizens be held accountable only to rules they authorize and understand,' to which we might add that they can for the same reasons demand to be held accountable only in the way and to the extent that they authorise and understand[20] (2012, p. 117).

There are potential problems with this line of argument familiar within contractualist theory, for example, about how to account for majority rule and the subjection of dissenting minorities to a general system of justice, as well as the necessary forms of consent, which will often in practice be implicit. The solutions to these problems are not uncontroversial, but I will suppose that contractualists can provide satisfactory answers to them. Even granting these assumptions, however, it seems that to work in the context of the claim of popular punishment the argument requires conflating the hypothetical and actual situations. Thus, traditional contractualism will impose a hypothetical contract situation on agents in which it might well require that their sentiments with respect to criminal justice count as reasons while constructing the social contract. But there is no reason to suppose that the actual (irrational, nonideal) sentiments of a population at any given time have any relation to the sentiments individuals would have in such a hypothetical situation.

In fact, the choice situation for the contract is typically constructed exactly so as to avoid certain biases that afflict the actual choice situation, Rawls's ([1971] 1999) imposition of the 'veil of ignorance' being the classical example. Furthermore, this version of the argument also seems better suited to the participatory than to the justificatory issue because, again, it seems it will be hard pressed to provide an impartial reason. It could, perhaps, be held to constitute an argument in favour of involving the public so as to provide them with the opportunity of con- or dissenting based on their actual, current preferences rather than idealised or hypothetical preferences, but it could not, it seems, provide them with *a reason for or against consenting* if they were involved in such a manner. As such, it cannot support the claim of popular punishment.

5. ASSESSING THE INSTRUMENTAL ARGUMENT

The last and perhaps most promising of the three arguments is the argument that the sentiments of the community can affect the way that other reasons play out and that in so far as we hold that these reasons influence the way we ought to punish, the sentiments must therefore be taken into account. I formulated this as the following attempt at filling out the second premise:

> (iia) When actual punishment P_a for O diverges from P, this imposes costs C_{Pa-P}; and (iib) we have reasons of beneficence to avoid imposing costs.

The first step for the argument is to make credible the notion that divergence will impose costs. Costs of divergence could arise in the form of non-compliance, loss of legitimacy and co-operation, increased vigilantism and retaliation, loss of communicative meaning including centrally censorious meaning, and sheer frustration, indignation, and anxiety as a result of the perceived inadequacy of justice (Gardner, 2007; Golash & Lynch, 1995, pp. 708–710; Robinson & Darley, 2007, pp. 18–31; Roberts, 2011, p. 111; Ryberg, 2010, pp. 152–159). It may even be possible to cover a version of the argument for popular punishment according to which the cost imposed is disrespect towards the victim of the offence, because the punishment does not meet what popular sentiments hold to be the appropriate punishment. So it seems that there are a range of potential costs, at least some of which should be acceptable to most moral theories. Does this mean that we should accept the instrumental argument?

At least some moral philosophers will be little impressed with the instrumental argument for the sole reason that they take it that costs and benefits cannot justify setting the level of punishment at any particular level. The severity of punishment, such absolutists could argue, must be determined solely by considerations of justice, and the relevant considerations of justice with regard to punishment is just deserts, that is, what the offender *deserves* to suffer by reason of his or her offence. For those who hold such a *Fiat justitia et pereat mundus* position, the instrumental argument is simply unavailable. But given the relative scarcity of absolutists in moral philosophy, it may be worth considering what those who are willing to grant at least some weight to considerations of beneficence in determining the justified level of punishment should think about it.[21]

In addition, it is worth noting that for some costs the instrumental argument can cut across the traditional divide between retributivist and consequentialist justifications of punishment. If, for example, the function of punishment is taken to be the fulfilment of our collective duty to express censure at the wrongdoing perpetrated by the offender, a $P–P_a$ discrepancy that causes the punishment to lose censorious meaning imposes a cost but one which is counted in the deontological currency of the loss of our ability to fulfil the duty of expressing censure at wrongdoing (cf. Roberts, 2011, pp. 112–114).

Several further objections remain. First, it is worth noting that on the most obvious version of the argument it assumes that the costs and benefits emerge from the distance between actual popular sentiments and the *perceived* level of punishment rather than the distance between sentiments and the *actual* level of punishment. Given that studies show that the difference between perceived and actual levels of punishment can be substantial, this is an important distinction.

It also opens the door to an objection based on the relative costs of changing actual penal practices and changing perceptions of penal practices (cf. Ryberg, 2010, pp. 157–158). Presumably, if the reasons at stake are reasons of beneficence, they cannot support changing penal practice if there is a better (more beneficial, e.g. because less costly) alternative available in altering perceptions of penal practices. In the most uncontroversial cases there will be no discrepancy between actual and desired punishment, only between actual and perceived punishment. Suppose, for example, that penal practices impose punishment of five months prison for offence O, that public sentiments demand at least five months prison for O, but that public perceptions of penal practices are that O is typically punished with three months prison, and that this divergence has the cost that the argument assumes. We can then either change penal practices, that is, increasing punishment until perceived punishment becomes five months, or we can change perceptions until perceived punishment becomes five months. If, plausibly, it will be easier and less costly to do the second, clearly this is what we must be taken to have a reason of beneficence to do. Studies suggest both that the problem is real and that the solution of adjusting perceptions is feasible (Bagaric & Edney, 2004; Hough & Park, 2002; Indermaur & Hough, 2002; Mirrless-Black, 2002, pp. 129–130).

However, since I have assumed that we are dealing with informed sentiments, this situation may be unlikely to arise. Presumably, an accurate perception of actual levels of punishment will be part of any realistically attainable maximum level of information. This leaves us with a further choice between changing actual punishments or changing popular sentiments. These may be harder to alter than the level of information, but there is no reason to assume that changing public attitudes in such a way is impossible (Robinson & Darley, 2007, pp. 52–66). Suppose however, as we should, that, while possible, doing so is itself costly. And suppose that we limit the discussion to situations where the costs of changing sentiments outweigh the costs of changing practice. Will there not then be reason to align punishment with sentiments?

At this point, I am willing to concede. Once we have narrowed the field in this way, I do not think we can raise further objections. It remains true that, on the occasions when the empirical conditions are met, those who hold that costs and benefits play a part in setting the justified level of punishment are forced on pain of contradiction to accept that there is at least a(n impartial, *pro tanto*) reason for punishing in accord with popular senti-ments. This is hardly surprising and may leave all parties to the traditional debates feeling comfortable. Absolutist deontologists will perhaps take it as further proof that consequentialists and threshold-deontologists are will-ing to take all the wrong factors into account all the while studiously ignor-ing the moral trumps that *really* matter, while their opponents should be able to happily agree that in cases where it will have beneficial consequences to adjust punishment so as to better align with popular sentiments, clearly, this gives us reason to do so.

The impact of popular sentiments should not be overestimated, how-ever. The reason is not decisive. The optimal punishment regime will depend on both normative and empirical facts: which costs go into the equation and how they increase or diminish in a concrete social setting ac-cording to changes in punishment. It might be true, for example, as Robin-son and Darley (2007) argue, that the greatest benefits produced by the criminal justice system depend on alignment between (the ordinal ranking of) the punishments that it metes out and popular sentiments, which amounts to the claim that the cost of not meeting popular sentiments out-weighs any individual competing cost. But it would remain an open ques-tion whether marginal deviations from perfect correlation between senti-ments and punishments would be an all-things-considered improvement (Robinson & Darley, 2007, p. 21; also see pp. 45–48; Golash & Lynch, 1995, pp. 709–711).

6. CONCLUSION

In the preceding I have attempted to clarify what we should understand the claim of popular punishment to (minimally) be, how an argument for the minimal claim of popular punishment must proceed, and how the difficult second premise of such an argument might be developed. I examined three versions of such an argument. There may be others, but I suspect that most or all of them will turn out to be variations on the ones at which I have looked, and will run into variations of the challenges that I have described. I have concluded that these challenges are strong enough that the first two versions of the argument, the epistemic and institutional, are unpersuasive, while there are circumstances under which the third argument will give those who accept certain normative presuppositions the reason required by the claim of popular punishment.

Is this a triumph for the proponent of popular punishment then? I have argued that we cannot refute the claim, since there is at least one version where under certain circumstances at least some ethical principles will support it. And if this is enough to satisfy the proponent, so be it. But it is a modest conclusion, and one that will be hard pressed to justify claims of popular punishment as they are typically made in practice, because it faces a heavy burden of proof in demonstrating that *this case*, in fact, happens to be one of those where it applies. There is a reason, then, why we should care what the public thinks. But for many proponents I suspect that this will be one of those cases where you get what you want only to find that it was not what you wanted after all.

REFERENCES

Audi, R. 2005. *The Good in the Right: A Theory of Intuition and Intrinsic Value*. Princeton, NJ: Princeton University Press.

Bagaric, M., and R. Edney. 2004. 'The Sentencing Advisory Commission and the Hope of Smarter Sentencing.' *Current Issues in Criminal Justice* 16(2): 125–139.

Bentham, J. (1789) 1996. *An Introduction to the Principles of Morals and Legislation*. Oxford: Clarendon.

Broome, J. 1994. 'Discounting the Future.' *Philosophy & Public Affairs* 23(2): 128–156.

Cohen, G. A. 1991. 'Incentives, Inequality and Community'. Tanner Lecture presented at Stanford University, May. http://tannerlectures.utah.edu/_documents/a-to-z/c/cohen92.pdf

Cohen, J. 1986. 'An Epistemic Conception of Democracy.' *Ethics* 97(1): 26–38.

Condorcet, J.-A.-N. C. de. 1785. 'Essai sur l'application de l'analyse à la probabilité des décisions rendues à la pluralité des voix'. Paris: l'Imprimerie Royale. http://gallica.bnf.fr/ark:/12148/bpt6k417181/f4.image

Cowen, T. 2001. 'What is the Correct Intergenerational Discount Rate?' Working paper, George Mason University, Fairfax, VA.

Cowen, T., and D. Parfit. 1992. 'Against the Social Discount Rate'. In P. Laslett and J. Fishkin (eds.), *Justice across the Generations: Philosophy, Politics, and Society*. New Haven, CT: Yale University Press, 144–161.

Crisp, R. 2006. *Reasons and the Good*. Oxford: Oxford University Press.

Duff, A. 2001. *Punishment, Communication, and Community*. Oxford: Oxford University Press.

Dzur, A. W. 2012. 'Participatory Democracy and Criminal Justice.' *Criminal Law and Philosophy* 6: 115–129.

Dzur, A. W., and R. Mirchandani. 2007. 'Punishment and Democracy: The Role of Public Deliberation.' *Punishment & Society* 9: 151–175.

Estlund, D. 2009. *Democratic Authority*. Princeton, NJ: Princeton University Press.

Gallup Politics. 2012. 'In U.S., 46% Hold Creationist View of Human Origins.' http://www.gallup.com/poll/155003/hold-creationist-view-human-origins.aspx

Gardner, J. 2007. 'Crime: In Proportion and in Perspective'. *Offences and Defences: Selected Essays in the Philosophy of Criminal Law*. By J. Gardner. Oxford: Oxford University Press: 213–238.

Golash, D., and J. P. Lynch. 1995. 'Public Opinion, Crime Seriousness, and Sentencing Policy.' *American Journal of Criminal Law* 22: 703–732.

Greene, J., R. B. Sommerville, L. E. Nystrom, J. M. Darley, and J. D. Cohen. 2001. 'An fMRI Investigation of Emotional Engagement in Moral Judgment.' *Science* 293: 2105–2108.

Haidt, J. 2001. 'The Emotional Dog and Its Rational Tail: A Social Intuitionist Approach to Moral Judgment.' *Psychological Review* 108: 814–834.

Hare, R. M. 1952. *The Language of Morals*. Oxford: Oxford University Press.

Hough, M., and A. Park. 2002. 'How Malleable Are Attitudes to Crime and Punishment? Findings from a British Deliberative Poll.' In J. V. Roberts and M. Hough (eds.), *Changing Attitudes to Punishment—Public opinion, Crime and Justice*. Cullompton, UK: Willan, 163–183.

Huemer, M. 2007. *Ethical Intuitionism*. London: Palgrave Macmillan.

Indermaur, D., and M. Hough. 2002. 'Strategies for Changing Public Attitudes to Punishment'. In J. V. Roberts and M. Hough (eds.), *Changing Attitudes to Punishment—Public Opinion, Crime and Justice*. Cullompton, UK: Willan, 198–214.

Kahneman, D., J. L. Knetsch, and R. H. Thaler. 2009. 'Anomalies: The Endowment Effect, Loss Aversion, and Status-Quo Bias'. In D. Kahneman and A. Tversky (eds.), *Choices, Values, and Frames*. New York: Cambridge University Press, 159–170.

Kahneman, D., and A. Tversky. 1974. 'Judgment under Uncertainty: Heuristics and Biases.' *Science* 185: 1124–1131.

Kahneman, D., and A. Tversky. 1979. 'Prospect Theory: An Analysis of Decision Under Risk.' *Econometrica* 47(2): 263–291.

Kahneman, D., and A. Tversky. 2009a. 'Choices, Values, and Frames'. In D. Kahneman and A. Tversky (eds.), *Choices, Values, and Frames*. New York: Cambridge University Press, 1–16.

Kahneman, D., and A. Tversky. 2009b. 'Rational Choice and the Framing of Decisions'. In D. Kahneman and A. Tversky (eds.), *Choices, Values, and Frames*. New York: Cambridge University Press, 209–223.

Lacey, N. 2008. *The Prisoner's Dilemma: Political Economy and Punishment in Contemporary Democracies*. Cambridge, UK: Cambridge University Press.

List, C., and R. E. Goodin. 2001. 'Epistemic Democracy: Generalizing the Condorcet Jury Theorem.' *Journal of Political Philosophy* 9(3): 277–306.

Lovegrove, A. 1998. 'Judicial Sentencing Policy, Criminological Expertise and Public Opinion.' *Australian & New Zealand Journal of Criminology* 31: 287–313.

McMahan, J. 2009. *Killing in War*. Oxford: Oxford University Press.

Mirrless-Black, C. 2002. 'Improving Public Knowledge about Crime and Punishment'. In J. V. Roberts and M. Hough (eds.), *Changing Attitudes to Punishment—Public Opinion, Crime and Justice*. Cullompton, UK: Willan, 184–197.

Morgan, R. 2002. 'Privileging public attitudes to sentencing?'. In J. V. Roberts and M. Hough (eds.), *Changing Attitudes to Punishment—Public Opinion, Crime and Justice*. Cullompton, UK: Willan, 215–228.

Murphy, J. G. 1973. 'Marxism and Retribution.' *Philosophy & Public Affairs* 2(3): 217–243.

Parfit, D. 1984. *Reasons and Persons*. Oxford: Oxford University Press.

Parfit, D. 2011. *On What Matters*. Oxford: Oxford University Press.

Pettit, P. 2002. 'Is Criminal Justice Politically Feasible?' *Buffalo Criminal Law Review* 5: 427–450.

Pratt, J. 2007. *Penal Populism*. London: Routledge.

Rawls, J. (1971) 1999. *A Theory of Justice*. Oxford: Oxford University Press.

Regan, T. 2004. *The Case for Animal Rights*. Berkeley: University of California Press.

Roberts, J. V. 2011. 'The Future of State Punishment'. In M. Tonry (ed.), *Retributivism Has a Past: Has It a Future?* Oxford: Oxford University Press, 101–129.

Robinson, P. H., and J. M. Darley. 2007. 'Intuitions of Justice: Implications for Criminal Law and Justice Policy.' *Southern California Law Review* 81(1): 1–68.

Robinson, P. H., R. Kurzban, and O. D. Jones. 2007. 'The Origins of Shared Intuitions of Justice.' *Vanderbilt Law Review* 60(6): 1633–1688.

Ryberg, J. 2010. 'Punishment and Public Opinion'. In J. Ryberg and J. A. Corlett (eds.), *Punishment and Ethics*. New York: Palgrave Macmillan, 149–168.

Sandberg, J., and N. Juth. 2010. 'Ethics and Intuitions: Reply to Singer.' *Journal of Ethics* 15(3): 209–226.

Schnall, S., J. Haidt, G. L. Clore, and A. H. Jordan. 2008. 'Disgust as Embodied Moral Judgment.' *Personality and Social Psychology Bulletin* 34(8): 1096–1109.

Singer, P. 1995. *Animal Liberation*. London: Pimlico.

Singer, P. 2005. 'Ethics and Intuitions.' *Journal of Ethics* 9: 331–352.

Tersman, F. 2009. *Moral Disagreement*. New York: Cambridge University Press.

Unger, P. 1996. *Living High and Letting Die*. Oxford: Oxford University Press.

NOTES

1. I am grateful to Kasper Lippert-Rasmussen, Martin Marchman Andersen, Thomas Søbirk Petersen, Sune Lægaard, Thom Brooks, Chris Bennett, Jesper Ryberg, Jakob Holtermann, Julian Roberts, Richard Lippke, and Paul H. Robinson for helpful comments.

2. An interesting question is whether it would make a difference to the argument for penal populism if it was based on the public holding such theoretically based and reflective beliefs. I believe that the criticism that I level at the claims of popular punishment based on public sentiments could be extended relatively easily to cover such cases, but since it seems to concern a claim that nobody in fact makes, nor is likely to make given the negligible probability of the general public attaining the requisite background knowledge of moral philosophy, I set the discussion and its attending complications aside.

3. Note that on the definition of a popular sentiment that I have proposed, to retain the quality of an intuitively formed belief while being increasingly informed, the information must be about empirical rather than normative matters. If in addition to informing someone of criminology, the law, the penal system and the crimes, criminals, and victims we informed them of the arguments, principles, and positions current in criminal justice ethics, we would presumably eventually end up with a belief that was the result of a reflective process and more or less identical to one of the existing positions. I shall assume that this is not what we understand by being informed.

4. Studies show a clear tendency for opinions to become more lenient with respect to sentencing the better informed they are. Roberts labels this tendency 'one of the most robust and often-replicated findings in the field' (2011, p. 105) Note also that Roberts advances a different argument for roughly the same position that I here adopt. (ibid., p. 106)

5. Once again, I think this is being maximally charitable to the proponent of the claim of popular punishment. In practice, this assumption is so difficult to work with, since counterfactual sentiments are well-nigh impossible to predict and the achievement of wide-spread maximal informedness is unfeasible, that most actual claims of popular punishment will have to find some way of working around it, that is, by basing the claim on less informed sentiments. But while this represents a genuine challenge to putting the claim into practice, I want to focus the current discussion on the strength of its foundation.

6. Robinson and Darley suggest that the diversity of intuitions about punishment may be less dramatic than is sometimes assumed. Empirical evidence, they argue, supports the claim that there is relative convergence on comparative judgements of offence seriousness, that is, 'offence O_1 is less/more serious than O_2'. (Robinson & Darley, 2007, pp. 9–11; cf. Robinson, Kurzban, & Jones, 2007). Intractable differences of intuition will then rather concern the anchoring points of the penal scheme.

7. This seems to be the point that Roberts has in mind when he rejects the 'direct importation' model of popular punishment, because 'one can easily imagine public sentiment turning against a particular category of offender or public hostility being aroused against a particular offense. If public views were followed, the result would be severity premiums for a particular kind of offender or some specific offense—which could not be justified by any retributive principles' (2011, p. 103). A different reading of Roberts' argument would not require a balance of reasons but set retributivist constraints on the influence of popular opinion. This reading is supported when Roberts's emphasises that 'a model that directly imports public views throughout the criminal justice system would lead to undesirable outcomes' (ibid.). The desirability of such outcomes would, on the balance of reasons view, be a function of the relative strength of all the reasons at stake, and it would therefore be an open question whether direct implementation or maintaining status quo would better fit the outcome deemed desirable on a balance of reasons in each case. Only on a constraint view could we say beforehand with any degree of certainty that the results would be undesirable. Overall, I believe the balance of reasons position is the more plausible view.

8. A requirement along these lines fits with general principles of metaethics accepted by many moral thinkers, such as Gerald Cohen's (1991) interpersonal test or Richard Hare's (1952) universalisability condition, but I need not make the controversial claim that impartiality is a general condition for a reason's being valid in moral or political reasoning. I shall stick to the simpler and less controversial claim that it suitably constrains the reasons at stake in the claim of popular punishment.

9. Some might argue that under this definition there can be no unreasonable beliefs about whether to perform an action, since there will always be at least one *pro tanto* reason for or against performing any conceivable action, or perhaps more modestly that this will as a minimum apply to any realistically relevant action. I do not have any firm belief about whether this is the case, but it seems to me that I could concede the point while maintaining the thrust of the dilemma with respect to the argument for the claim of popular punishment.

10. Some may prefer to speak of 'making a decision of whether to φ' and letting beliefs affect our 'decision', for example, because the phrasing that I have employed may seem to suggest moral internalism, where normative beliefs are themselves motivating or even determinate of an agent's actions, which many thinkers would prefer not to assume. I believe that the dilemma holds on either version and so do not mean to imply a particular stand with respect to the internalism/externalism debate. Furthermore, and in a similar vein, some may wish to read 'a belief about whether to φ' as 'a belief about whether we ought to φ', or, even more elaborately, 'a belief about whether all things considered we have reason to φ'. I take the three to be identical in the context of the dilemma and so have used the simplest formulation.

11. Some might object that I have defined such sentiments as intuitive and that the process of weighing reasons is reflective. This is true on a more narrow understanding of intuition sometimes applied in moral philosophy but not on the looser meaning that I employ here. It seems to me that much—but not all—of our practical reasoning consists of weighing reasons in a way which is spontaneous, fast, and unreflective, so that we are not conscious of the details of the process and would struggle to put it into words.

12. The alternative is to shift to a reflective process of deductive reasoning. But once we do that we are no longer dealing with the type of belief at stake in the claim of popular punishment.

13. Other notable candidates well described in the literature include, for example, availability and representativeness, the first of which concerns the tendency to overestimate the relative weight of prominent or emotionally charged factors and the other, the tendency to overestimate the relative weight of common or average factors. We might suppose, for example, that the first influences perceptions of offences or punishments based on the degree to which they can be visualised and become emotionally significant when so imagined and that the second influences perceptions based on the degree to which the particular state of a moral factor is considered 'normal'. Another prime candidate drawn from the philosophical literature is pure time discounting, which is highly intuitive to most persons but extremely hard to justify. (Broome, 1994; Cowen & Parfit, 1992; Cowen, 2001; Parfit, 1984).

14. A somewhat similar objection concerns the difficulty of establishing empirically what the intuition responds to. (Golash & Lynch, 1995, pp. 720–725) The objection differs, however, in that it does not fundamentally challenge whether intuitions track the relevant features of the situation but only our ability to identify which features of the situation are being picked out by any particular intuition and hence our ability to formulate general principles from composite judgements of individual cases.

15. An objection at this point might be that I have already, for charitable reasons, assumed that a number of potential sources of error were not present in the sentiments at stake. I have assumed, recall, that these sentiments are informed, consistent, and weighable. Could we not simply adopt similar charitable assumptions at this point? I think not. While there is no sharp distinction between the sources of error at stake, it seems to me that we could narrow the field and educate the public to derive a set of actual sentiments that met the first

three assumptions, while no such possibility exist for the problems sketched in this section. While it is perhaps theoretically possible to avoid cognitive biases and distorting influences (see below), it seems to me unrealistic to expect that we could achieve it with public sentiments in practice. A different way of putting the point is that we *could* adopt such 'charitable' assumptions for these problems too but doing so would make an argument based on them vacuous since it effectively empties the field of candidate sentiments and thus would hardly be a service to the proponent.

16. Some might object that this seems an example of disgust affecting the weighing of reasons rather than introducing a reason. There is some difficulty, I think, in distinguishing the two in cases like this. A related experiment by Haidt (2001) is perhaps more suggestive, since it introduces the factor of disgust directly into the scenarios that persons are asked to assess and shows equally strong intuitive responses, indeed responses so strong as to be maintained when test subjects are pushed to admit that they cannot explain why their disgust-response should constitute a reason.

17. Contemporary defenders of intuitionism include Robert Audi (2005), Roger Crisp (2006), Michael Huemer (2007), and Derek Parfit (2011). Generalizing, one common line of defence is that there are certain fundamental intuitions which we can justify as reliable in the face of otherwise confusing factors, such as the intuition that welfare is good while harm to welfare is bad, or the intuition that we have reason to promote welfare. It seems safe to say at least that the position has not been abandoned yet.

18. Slightly earlier and in the same vein Roberts argues: 'Seriousness ratings and sentencing factors (for example) should reflect public opinion not for instrumental reasons—because the public will have more confidence in or respect for sentencing—but because community views constitute an inherent element of crime seriousness' (2011, p. 114). However, Roberts' point may perhaps be better understood as concerned with the participatory issue and advocating the use of popular sentiments through some form of public input—Roberts favours sociological research over democratic participation—to properly calibrate punishments so as to achieve the ends determined independently. This seems to me a more persuasive point. In any case it is not clear to me and I do not mean to suggest that he advocates the contractual argument in the shape that I here present it.

19. Note that the claim need not be, and plausibly should not be, that punishment is thereby all things considered unjustified. It can be unjustified in the limited sense of there being a *pro tanto* reason against it, which is all that the minimal claim of popular punishment requires.

20. Note that Dzur takes this to be an argument against institutional insulation. Whether it is depends on whether one believes that it is explicit or potential consent that does the normative work. If the former, institutional involvement is required to meet the condition; if the latter, it suffices that the solution arrived at is one that citizens *would* consent to, that is, that it aligns with their sentiments. Also note that the argument here is related to but is different from the form of retributivism which takes punishment to be the rectification of a balance of benefits that has been disturbed by the unfair advantage the criminal

has gained through enjoying the protection of the law while refusing the restrictions of liberty that granting that protection to other members of society would constitute (Murphy, 1973; for criticism of using this as the basis of the claim of popular punishment, cf. Golash & Lynch, 1995, pp. 715–716).

21. I believe that the majority of retributivist thinkers will want to be nonabsolutists and must therefore face the argument, especially of course those that accept Hart-style mixed theories, such that the institution of punishment can be fundamentally justified by its beneficial consequences. But not much depends upon whether this is true: absolutists can reject the argument at the cost of certain other difficulties, while nonabsolutists can avoid the difficulties that absolutism raises at the cost of having to face the argument. Whether one or the other is overall the more defensible position is probably a matter on which thinkers can reasonably disagree.

7

Public Opinion and Democratic Control of Sentencing Policy

Christopher Bennett

In this chapter I consider some of the reasons one might have for wishing to introduce public opinion into sentencing.[1] I begin by attempting to say what is wrong with penal populism, and I argue that the reasons against appealing to public opinion leave some scope for a more positive assessment of public input. This raises two questions: on the one hand, what reasons might we have for giving the public some input into sentencing matters; and on the other hand, what form should that input take? The answers to these questions are likely to be connected: perhaps we will not be able to say *what sort* of public input would be valuable until we know *why* it is valuable. I look at three reasons that might be thought to justify public input of some sort into sentencing. First, *public confidence* in the justice system is surely important, and public input might be necessary to sustain such confidence. Second, public input might be thought, under certain conditions, to lead to *better or fairer sentencing outcomes*. Finally, it might be thought independently valuable for there to be genuine *democratic control* over sentencing. I will argue broadly in favour of such reasons and so will in the end turn to the question of which institutions would be most suitable for public input. I am concerned in particular with the argument one might make for a certain model of public control over sentencing: the determination of sentences by jury rather than judge.[2]

1. WHAT IS WRONG WITH PENAL POPULISM?

First, what is wrong with penal populism (Pratt, 2007; Roberts, Stalans, Indermaur, & Hough, 2002)? One thing that might be wrong with it, of course, is that it produces harsher sentences than can be justified. That means not only that offenders suffer more than they ought to but also that they are done an injustice. But there are some other aspects to penal populism that are unsavoury. In the accusation of penal populism, there is also an implication that all parties concerned ought to know better. The politicians ought to know better in that they should be courageous enough to be prepared to be honest with the public. But such courage is required of politicians collectively. When penal populism is regarded as a legitimate tactic by at least one party, the honest politician is vulnerable to a rival who will undercut him or her, as it were, appealing to a simple, eye-catching, or gut-grabbing, vision of black and white justice (in this there are parallels to the way in which workers who attempt to maintain a dignified refusal to work for less than a decent wage, are vulnerable to being undercut and therefore losing everything: a race to the bottom) rather than a more complex but more adequate picture. Democracy, conceived as a market in votes, might lead, like advertising, to an appeal to and reinforcement of an unthinking or immediate response to crime. Penal populism is problematic not only because of its effects on offenders and the injustice done to them but also because it involves the cynical (or sometimes idealistic) manipulation of the public by politicians in the pursuit of power, in which the public is kept in partially complicit ignorance.

One question that arises out of this is whether or to what extent these considerations demonstrate that public opinion and sentencing policy do not mix. For instance, it might be said that on any view that gives public opinion a role in determining sentences, there will be a risk that offenders end up being treated more harshly than they ought to be. However, in response, three things might be said. First, it is also at least possible that they will be treated *less* harshly. Second, even if responsibility for sentencing is given to judges informed by sentencing guidelines, there is still the possibility that offenders will end up being treated more harshly than they ought to, since it is not the case that sentencing judges or guidelines are infallible. Indeed, an argument would need to be given as to why they should be taken to be more accurate than public opinion (I am not saying that such an argument could not be given, simply that would need to be such an argument. This issue will be considered below.) Third, we often think that wrong decisions are made through democratic procedures but that the decisions should nevertheless stand. This has been called the paradox of democracy (Wollheim, 1969). Not really a paradox, it is simply the fact that, when one is committed to decisions being made democratically, one might often end up with two conflicting views about 'what ought to be done:' on the one hand, the course of action one takes to be supported by the actual reasons, and, on the other, the course of action decided by the vote. If one is committed to democracy, therefore, one might believe that the democratic decision made about sentencing is wrong but nevertheless think that it ought to be followed, even though it will mean that the offender suffers more than he or she ought to and is to that extent done an injustice.

However, giving public opinion a greater role in sentencing decisions might extract some of the other poisons from penal populism. If politicians were not the ones deciding on sentencing policy, there would be no votes in claiming to be tough on crime. And taking responsibility for sentencing might force members of the public to become better informed about criminal justice issues. That might, of course, seem like mere idealism. At any rate readers will need a good deal of argument to convince them that this is an option worth pursuing. The present chapter will not be able to fill that argument out fully, of course. It only aims to provide some reasons to think that further thought on the topic might be worthwhile.

To begin, let me highlight some of the questions that we would have to deal with before we can claim to have a considered answer to the overall question of whether public opinion should have a role in determining sentencing levels:

- What is the justification of punishment or the purpose of sentencing?
- What are the reasons for giving public opinion a role in sentencing?
- What form will the introduction of public opinion take?
- What is the nature and importance of proportionality in sentencing and how can that be made compatible with allowing public opinion some influence over sentencing?

It might not be obvious at first glance why the first question is relevant to this list. However, as will become clear, the justification that one accepts for punishment and the institution of criminal justice will influence the reasons one thinks might count for giving public opinion some role in sentencing—for instance, what it would be for public opinion to further the aims of punishment or contribute to its legitimacy. It also influences the reasons one might have for thinking that proportionality matters, what it consists in, and hence, how public opinion might be made compatible with proportionality.

The first thing to do, however, is to ask ourselves what the reasons are for giving public opinion a role in sentencing.

2. WHY GIVE PUBLIC OPINION A ROLE IN SENTENCING?

In the following sections I consider a number of reasons that might be put forward for giving public opinion a role in sentencing policy. In thinking about these reasons we will inevitably have to say something about the wider question of the justification of the criminal justice apparatus and the shape that the introduction of public opinion might take.

Increasing Public Confidence in Justice

Considerations like this have been put forward by Julian Roberts, who claims that 'if sentencing practices diverged widely and consistently from public opinion the legitimacy of the judicial system would be compromised' (cited in Ryberg, 2010, p. 153). There are a number of things to note about this view. First, there are various things that can be meant by 'legitimacy'. Legitimacy, or its lack, in the sense in which we are interested here, is a property of the occupier of a hierarchical social position, a property of a person or body in some sort of practical authority. But given that basic idea, legitimacy might be understood in a number of different ways. For instance, it might be thought of as the claim that the person or body's claim to have the right to wield the power they do is a justified one. Or it might be the claim that there is a good justification for the existence of their hierarchical role, with its rights and responsibilities, and their occupation of it. Thus if an authority is legitimate, on this interpretation, the authority's claim to make the decisions that it does—to impose duties on its subjects and to wield power over them—is a justified one. On this interpretation of legitimacy, however, it is not (or need not be) a condition of legitimacy that there is any particular relation between the authority and public opinion: thus, on Joseph Raz's celebrated justification of political authority, the authority is justified if it makes it more likely that its subjects will comply with the reasons that apply to them (1986, p. 53). This condition might be met without the authority having any particular relation to public opinion.

Sometimes, however, the idea of legitimacy is understood specifically as having to do with *being recognised as being legitimate* or of having the confidence of the public. Here the issue is not so much *justification* as *credibility*. It is this variant of the idea of legitimacy that appears in the quote from Roberts: the legitimacy of the judicial system would be compromised if it were too far out of line with public opinion in the sense that it would no longer be regarded as being legitimate. There are two ways of understanding the idea of legitimacy that Roberts is invoking here. On the first, legitimacy simply is the property the occupier of a hierarchical social position might have of actually being supported by those over whom he or she rules or whose lives he or she affects.

On this interpretation, there is no distinction between being legitimate and being judged to be legitimate. On the second interpretation, the perception of whether someone in authority is legitimate might be justified or unjustified, accurate or inaccurate. The first interpretation is problematic since it makes legitimacy simply a matter of gaining acceptance. What matters for legitimacy is surely that there is acceptance for the right reasons. In which case we need to ask what the right reasons are—in which case we are asking whether the claim of the authority to be legitimate is a justified one, something that has to be settled by looking at the rationale for having that position occupied by that person or body and not simply at the public perception thereof.

The perception of legitimacy might still be very important, of course: for instance, given a social control or deterrence model of criminal justice, for the sentencing process to be effective as part of an apparatus of social control or maintenance of public order, people must believe in the process in a certain way, thinking that it is effective and that it gives them good reason to abide by social order. This might give those designing criminal justice institutions reason to make them responsive to public perceptions. Even on a more retributive view, it might be important, not just for justice to be done, but for it to be seen to be done. However, it might be thought that on a retributive view, the impetus is not so much to make the justice process responsive to public perceptions but to make it clear that the justice embodied in the process is recognised by the public. This raises an important issue about the direction of travel between public opinion and criminal justice: which should be moulded by which? What I called the 'second interpretation' in the preceding paragraph insists on the importance of public recognition to legitimacy—rejecting the idea that legitimacy consists simply in nothing more than justified authority. On this view we might say that legitimacy is *justified credibility*.

This is an apt moment to raise another question about what exactly the relation between public opinion and sentencing is supposed to be on this 'public confidence/legitimacy' approach. One thing that one might have in mind if one worries about public perceptions of criminal justice is whether the *outcomes* of judicial or sentencing decisions are in line with public opinion. Another thing one might be worrying about is whether there is public support, not necessarily for the outcomes, but for the *processes* and *procedures* by which those decisions are made: the outcomes may sometimes look strange to the public, but do they have confidence in the officials who make them and the procedures that they follow in doing so? If so, they may be prepared to accept some outcomes that appear to be out of line. A third way to read the aspiration to bring public opinion into sentencing, however, would be to stress the need for public control over sentencing, either in a direct or an indirect way. The first two options rely rather on the idea that public opinion should be in a position to *endorse* either outcomes or procedures, but it is not necessary that the public should be able to exercise *control*, whereas on the latter view some sort of control and a particularly direct form of accountability is necessary. Presumably for shoring up public confidence, it may be the case that only the endorsement of outcomes or procedures is necessary. However, it might be the case that, where confidence has got to such a low ebb, the public has to be given greater control over the process to restore confidence. If the public takes control of the process then, even if it delegates responsibility for making decisions to representatives in a bureaucracy, it might then become important that the outcomes or procedures be in line with public opinion.

However, the approach to introducing public opinion canvassed at the end of the last paragraph sees any potential accountability of sentencing decisions to public opinion as merely a means to the end of making criminal justice effective. It is not a matter of right. If one could have stable social control without public participation or the alignment of sentencing decisions with public views, on this view, that is what should happen. However, on a more ambitious view, on which matters of the rights of the public are invoked, it might be said that the reason sentencing decisions should be aligned with public opinion is that it is only then that they become truly justifiable—for instance, because it is the public's right in some way to be part of the process. Is there something that might justify that claim that the public has a right to be involved in sentencing decisions?

Better, Fairer Outcomes?

One argument for paying more attention to public opinion in deciding sentencing outcomes, or even for giving the public greater control over sentencing decisions, might be that this will lead to better quality sentencing decisions being made. There are various ways in which this claim might be made, some perhaps more plausible than others, depending on one's view of the purposes of sentencing. It might be less plausible if one thinks that the purpose that determines sentencing is deterrence or incapacitation of the dangerous. It might seem clear here that what is required to make a good decision is expert knowledge, either of the behavioural tendencies of the offender or the effect of the offender being punished on the behavioural tendencies of the population as a whole. The reliance on experts might be doubted, of course. We might doubt the purported wisdom of psychological experts. If that could be made plausible, it might open the way for an argument that, if we are attempting to make an intuitive assessment of a person's likelihood of offending or of the deterrent effect on others of publicising a certain punishment, a collective decision is likely to be better than an individual one. This argument in turn could be made in two ways. One would appeal to the Condorcet jury theorem, which says that simply as a matter of mathematics, the majority decision of a large group is more likely, across a series of decisions, to approximate to the truth than individual decisions across the same series.[3] Another would appeal rather to the possibilities of deliberation that precede a collective decision being made, arguing that such deliberation can correct for obvious mistakes and biases, can pool information, can lead to a number of perspectives being taken into account, and so on (Aikin & Clanton, 2010). Nevertheless, although this argument might be made, deterrent theorists might be unwilling to accept that this method is more likely to lead to correct outcomes than reliance on expert opinion. In the end, predictions of deterrent effect are complex probabilities relying on hard-to-ascertain matters of empirical fact, and it might plausibly be said that members of the public are simply not competent to make such decisions.

However, matters might be different if we take up instead a nonempirical sentencing rationale such as retributivism. For the retributivist, the severity of punishment should be determined by the seriousness of the wrong. But this simple formula notoriously leads to difficult questions. For a start, there seems no simple way to categorise the seriousness of wrongs. Is 'wounding with intent' always a less serious offence than 'manslaughter'? Now, on one strand of retributive sentencing theory, it is taken to be a sine qua non of retributivism that there must be some sort of determinate answer to such questions: an ordinal scale of offences at the very least (von Hirsch & Ashworth, 2005, Chapter 9). However, others are sceptical about this possibility.[4] Will not the seriousness of these two actions depend on the precise and detailed nature of the offence and the offending circumstances? Where the wounding is caused maliciously, with the intent to cause serious and prolonged pain, whereas the manslaughter results from a stupid but minor lapse in attention, although the act of wrongful killing is far more serious than the act of wounding and its consequences more dreadful, it might be said that the culpability involved in the latter is far greater. How should those elements of the act itself; its intention, motivation or culpability; and its harmful consequences be weighed in assessing 'the seriousness of the wrong'?

Even assuming, however, that despite these problems we do have some grasp on ordinal proportionality—that is, which wrongs are more serious than others—if we move on to the question of cardinal proportionality—which wrongs are equivalent to or fitting to which punishments—again it might seem hard to see a simple answer. How is the ordinal scale to be 'anchored' with certain punishments being judged appropriate to certain crimes?

The retributivist might acknowledge these difficulties but deny that they lead to the conclusion that there is no determinate answer to questions about proportionality. He or she might accept, however, that there is no simple way to determine what these answers are. Rather, as with many complex questions where we find it hard to specify an answer in advance of inquiry, the retributivist might say, what we have to do is rather to give an account of what an inquiry would have to be like for an adequate answer to be discovered. Then it might be said that, as an epistemic matter, we have no better grasp of the concept of an adequate, for example, conception of the seriousness of a particular wrong or of a punishment fitting to a particular crime than the answer (or, perhaps, range of answers) that might be given at the end of such an inquiry. For instance, one recent, broadly pragmatist approach to epistemology argues that we have no better grasp on the notion of truth than the outcome of a well-conducted inquiry and that we have no better grasp on the notion of a well-conducted inquiry than one that involves the possession and exercise of an appropriate range of epistemic or intellectual virtues (curiosity, conscientiousness, attentiveness, imaginativeness, etc.).[5] The range of virtues that an inquiry would have to display to be well conducted would no doubt differ with the particular domains into which are being inquired. But the basic thought is that they are virtues that involve the pursuit, appreciation, and correct weighing of relevant considerations and the removal or overcoming of bias. Whether one accepts that pragmatist account of truth as such, one might well think that in a domain of inquiry such as that of retributive justice (if one accepts that there is such a thing as legitimate inquiry in this domain), we have no better grasp of a standard of correctness or adequacy for our judgements than that just given. Further, one might argue that it is quite likely that a group is more likely to possess and be able to exercise these virtues than is any individual working in isolation.

If the considerations of the last few paragraphs are plausible, one might argue for a version of the claim that public opinion should have an input into sentencing: on a retributivist view, it might be claimed that sentencing decisions about proportionality are better made by a jury of citizens rather than a sentencing judge or magistrate. (Furthermore, for reasons having to do with the relation, on a plausible retributivist view, between the need for punishment and the need for apology and reparation, it might be that the participants in the jury ought to include the victim and the offender, if they are so willing.[6]) Having said this, however, it seems reasonably clear that a jury would benefit from some guidance or direction from a judge for a number of reasons: (a) information about decisions in like cases might be epistemically useful as a starting point to fix standards or to make clear the need for argument about the relevant differences of the case in hand; (b) it is essential that the sentencing be for the wrong as captured in the legally defined offence rather than the wrong as such, and the jury would need guidance on the difference between those two; and (c) a virtue of a sentencing system is parity across like cases, and some guidance would need to be given to the jury to ensure that due consideration was given to that. But if a jury makes it clear in its judgement that it has taken such direction and guidance into account and shows evidence that it has given each of these points due consideration, it might be that we have no better epistemic standard of what punishment crime deserves.

Democratic Authority

However, for some people, for all that some of these considerations might be helpful and persuasive in some respects, we have not yet got to the heart of what drives the argument for public control over sentencing. For them, the crucial question is not just about the quality of the outcomes but rather about who is in charge. It is a question, not simply about how the make the best decisions, but who gets to make the decisions. It is a question, in other words, of authority.

On some views, it follows straightforwardly that a body that is best placed to make decisions that have good outcomes ought to be in charge. But even on those views, a concern for authority is something different from a concern for outcomes. Authority is a matter of having the right to make decisions, to have those decisions followed and implemented by those who are governed by the decision (those under the jurisdiction of the relevant body), to have those decisions treated as settling the question of what those governed by the decision should, as a group, do. There is a question of what justifies anyone having this hierarchical position. And on the range of views that we are considering in this paragraph, this is settled straightforwardly by the fact that a particular body is more likely, on the whole, to make good, well-informed, and effective decisions than any other body and so that being governed by that authority will cause those governed to act more in line with the reasons that apply to them than they would have otherwise.[7]

Now even on this type of view, there must be more than wisdom that qualifies a body to be an authority. There is no point in having wisdom, for instance, unless when one speaks others will actually follow. So another necessary condition of the justification of some authority would have to be efficacy or the ability actually to coordinate the action of a group by means of one's dictates. But there are some further, more serious problems with this sort of view. We can group these problems into two importantly different types. But addressing these problems might be thought to lead us in the direction of greater democracy and greater incorporation of public opinion.

First, there are concerns about epistemic access to the reasons governing the domain over which the authority rules. If we take the example of an authority setting laws to govern the whole of a political society, it seems clear that decisions will invoke normative matters. Now, while many theorists will reject pure subjectivism about normative matters, assuming that there at least some well-ordered practices of inquiry by which we can make headway in coming to determinate answers about practical questions, many think nevertheless that the notion of one body having wisdom in a certain area is problematic on the grounds that the considerations involved and the process of weighing such considerations are hugely complex. Reasonable humility should, on this view, lead any person or group to be wary of imposing their view on others, just because no one is infallible, and in such a complex area of thought it is very easy to go wrong.[8] Some, indeed, go further and assert not just that true claims about normative matters are hard to discern but that values are plural and incommensurable and that there simply are always going to be a range of equally satisfactory answers to at least some normative questions (Berlin, 2003). In which case it might be important for anyone making authoritative decisions on normative matters to take public opinion into account for the reason that they should accept that there are likely to be a range of epistemically reasonable positions on any one question, and reasonable humility dictates taking the view that there may be no good way of telling for certain whether the view to which one inclines oneself is in the end more adequate than an opposing view.

Of course, even on this view, these considerations do not entail that officials should simply take public opinion on a particular question for granted, that they should translate it uncritically into public policy. Public opinion should be taken as a guide only insofar as the best explanation for the content of the public's views is engagement with the relevant issues. Where the content of the public's view can be convincingly 'explained away' as a result of lazy thinking, political rhetoric, manipulation, prejudice, and bias (as in the case where 'penal populism' inflames and distorts public opinion for certain ends), then on this line it need not be taken seriously. This is because the fact that a person espouses a certain view is not credible as a source of evidence about how things are, normatively speaking, if there is reason to think that they hold that view for nonepistemic reasons. It may be that we should have a certain degree of faith in people's intellectual seriousness or at least their willingness to be intellectually serious when properly engaged. And we should have a certain degree of willingness to accept a person's assurances that they have thought seriously about a matter when they say that they have. But neither of these points entail that, on the view being discussed in this paragraph, public opinion should be taken uncritically as a guide to public policy making. Nevertheless, it may be plausible to think that, even after we take away those views that are ill considered, biased, or prejudiced, there will remain a range of serious public opinion and that reasonable answers to many of our pressing practical questions will not point in just one direction. Furthermore, and crucially for the example of the jury, we might think it plausible that we can design ideal deliberative fora in which individuals who might in many circumstances be tempted into lazy thinking are enabled to engage instead with depth and seriousness: for instance, where it is clear that something important is at stake and that they have a serious responsibility over someone's interests and where the problem they are asked to solve is one that it is within their powers to solve (i.e. that it is reasonably focused, not overwhelming, etc.).

On the basis of the considerations of the past two paragraphs, we might think that it would be problematic to allow any particular body or class of individuals (or ruling elite, drawn largely from a particular class, ethnic group, and educational background) to be given responsibility for authoritative decision making in a particular normatively charged domain and that it would be more satisfactory if we attempted to find some compromise based on the range of serious public opinion, something that a citizen jury might be an attractive mechanism for bringing about. Thus even if one thinks that all that matters in the justification of authority is the quality of the guidance given by a particular authority's directives, one might be inclined towards democratic decision making.

Second, however, the idea that wisdom confers (political) authority might be disputed on the basis of concerns about whether there really is nothing more to the justification of authority than the quality of guidance. For some, as well as concerns about the quality of the outcomes of decision-making, there are also concerns about the fairness of the procedures themselves (e.g. Waldron, 1993). In particular, there is a concern that the procedures should be compatible with the equality of each person as a citizen and as a joint author of the actions of the state. On this view, anything that the state does ought to be capable of being seen as an act taken on behalf of the people as a whole. But if the people as a whole is in charge, that means that each person should have exactly the same say in determining how the state should act, that is, what its determining principles and policies are. In this case we can say that procedures by which policy decisions are made—including decisions about sentencing policy—have to be such as are compatible with the equality of each citizen, specifically the equal right of each to have a say in determining what those policies are.

Now there are two immediately pressing questions. One is about the value of democracy. Why should we think that a form of government is particularly important if it gives each (adult) member an equal say?[9] Of course, there is much to say about this, but the basic intuition, which might be cashed out in various different ways, is that in the context of political life no one should be treated as being more important than anyone else, that the dignity of each requires that they not be required publicly to accept a second-class status, and that they would have to accept a second-class status if some were given a right to greater say in decision making than others. The upshot of this is that, regardless of the inevitable variations in epistemic acuity, each person has the same right as any other to determine what the policies of the state ought to be.

Even if that is convincing, however, a second pressing question concerns the practical implications of the value of democracy: what does it actually mean for procedures to be compatible with the freedom and equality of each citizen? On this point, we could return to the distinction that we made earlier between: on the one hand, the importance of public endorsement, either of sentencing outcomes or the procedures by which those outcomes are decided upon, and on the other, public control over those outcomes. The importance of public endorsement might be kept in view by a set of benevolent officials who are committed to implementing only publicly endorsed policies but where the public has no control, direct or indirect, over the way in which these officials act. This benevolent dictatorship is often thought to be problematic on the grounds that it is empirically unlikely that such an insulated group would remain committed to taking public views seriously. So some sort of mechanisms of accountability to the public might have to be introduced, by which the public exercise control and determine for themselves that their will is being followed.

If this is so, however, there is a question of how much control is necessary. A central debate on this point is between those who believe that democracy is compatible with at least some significant decisions being made by representatives and those who believe that true democracy has to be direct. Even on the direct democracy view, however, the democratic input is often taken to be most important in the decision making, and there can be room for plenty of delegation of powers to those who will implement those decisions. For instance, if there was democratic control of sentencing, at least one possibility would be that, although a group of citizens made the decisions, responsibility was delegated to a group of specialists to implement the decision. Furthermore, there might also be a specialist role for oversight of the implementation of the decision. Ultimately, of course, those who implement the sentence would be accountable to the jury, or to the public as a whole, for their carrying out the task. But the responsibility for day-to-day oversight and accountability might be something that it is compatible with democracy to delegate to a specialist. Of course, this might be denied: it might be argued that democratic control is only genuine when the sentence is implemented in and by the community itself. This might have certain benefits—it might build social solidarity and encourage victims, offenders, and others to engage with one another and develop important character skills by taking responsibility for these tasks rather than leaving it to the experts. However, it might be argued that democratic authority is not the only important value and that offenders will be treated better and more effectively when a team gets the opportunity to specialise in that role rather than doing it in their spare time as public service. An argument for the more participatory model could either be made on empirical grounds, claiming that the trade-off between these values favours the punishment-in-the-community model, since the benefits to be gained for individuals and the community as a whole outweighs the costs. Or it could be made by insisting that the importance of democratic authority outweighs whatever costs that community implementation might have.

If it is accepted, however, that some degree of representation or delegation is compatible with democratic authority, what are the reasons to favour decision making on sentencing by a citizen jury rather than by a group such as judges who are at least indirectly accountable to the public (e.g. through the control of the legislature over sentencing guidelines)? I have mentioned a number of relevant considerations already: for instance, the epistemic value of a collective deliberative mechanism in tricky evaluative questions; such collective deliberation might be impossible to organise amongst the whole electorate for every sentencing decision, of course, but it would be possible to organise a group of citizens picked more or less at random for each decision (or the day's or week's decisions). Furthermore, it might seem preferable, from what we have been saying, to have a small group of collective deliberators who are able to pay attention to the details of each individual offender's case rather than democratic control over some more abstract sentencing priorities that are then implemented mechanically by those to whom power to set sentences has been delegated. There is also the consideration that any group of representatives comes to have its own vested interests that might bias its decisions and might break the link with democratic control. And it is also very important to acknowledge that the citizen jury has an important symbolic value: it says very directly that the public is in charge.

3. CONCLUSION: FURTHER QUESTIONS

In this chapter I have attempted to sketch out a route, or a number of routes, by which one might seek to justify introducing public opinion into sentencing policy in a specific way—by having sentencing decisions made by a jury—and to provide some evaluation of those arguments. But there are important questions that I have left unaddressed. For instance, I have suggested that the argument for sentencing by jury would likely be at its most plausible if it is accepted that sentencing has an essentially retributive- or desert-based component: given the complexity of situations of criminal wrongdoing that cannot be captured by rigidly applied sentencing guidelines and given the superiority of group over individual deliberation, there is at least an argument to be made that a jury would be best placed to decide on what that the retributive sentence should be. But what if one thinks that sentencing should be determined either in part or in full by considerations about deterrence or incapacitation? It might be said that in these domains expert knowledge trumps untutored collective deliberation. Even here, however, it might still be said that the final authority to make decisions rests with the people on the grounds that the most important value for public policy is that it should be an expression of the will of (all) the people. If we find that thought plausible, perhaps the public should be advised by the experts, appearing as it were as witnesses, but the jury should make the final decision.[10]

Another large question, however, is how far we think democratic decision making in sentencing is of value and how far we ought to prioritise democratic processes if they come up with decisions that are plainly wrong. Even on the strongest defence, democracy remains only one value amongst others. Therefore, it might be said that defence of other values sometimes requires anti-democratic intervention to correct gross injustices that would otherwise be inflicted. Furthermore, democracy has certain foundational values—for instance, respect for the equality of citizens as self-determining beings—but a democratically constituted decision-making body might make a decision that contravenes those values. In these cases there could be a strong argument that democracy itself requires that the democratic decision be constrained (Brettschneider, 2007). However, we need an account of a mechanism by which that constraint could be brought about. I have already suggested that a sentencing jury should have a legal adviser: should a legal official have the power not just to advise but in extremis actually to strike down a sentencing decision or ask the jury to think again? Could the offender him- or herself appeal the decision? If so, to whom should the appeal be referred?

I should also note that sentencing by jury is not the only model of democratic control over sentencing that is worth considering. An alternative would be the model proposed by Paul Robinson (this volume), on which psychological experiments are used to make precise assessments of public opinion on questions of ordinal and cardinal proportionality, the results of which are used to formulate sentencing guidelines applied by judges. Proper assessment of this model is not possible here, but it is worth noting a number of advantages of the jury system. First, the jury system puts the public in a position not just to endorse sentencing outcomes but actually to control them. (Whether this is important depends on one's views about the extent to which it is legitimate for the public to delegate decisions to representatives.) Second, an aspect of my argument for the jury had to do with the epistemic value of decisions made by the public given the irreducible complexity of particular situations. I suggested that a group of deliberators might be better able to come to a view about the significance of the situation of wrongdoing as a whole. This would be lost if it were simply the case that a sentencing judge were required to respond more or less automatically to the presence of a certain feature in the criminal act.

Third, and relatedly, a jury with control over the sentencing decision is able to respond to the offender as a human being rather than simply categorising him or her according to the guidelines, and this can be an important factor in reducing the likelihood of disproportionately punitive sentencing decisions. When members of jury have the offender in front of them and they realise that they have responsibility for the future direction of that person's life, there is at least a possibility that this situation of human contact should have a transforming effect on those judging—as is quite widely reported in restorative justice 'sentencing circles'—an effect that it is hard to see could be brought about if retributive responses are being measured by responses to cases in laboratory conditions. On this last point, however, it is worth noting that my response assumes that the jury would indeed have the offender in front of it as a judge does in passing sentence: a full consideration of these issues would have to consider whether that is more attractive than the alternative that sentencing decisions should be made in anonymous conditions where, for example, the race, appearance, gender, and other potential sources of bias surrounding the offender are removed from the jury's ken.

Other questions to be considered in a development of the arguments canvassed here might include: How long should citizen juries serve? Should it be something more like a commission that lasts for six months or a year? Should it have exclusively lay membership? How would its membership be determined? On the latter question, it seems clear that it would be better for the purposes of genuine deliberation that jury members are appointed rather than elected on a platform, so that they have no manifesto commitments to defend or public perceptions to take into account. However, if appointment is the way to go, is random selection best or should there be an expert element to each jury (should there be e.g. an ex-offender on each jury?)? If randomisation is chosen, is it nevertheless important to ensure that the make-up of the jury reflects social diversity to a reasonable degree?[11] These are questions to be dealt with at a later date. I hope, however, to have made at least some headway in thinking constructively about how to improve the relationship between public opinion and criminal justice.

REFERENCES

Aikin, S. F., and J. C. Clanton. 2010. 'Developing Group-Deliberative Virtues.' *Journal of Applied Philosophy* 27: 409–424.

Arneson, R. 2004. 'Democracy Is Not Intrinsically Just.' In K. Dowding, R. Goodin, and C. Pateman (eds.), *Justice and Democracy: Essays For Brian Barry*. Cambridge: UK: Cambridge University Press.

Bennett, C. 2008. *The Apology Ritual*. Cambridge, UK: Cambridge University Press.

Berlin, I. 2003. 'Alleged Relativism in Eighteenth-Century Thought' in H. Hardy (ed.), *The Crooked Timber of Humanity: Chapters in the History of Ideas*. London: Pimlico.

Brettschneider, C. 2007. *Democratic Rights: The Substance of Self-Government*. Princeton, N.J.: Princeton University Press.

Duff, R. A. 2001. *Punishment, Communication and Community*. Oxford: Oxford University Press.

Dzur. A. W. 2012. 'Participatory Democracy and Criminal Justice.' *Criminal Law and Philosophy* 6: 115–129.

Estlund, D. 2008. *Democratic Authority*. Princeton, N.J.: Princeton University Press.

Gardner, J. 1998. 'Crime: In Proportion and In Perspective.' In A. Ashworth and M. Wasik (ed.), *Fundamentals of Sentencing Theory: Essays in Honour of Andrew von Hirsch*. Oxford: Oxford University Press, 1998.

Loader, I. 2000. 'Plural Policing and Democratic Governance.' *Social and Legal Studies* 9: 323–345.

Pratt, J. 2007. *Penal Populism*. London: Taylor and Francis.

Rawls, J. 1993. *Political Liberalism*. New York: University of Columbia Press.

Raz, J. 1986. *The Morality of Freedom*. Oxford: Clarendon.

Roberts, J. V., L. J. Stalans, D. Indermaur, and M. Hough. 2002. *Penal Populism and Public Opinion: Lessons from Five Countries*. Oxford: Oxford University Press.

Ryberg, J. 2010. 'Punishment and Public Opinion.' In J. Ryberg and J. A. Corlett (eds.), *Punishment and Ethics: New Perspectives*. Basingstoke, UK: Palgrave Macmillan.

von Hirsch, A., and A. Ashworth. 2005. *Proportionate Sentencing*. Oxford: Oxford University Press.

Waldron, J. 1993. 'A Right-Based Critique of Constitutional Rights.' *Oxford Journal of Legal Studies* 13: 18–51.

Wollheim, R. 1969. 'A Paradox in the Theory of Democracy.' In P. Laslett and W. Runciman (eds.), *Philosophy, Politics and Society (Second Series): A Collection*. Oxford: Blackwell.

Zagzebski, L. 1996. *Virtues of the Mind: An Inquiry into the Nature of Virtue and the Ethical Foundations of Knowledge*. Cambridge, UK: Cambridge University Press.

NOTES

1. A version of this paper was discussed at a symposium on punishment and public opinion organised by Julian Roberts and Jesper Ryberg in October 2012. I am very grateful to the organisers for inviting me to be involved and for the comments that I received at the workshop. I would particularly like to thank Paul Robinson, Albert Dzur, and Richard Lippke.

2. For a paper with somewhat similar aims, see Dzur (2012).
3. 'If voters are only a little better than random, and choices are between two alternatives, then majority rule would be nearly infallible' (Estlund, 2008, p. 15).
4. Cf. Duff: 'The cost of [the von Hirsch approach] is a kind of generalisation, of abstraction from the concrete particularities of different kinds of crime, which threatens to separate the law's definitions of crimes from extralegal moral understandings of them as wrongs. These moral understandings are more complex, particularised, and concrete than are the understandings available within such a legal framework. They preclude any unitary ranking of all crimes on a single scale of seriousness, since they connect the wrongfulness of different kinds of crime to different kinds of value that cannot without distortion be rendered rationally commensurable' (2001 p. 136). See also John Gardner's (1998) critique of von Hirsch.
5. Because of the central role it gives to virtues in knowledge, this approach has been called 'virtue epistemology'; see Zagzebski (1996).
6. See my discussion of the 'limited devolution model' in the final chapter of Bennett (2008).
7. Cf. Raz's (1986) 'normal justification thesis'.
8. See, famously, on the 'burdens of judgement': Rawls (1993).
9. This has been recently denied by Arneson (2004).
10. Cf. the M'Naghten Rules on the use of the insanity defence, where it remains the jury's responsibility to determine whether the defence should be accepted, on the basis of expert testimony.
11. Cf. the considerations about democratic control of the police through police commissions in Loader (2000).

8

Criminal Prosecutors: Experts or Elected Officials?[1]

Richard L. Lippke

Contributors to this volume approach the normative role of public opinion in criminal justice policy and practice from a number of different perspectives, some theoretical, others more applied. Here the question is explored by considering the role that the public might play in regulating the exercise of discretion by a critical actor in the criminal process: the prosecutor. Specifically, the essay examines the practice in the United States of requiring prosecutors to stand for election.

One of the unique features of the US criminal justice system is that not only must prosecutors in some jurisdictions submit to the electoral process so must police chiefs (or in rural areas, sheriffs) and judges. Although the character of these elections and their frequency varies, whatever form they take, they would seem to necessitate some degree of responsiveness on the part of the officials involved to the concerns of the democratic electorate. If it is assumed, as it often is, that the electorate is, with some frequency, whipped into a frenzy (by the media or by politicians holding or running for public office) about crime, it will seem that elected police chiefs, judges, and prosecutors must cater to demands for the severe punishment of offenders. Those officials also might be tempted to give into to voter scepticism about the value of the many procedural protections afforded individuals suspected or accused of crimes and thus be led to ignore or evade those protections. Given the extent to which legal punishment of all kinds is inflicted upon citizens of the United States, it is natural to cast the democratic election of key criminal justice officials as a worrisome feature of a system that appears in other respects to be running amok.

There is, I would acknowledge, something quite compelling about the line of argument just sketched. Yet it is one that rushes rather too quickly to its conclusion. My focus in the discussion that follows will be on prosecutors. The merits and demerits of electing police chiefs or judges are topics for another time. The first thing to note, then, is that most prosecutors in the United States are not directly elected. Only chief prosecutors in the 2,300 or so local or regional legal jurisdictions within states are elected; federal prosecutors are not elected and subordinate prosecutors within local or regional jurisdictions are appointed by chief prosecutors and serve at their discretion.[2] It would be a mistake to infer that subordinate local and regional prosecutors are thereby insulated from the demands of the democratic electorate. Clearly they are not; if their bosses are sensitive political animals, as some of them will be, subordinate prosecutors will have to take into account the politically motivated wishes of their superiors. But chief prosecutors will undoubtedly vary in the degree to which they grant autonomy to those who work for them, and this might open up space for subordinate prosecutors to ignore or downplay the wishes of the electorate. Furthermore, chief prosecutors will likely have some ability to shape the public's perceptions of what their offices should be doing with respect to combating crime. In short, we should be cautious about assuming that chief prosecutors are simply conduits for the public's demands about how crime is to be controlled effectively.

Despite these complications, it might nonetheless seem more likely than not that the election of chief prosecutors will, to a significant extent, expose the criminal justice process to the views of voters who are rather 'inexpert', as it were, concerning the causes of crime, the costs and consequences of legal punishment, and the vital role procedural protections afford those suspected or accused of crimes. Indeed, as we will see, there is a tempting line of argument according to which we should be prepared to limit, quite dramatically, the input that the democratic electorate has concerning the operations of the criminal justice system. According to this line of argument, the investigation, prosecution, and punishment of crimes is a domain appropriately guided by specialised forms of knowledge that it is unlikely most of the citizens of democratic societies possess. As such, these important tasks should be carried out by more knowledgeable individuals who are effectively insulated from the demands of the democratic electorate. How far proponents of this view would be prepared to take it is unclear. But if the pursuit of criminal justice in the United States is too democratic, the 'expertise account', as I shall term it, provides us with a vision of a society in which it might not seem democratic enough.

The discussion proceeds as follows: In Section 1, I lay out the extraordinary discretion that prosecutors, and especially chief prosecutors, in the United States have. In light of this discretion, it is plausible to claim that the democratic electorate has some legitimate interest in monitoring and guiding their activities. Yet there is empirical evidence suggesting that democratic elections are ineffective devices for checking the power of chief prosecutors. Although such elections might be improved, there is reason to believe that they can never do more than give citizens the power to remove chief prosecutors from office, rather than replace them with better ones. Moreover, there is a principled argument to the effect that it is inappropriate to subject the prosecution of crimes to any form of direct electoral control. This is the expertise account, which is developed in detail in Section 2. In elaborating it, we are confronted with various problems. First, we must explain the ways in which the prosecution of crime is an activity involving specialised forms of knowledge or skill. Second, we must explain why citizens in democratic societies ought to be prepared to turn over the prosecution of crime to the experts. Even assuming that these questions can be answered to everyone's satisfaction, we might doubt that turning the pursuit of criminal justice over entirely to the experts is a sound idea.

In Section 3, I summarise the respective strengths and weaknesses of electing prosecutors compared with having them trained and promoted within professional bureaucracies that insulate them from democratic politics. Although the balance of reasons favours regarding prosecutors as experts rather than elected officials, democratic values might still seem to auger for their election. However, I conclude that public input of other kinds into the criminal justice system is preferable to the direct election of prosecutors.

1. DEMOCRATIC CONTROL OF US PROSECUTORS

It is well-established that the prosecutorial function in the United States is multifaceted and that prosecutors have considerable discretion in performing their various tasks (see Wright, 2008–2009, pp. 584–588; see also Davis, 1969; Gold, 2011; Vorenberg, 1981). This is especially true of chief prosecutors. Although it exaggerates things to say that the criminal code exerts no pressure on charging decisions, the proliferation of criminal prohibitions in the last fifty years has provided prosecutors with a veritable smorgasbord of possible crimes with which they can charge individuals (see Stuntz, 2001, pp. 508–509). Most of the charging discretion that chronically underfunded and overburdened prosecutors have is utilised in trying to convince individuals suspected of crimes to plead guilty, quite often by overcharging them and thereby menacing them with such long sentences that they quickly cave in and agree to enter guilty pleas in exchange for some charging or sentencing lenity (Stuntz, 2001, pp. 519–520; Vorenberg, 1981, pp. 1524–1537). Decisions about who to charge with crimes, with what to charge them, which charges to add or drop once some have been lodged, and what charge reductions to offer accused individuals to induce them to plead guilty are left almost entirely to the discretion of prosecutors. Judges do not rigorously oversee the charging process, and the victims of crimes have little formal legal recourse if prosecutors decide not to lodge charges at all or to reduce them to what they believe will convince defendants to plead guilty. Sentence discounts in plea bargaining are subject to some oversight by the courts, but most experts agree that judges are reluctant to veto sentence bargains once they have been struck by prosecutors and defence attorneys (Heumann, 1977, pp. 127–418; Pizzi, 1993, pp. 1358–1359). In the relatively few cases that go to trial, prosecutors typically have more resources at their disposal than the accused, especially since the indigent defence system in the United States is chronically underfunded (Lefstein, 2004). It is therefore not surprising to discover that prosecutors win over 80 per cent of the felony cases that go to trial (Stuntz, 2001, p. 570). Defendants who lose at trial are not only denied the charge or sentence discounts that their guilty-pleading counterparts receive, but might also encounter sentence recommendations from prosecutors that are vindictively motivated—so-called trial penalties.[3] The higher courts have upheld such penalties (see *Bordenkircher v. Hayes,* 1978). Trial judges too have been known to exact them from defendants whom they believe have wasted everyone's time by insisting on the ritual of a trial (Heumann, 1977, pp. 144–148).

Since convictions in over 95 per cent of criminal cases in the United States are the products of plea bargaining, voters who wish to evaluate prosecutorial performance would be well-advised to focus their attention on plea-bargained outcomes. Most prosecutors will be successful at amassing convictions, at least in the aggregate. Indeed, legal observers worry that US prosecutors are conviction maximisers, meaning that they are concerned with getting convictions whether or not charged defendants are guilty or, perhaps more often, whether or not the charges ultimately agreed to match the crimes that those who plead guilty actually committed (Bowers, 2007, p. 1141). Voters presumably should be interested not only in prosecutorial success in gaining convictions and more interested in this when the crimes in question are serious but also in whether the sentences ultimately agreed to by prosecutors (and ratified by judges) match the seriousness of the crimes committed by individuals. Unfortunately, it will be difficult for voters to discern whether plea bargained outcomes accurately reflect the criminal activities of those who fall under the purview of the criminal justice system. It has been suggested that prosecutors' offices should provide the public with records of any and all charges lodged in cases (Gold, 2011, pp. 97–98). By comparing charges initially filed with those ultimately agreed to in plea negotiations, the public might be better able to gauge how willing or unwilling prosecutors have been to acquiesce in reduced punishment to gain convictions. This might provide the public with some sense of prosecutorial performance in assigning appropriate sanctions to crimes.[4]

Beyond the absolute or noncomparative justice of the sentences effected by prosecutors' offices, voters should also have some interest in the comparative justice of plea bargained outcomes. Although it is difficult to compare cases and negotiated outcomes will often turn on slight differences in offenders' criminal actions and their previous records, voters do have some legitimate interest in having like cases treated alike.[5] This will especially be true if certain individuals in society are routinely offered more attractive plea deals than others despite scant differences in their crimes or other relevant sentencing features.

Beyond the comparative and noncomparative justice of plea bargained outcomes, voters have a significant stake in the conduct of prosecutors in other respects. They might scrutinise the profile of crimes processed by a prosecutor's office. Are convictions for certain kinds of crimes pursued more often than convictions for other kinds?[6] Also, are serious crimes given appropriate weight by the office, such that more resources are expended on them than on convictions for mid- or low-level offences?

The public also has a significant interest (whether it always realises it) in the extent to which prosecutors' offices respect and uphold the requirements of procedural justice. Does the office 'play fair' with defendants and their attorneys, or does it use every bit of leverage that its charging discretion affords it to extract guilty pleas? Does it reliably disclose exculpatory evidence or do so only grudgingly? In cases in which convictions appear unsafe because key pieces of evidence have been shown to be unreliable, does the office cling to convictions come what may, or does it gracefully concede that injustices may have been done? These are questions with which the public should be concerned about getting some answers to, as they would tell it much about the office's attitude towards the use of its considerable power to adversely affect citizens' lives.

Finally, since chief prosecutors are ultimately responsible for staffing and running their offices, voters should have some interest—although one would think a lower priority interest compared with the ones just discussed—in how well they perform these 'office management' tasks. This interest might lead them to inquire into the following: Do subordinate prosecutors have clear guidelines for deciding how to allocate their resources and the kinds of plea deals to offer? Also, how efficiently run is the office? Are charges and legal motions filed in a timely fashion or are cases often botched due to avoidable delays in executing these tasks? How effective is the office at investigating crimes once an initial case record has been turned over to it by the police? Does the office have a good working relationship with the police and investigators who do the initial work on crimes? Does the office have a good working relationship with local judges who perform plea colloquies or try cases? Further, does the office have competent individuals to try the relatively few cases that cannot be resolved through plea bargaining? Or does it routinely lose cases that go to trial? Admittedly, trial success or failure has to be interpreted carefully, as even skilled attorneys can lose cases for reasons that are largely beyond their control. But a record of persistent success or failure at trial likely tells us something about the competence of a prosecutor's office.

Given the enormous power that prosecutors' offices in the United States have and the relative paucity of institutional checks and balances on exercises of that power, it is not preposterous to suggest that we might subject the individuals who manage those offices to close oversight and, perhaps, electoral control (Pizzi, 1993). Someone ought to be monitoring the performance of prosecutors to ensure that they are acting appropriately. In the absence of oversight by other agencies or qualified officials, the voters in a given jurisdiction might be assigned the task of monitoring whether prosecutors' offices are producing comparatively and noncomparatively just outcomes in criminal cases, processing an appropriate mix of criminal offences, competently investigating and efficiently processing criminal cases, interacting effectively with the other legal officials on whom their success depends, and robustly adhering to due process standards. If there is a convincing argument for the election of chief prosecutors, this is it.

Unfortunately, there is empirical evidence suggesting that the democratic electorate is not doing a very good job—or, perhaps more fairly, is not in a position to do a very good job—of using the power of the vote to evaluate the performance of prosecutors' offices. This has to do in part with the relatively uncontested nature of many of the elections involving chief prosecutors. A recent study (Wright, 2008–2009) reports that the overwhelming majority (85 per cent) of prosecutorial elections with an incumbent are uncontested. Also, of the incumbent prosecutors who run for reelection, 95 per cent win. Of course, it could be that most chief prosecutors are deemed to be performing so well that few rivals see any need to challenge them or the public sees little reason to replace them. Alternatively, the unwillingness of the electorate to remove chief prosecutors from office might indicate a high degree of indifference to the task of monitoring and controlling prosecutors' offices. Such indifference would pose a challenge to the notion that the legitimacy of the operation of those offices depends vitally on close public oversight of their performance. Before reaching that conclusion, however, it should be noted that substantial barriers exist to running against incumbent chief prosecutors.[7] Moreover, where there are contested races, the public is often not in much of a position to evaluate the incumbent's performance or compare it to that of a challenger who will, after all, very likely have no track record as a chief prosecutor. If voters are to do a good job of evaluating the performance of prosecutors' offices, they will need quite a bit of information about the operations of those offices. Even assuming that they could acquire such information and process it, they will often find themselves in the position of not knowing whether or in what ways a challenger would run a better office. These kinds of comparative and noncomparative information deficits might most convincingly explain why most prosecutorial election contests focus primarily on claims about the character or experience of the contestants, well-known cases that have gone to trial, relationships with subordinates or the police, or promises by one or both of the contestants to more vigorously pursue one or another type of criminal offence (Wright, 2008–2009, p. 601).

Proponents of electoral control over prosecutors' offices contend that we should attempt to provide voters with more and better information about incumbent performance (Gold, 2011, pp. 94–99; Wright 2008–2009, pp. 606–610). Our aim should be to improve prosecutorial elections, not abandon them. They might also argue that voters are not notably more informed when it comes to the election of other public officials—mayors, legislators, governors, and even presidents. Many democratic elections turn on something other than careful analyses of incumbents' track records and comparisons of those records with those of challengers. Why should the election of chief prosecutors be expected to meet a higher standard?

I am pessimistic about improving prosecutorial elections, although I am not opposed to trying to do so. We could provide voters with enhanced information about the performance of prosecutors' offices. But without that information being processed and packaged into some manageable form by some reliable individual or organisation—one not overly narrow or biased in its concerns—I suspect that most citizens will be overwhelmed by such information in its 'raw' forms.[8] To address this problem, we might envision the emergence of special commissions charged with evaluating and issuing reports on prosecutorial office performance along the dimensions outlined previously.[9] Of course, such commissions would have to be formed and staffed in ways that earned the trust of citizens. Moreover, we would have to hope that their reports were actually heeded by the voting public.

Even if the preceding conditions were satisfied, such commissions would presumably not be able to provide comparable reports on how rival chief prosecutorial candidates would operate their offices. This means that prosecutorial elections would mainly involve the exercise of veto power by citizens, in the sense of removing from office chief prosecutors whose job performance was deemed unsatisfactory. Even that might be a laudable improvement and be seen by some as an appropriate exercise of democratic authority. Yet we are a long way from having commissions of experts to aid us in evaluating prosecutorial performance, and it might be claimed that there is no clear path in the United States to getting us there.

With regard to the dismal conduct of voters in other electoral contests, although the point must be conceded, there are some salient differences between prosecutors and other elected officials that weaken its force. Most of what we vote for when we elect mayors, governors, legislators, and presidents are the priorities that they reveal by their party affiliations or campaign platforms. Granted, if they have demonstrated records of incompetence, those will also matter. But competency or the lack of it will, in such contests, be contested, in the sense that judgments about it are apt to reflect voter values and political ideologies. In light of all of this, it makes sense to let electoral politics determine who prevails in such elections and who does not. It might not be accurate to say that what constitutes good or bad performance of the prosecutorial function is value neutral. However, it does seem plausible to argue that much of what prosecutors are expected to do is less deeply contentious. Most everyone has an interest in criminal offenders being punished (both comparatively and noncomparatively) justly, in the effective and efficient management of prosecutors' offices and in the upholding of due process values in the investigation and adjudication of criminal charges. Maybe these are not objective or neutral values, but they are ones on which individuals in democratic societies who otherwise have opposing beliefs and values are apt to converge.

The preceding point takes us some way towards what I earlier termed the 'expertise account'. Some might argue that even if the prospects of improving prosecutor elections are less dim than they appear to be, there is a principled argument against having such elections: decisions about which crimes to prosecute and how to do so are not ones that we should subject to the tumult of electoral politics. It is not clear to me that anyone subscribes to the expertise account in unvarnished form. Those who lean towards criminal prosecution as an area of expertise might concede that there are numerous ways in which democratic majorities have defensible roles to play in determining how the criminal justice system is set up and operates. But they might insist that the prosecutorial function is not one over which democratic politics should have much influence.

2. THE EXPERTISE ACCOUNT

Michael Tonry will serve as the inspiration for the expertise account of prosecutors (2004a, pp. 9–10; 2004b). In fairness, it seems clear that he does not take it to the extreme that I push it.[10] But he does in various places lament the intrusion of electoral politics into the criminal justice process, including the prosecutorial function, worrying that it inclines criminal justice officials to give too much weight to the (often irrational) emotions of the democratic electorate and to their short-sighted views about crime. One consequence of this, as Tonry sees it, has been the gradual ratcheting up of sentences in the United States. Other consequences include the adoption of forms of punishment and alterations in liability to punishment that have made the United States one of the most punitive societies in the world.[11]

But if the public's responses to crime are unreliable in these respects and if the democratic election of prosecutors facilitates their being translated into criminal justice policies, what is the alternative to bending the prosecutorial function to the democratic will? The answer might be to select and train prosecutors as other countries in the world do. In European countries, prosecutors are not elected but are instead highly trained members of government bureaucracies (Frase, 1990; Pizzi, 1993, pp. 1331–1336). They have chosen careers in criminal prosecution after having already received education in the law. They have then been provided additional training and education, at which point they become members of professional bureaucracies in which advancement is based on careful assessments of their performance. The extensive legal training of prosecutors in these countries inculcates in them specialised knowledge of the criminal law and its procedures and a set of attitudes supportive of their acting on that knowledge. Both the specialised knowledge and supportive attitudes are not things possessed by the public at large. In this respect, prosecutors in many countries are not unlike scientists who have specialized knowledge of their fields and the skills and dispositions needed to extend that knowledge. None of this should be taken to suggest that either prosecutors or scientists are mindless automatons or that they will not harbour any differences of opinion about how they are to conduct themselves in their respective fields. However, these differences of opinion are apt to be confined within a fairly narrow range.

Prosecutors educated and trained in these ways will be strongly inclined to make decisions about what charges to lodge against suspected offenders based on the evidence that the police have turned over to them or that they have been able to turn up on their own. If they determine that charges should be filed, they will attempt to do so in ways that capture the criminal event fully and accurately given the provisions of the criminal code under which they operate. As we have seen, prosecutors in the United States have considerable discretion in determining which crimes to pursue and how to pursue them. This unchecked discretion in wielding their power makes it appear sensible to try and subject them to democratic control. But quite independently of doubts that we might have about the effectiveness or wisdom of democratic control over prosecutorial power, there are persuasive arguments for limiting the discretion that US prosecutors have to engage in plea bargaining (Lippke, 2011). Prosecutorial abilities to manipulate the sentencing differentials defendants face as between plea bargained and trial outcomes produce enormous and arguably unfair pressure on defendants to plead guilty. One result of this is that there will be a less reliable relationship between what crimes individuals have committed and their sentencing outcomes. Also, free-wheeling plea bargaining has the potential to produce sentencing inequities of significant proportions (Bibas, 2004).

Although many European countries have forms of plea bargaining or, perhaps more accurately, offer charged defendants sentencing concessions if they plead guilty or confess, they do not give prosecutors anywhere near the discretion that US prosecutors have to bargain about charges or sentences (Langer, 2004; Ma, 2002). Thus, assuming a veridical set of charges, ones based on the evidence, and assuming the availability of only modest sentence discounts for defendants willing to admit their guilt, the problems of ensuring noncomparative and comparative justice in sentencing are greatly reduced. Further, prosecutors in many European countries have much less discretion than US prosecutors in determining which crimes to prosecute. Although it exaggerates things to say that prosecutors in European countries are required to prosecute all crimes brought to their attention, there is nonetheless more of a presumption that they will do so, one enforced by the oversight of their superiors in prosecutorial bureaucracies and by the right of victims to petition the courts if they believe that prosecutors have not acted appropriately in making determinations about how to proceed with cases (Pizzi, 1993, p. 1333). With prosecutorial discretion pared back and constrained in these ways, there is, arguably, less need for electoral checks on its exercise. Also, prosecutors working in government bureaucracies face scrutiny of their performance by their peers and superiors—scrutiny that is presumably more informed and professional than that which democratic voters can hope to provide. Hence, prosecutors who are not efficient in the deployment of their resources, do not interact effectively with the police and other agencies, or who make poor decisions or are neglectful of their duties will be less likely to be promoted and might even be forced to resign from the prosecutorial service. At the same time, this scrutiny by peers and superiors insulates prosecutors from political pressures, as they are most directly answerable to others educated and trained like them, not the electorate. Even their superiors will not often be elected, although at the highest levels they might be appointed by and thus answerable to elected political officials.

Indeed, what is so striking about prosecutors in the United States is not solely the fact that some of them are elected, it is also that they receive much less formal training than their counterparts in other countries (Frase, 1990, p. 561–562). Many chief prosecutors in the United States were legal practitioners in other areas before running for elected office. Many of the subordinate prosecutors that elected chief prosecutors appoint are fresh from law school, with little experience in criminal prosecution (Frase, 1990, pp. 562–563). They learn on the job, as it were, and under the guidance of chief prosecutors whose commitments to procedural and substantive justice might or might not be commendable. Add to this the extraordinary discretion that prosecutors in the United States have to arrange guilty pleas, and there is what looks like a perfect storm of factors designed to produce questionable criminal justice outcomes—poorly trained prosecutors who are given formidable tools with which to operate and lax oversight of their conduct by other criminal justice officials and the democratic electorate. It seems preferable to trim prosecutors' discretion, provide them with more education and training, and subject them to close supervision by individuals who thoroughly understand and are steeped in the values of due process and the rule of law.

Still, we might wonder why citizens of democratic societies should be willing to turn the prosecution of crimes over to experts. Granted, the members of prosecutorial bureaucracies will undoubtedly know a lot more about the criminal law and procedure than ordinary citizens and be committed to the values of substantive and procedural justice in ways that ordinary citizens might not be. But why should not ordinary citizens view this 'rule by experts' with some unease? More precisely, what reason is there to believe that the experts are not imposing policies of their own choosing on ordinary citizens, policies that in democratic societies should instead by chosen by the majority through their elected representatives?

In response, it might be argued that these criminal justice experts will be attempting to ensure the implementation of policies of particular kinds, ones that long history and experience have shown give all of us what we want from the prosecutorial function—namely appropriate punishment of the guilty conjoined with nonpunishment of the innocent.[12] The presumption of innocence for criminal defendants, the burden of proof on the state, the high standard of proof in criminal cases, and the entire array of evidence rules governing charge adjudication have all been crafted, over centuries, to ensure that the criminal justice process screens out the innocent from amongst those suspected of crimes, leaving us with the guilty. Mistakes are still made, of course, but it is better that experts, rather than nonexperts, control the process. Indeed, discomfort with the election of prosecutors stems, at least in part, from the concern that nonexperts are asserting too much authority over the criminal justice system, thereby distorting or corrupting the process.

Although the preceding account takes us some way towards addressing the concern that deference to prosecutorial expertise does not sit well with some of the basic assumptions of democratic theory, a deeper and more compelling story might be told. It is one according to which the rules and standards of due process are necessary to safeguard the human rights of those suspected or accused of crimes. Human rights, we might say, carry with them presumptions against their infringement by state authorities. Those presumptions can be rebutted, but only if individuals are authoritatively shown to have violated legal rules that, in part at least, are designed to safeguard the rights of all citizens (Bassouni, 1992–1993). Such an authoritative showing is achieved if those accused of crimes are given rigorous due process. Prosecutors, it might then be claimed, are experts in due process, and thus the standards and procedures which must be adhered to if the rights of criminal offenders are to be justifiably curtailed or infringed by legal punishment.

There are complications with the preceding account that should be noted, although there is not the space here to pursue them.[13] Assuming that these complications can be addressed, why would it further the legitimacy of prosecutorial expertise to link it with the protection of human rights? The answer to this question is that it has long been understood that democratic rule is appropriately limited by the need to protect the human rights of all citizens. Even in the United States, the country perhaps most committed to direct democratic control over the prosecution of crimes, the Constitution places significant limits on the ability of the electorate to trample certain rights of citizens (Sherry 2006–2007). The majority might want to abolish the right against self-incrimination or permit searches and seizures at the whim of the authorities, but the Constitution does not permit such things. More generally, if it can be argued that expert prosecutors are not simply pursuing their own idiosyncratic agendas but are instead governed by rules and loyal to procedures that are designed to protect the human rights of all citizens, that should be a powerful antidote to the concern that turning the prosecutorial function over to experts is somehow at odds with a commitment to democracy.

But that brings us to a further question: why think that it is only the prosecution of crimes that is a matter of expertise, such that citizens in democratic societies should be content to turn it over to those individuals who are apt to have it? Tonry's concern that the democratic electorate will interject too much emotion into the prosecution of crimes if permitted to elect prosecutors might seem to have implications for other areas of the criminal justice system. Tonry (1993) himself believes that in devising sentencing schemes, we might appropriately defer to experts in the form of sentencing commissions. Such commissions are typically made up of individuals with various kinds of specialized knowledge of the criminal law, the effects of punishment on individuals, or the sociology of crime. But why stop there? Why should we not defer to experts when it comes to the substantive provisions of the criminal law itself? The Model Penal Code, to take one well-known example, arguably offers a more coherent and sound basis for criminalising conduct than most elected state legislators are apt to hit upon. If we want a criminal code that adequately secures the human rights of all citizens, we could do worse than defer to those individuals (political philosophers and legal scholars?) who have a thorough grasp of what human rights require in the way of legislation and who understand the pitfalls and nuances of devising legal rules to secure such rights. Then there are the well-known problems with citizen jurors in criminal trials, individuals who are called upon once or twice in their lifetimes to serve on juries and, somewhat preposterously, expected to perform ably although they are offered meagre guidance (Laudan, 2006, especially chapter 6). Surely we might do better to turn critical decisions about the guilt or innocence of criminal defendants over to professional judges or perhaps mixed panels of professional and lay judges, individuals who can be expected to accept the presumption of innocence, understand the standard of proof, and grasp the kinds of considerations that properly go into determining guilt or the lack of it with respect to criminal charges.

It is not clear, in other words, once we start deferring to expertise in the realm of criminal justice, where exactly we should stop doing so. If we go all the way, as it were, and there are some countries (e.g. Germany) whose criminal justice systems go pretty far in the direction of deferring to experts, we must worry, once again, about how the criminal law and its allied institutions can be made to seem legitimate to the democratic electorate or as effectively expressing their wills as equal members of society. There might come a point at which citizens in democratic societies will view a criminal justice system entirely devised and administered by experts as rather far removed from their interests and concerns. It is hard to see how that would be a good thing.

We butt up here against one of the interesting problems of democratic theory, one succinctly outlined by Thomas Christiano (1996, pp. 125–126). There is, in modern societies, a necessary division of labour. Most of us cannot be experts about many of the topics with which democratic governments concern themselves. In fact, few of us, including most elected representatives, are experts about more than one of these topics. Yet if we cannot do without the experts, and many of the problems with which democratic governments must contend require expert knowledge, how is there any room for meaningful voter participation in governance? Simply put, should we opt for rule by experts and be done with democracy?

Christiano sensibly argues that democratic citizens should be conceived as choosing the aims of society overall, or what he terms the 'collective properties' of the social order in which they live (1996, p. 169). It is properly left to citizens to decide such large issues as whether and to what extent they will ensure health care for all citizens or collective provision for the elderly and how to weigh and balance the provision of such goods against the provision of other goods (e.g. security). These are matters concerning which free and equal citizens are entitled to form and express their views by, amongst other things, voting. Once democratic majorities have set these overall aims, it will usually be up to policy experts to decide how best to achieve them.

Christiano's approach is, as he recognises, controversial. Amongst those who might challenge it are proponents of deliberative democracy. They might argue that the gap between expertise in any area and the deliberations of citizens about their society's collective properties and the means to achieve them is to be lamented. What we ought to do is find ways to enable citizens to acquire more expertise and thus deliberate effectively about matters of public policy (Fischer, 2009). Even if we concede this point, it still makes sense to ask which features of the criminal justice system are best left to expert determination or, perhaps, insistent advice and which are ones that citizens of democratic societies ought to more directly affect through their votes. A further question is what form democratic influence should take when it is appropriate for it to do so. In addition to summarising what can be said for and against the election of prosecutors, I offer some brief and tentative answers to these questions in Section 3.

3. CHOOSING BETWEEN THE TWO APPROACHES

It is tempting to portray the US criminal justice system, with its direct election of chief prosecutors, police chiefs, and judges in many jurisdictions, as being more democratic than it really is. However, only a few of these officials must stand for election and then only periodically. The day-to-day decisions of these elected officials are rarely subject to democratic oversight; instead, it is their collective decisions over the course of several years that the electorate is supposed to evaluate. And that is presumably a good thing. There is very little democratic micromanagement of the US criminal justice system. Expertise does prevail throughout much of the system, although perhaps it is kept on a shorter leash in the United States than elsewhere.

More expertise might be infused into the US system if, as suggested earlier, some trusted organisation could be instituted and charged with providing evaluations of prosecutorial performance. If voters heeded these performance evaluations—and it is worth noting that there is no guarantee that they would do so—they might reproduce some of the monitoring and oversight of prosecutors that is typical within prosecutorial bureaucracies.

The two systems, one that treats chief prosecutors as elected officials and the other that treats them as experts, might thus begin to converge. Nonetheless, prosecutorial elections aided by 'objective' performance evaluations would, at best, enable voters to defeat incumbent chief prosecutors perceived to be incompetent or untrustworthy. They would not ensure that those elevated to chief prosecutorial positions were the 'best and brightest'. In this regard, professional bureaucracies appear to have an edge, especially if they closely adhere to merit-based rules of evaluation and promotion. Also, professional bureaucracies retain the significant advantage of providing prosecutors with specialised training and acculturation to the norms of responsible criminal prosecution. It seems one of the signal failings of the US system that the individuals who wind up overseeing prosecutorial offices or working within them may have had little training in the complex tasks that they are expected to perform. Finally, subjecting chief prosecutors to electoral contests, even more informed ones than are currently the norm, will inevitably, it seems, inject more political considerations into the prosecution of criminal cases. To the extent that we regard such considerations as regrettable, the bureaucratic expertise approach, with its greater insulation of prosecutors from politics, seems superior.

Nevertheless, there is something to be said for the notion that since prosecutors are entrusted with and potentially exercise significant power over the lives of citizens, their activities ought to be subject to electoral oversight and control. One respect in which such oversight and control might seem especially apt is with respect to the overall mix of offences pursued and punished by the authorities. It might be thought that the mix will be determined by the criminal code itself, perhaps in conjunction with its attached sanction scheme. In particular, more serious offences would seem to warrant more attention from the authorities than less serious ones. Although correct in theory, prosecutorial practice might not fall into line in ways that the code and its attached sentencing scheme would seem to dictate. More to the point, the authorities will almost always have somewhat limited resources at their disposal and so will have to make decisions about which kinds of crimes to pursue vigorously and which ones to ignore or pursue less vigorously. This will especially be true when the crimes in question are middle- or lower-level offences (Bowers, 2007, pp. 1135–1139; Vorenberg, 1981, pp. 1524–1537). Even if citizens in democratic societies have no defensible role in second-guessing specific decisions made by the authorities, they arguably ought to have some say about the overall profile of offences being processed by the criminal justice system. If, for instance, the crimes of the rich or powerful are routinely passed over by prosecutors or if crimes against certain persons in society are not assiduously prosecuted because the victims are members of despised or distrusted minorities, citizens should be able to express their concerns to the authorities about these matters in ways that the authorities cannot simply ignore.

The problem is that little follows from this point about what specific form that oversight and control should take. Again, in European countries that subscribe to the expertise model, the heads of prosecutorial bureaucracies, while not themselves elected, typically answer to officials who are elected or serve at the pleasure of officials who are elected. If the public perceives that the prosecution service is incompetent, biased, or corrupt, it likely will be able to bring pressure to bear on the elected officials who oversee the service. Moreover, it seems a mistake to assume that prosecutors who are professional bureaucrats will be wholly out of touch with community sentiments about their performance and thus unaffected by such sentiments. Their greater degree of insulation from the distorting influence of politics does not mean that prosecutors will conduct their official activities in complete and splendid isolation from their social surroundings (cf. Tonry, 2004a, p. 209). Whether greater democratic input on the performance of their tasks than this is needed to ensure the legitimacy of their exercises of official power is, I would submit, unclear.[14]

If the preceding seems too dismissive of the public's role in guiding and constraining the operations of the criminal justice system, it should be noted that it is clear that there are crucial features of that system that are appropriately subject to more direct forms of democratic input and control. Moreover, these are features of the system that are likely to determine that system's direction and operations in more profound ways than the decisions of prosecutors working within professional bureaucracies. First, it is entirely appropriate for citizens in democracies to determine the amount of public funds to be allocated to criminal justice as a whole or to subdivisions of it (e.g. policing vs. the courts), especially if we bear in mind that such decisions will involve balancing the pursuit of criminal justice against such things as the provision of education, health care, public highways, and eldercare. These are decisions about society's ultimate priorities and, as such, are ones that citizens in democratic societies, with their differing views and commitments, ought to determine by voting, at least within limits (the limits arguably set by an account of the human rights that the society is committed to realising). Of course, saying this is consistent with such decisions being delegated to elected representatives, as they currently are.

Second, there are the provisions of the criminal code itself. The kinds of actions that should be criminalised might seem to be ones for the democratic electorate to determine. Granted, to some it will seem doubtful that society is well-served by relying solely on the choices of elected representatives in this regard. For one thing, such representatives might not be skilled at crafting a coherent or clear set of provisions. They would do better to accept the advice and counsel of legal and criminal justice experts, much as a majority of states in the United States did following promulgation of the Model Penal Code by the American Law Institute. For another, there is no guarantee that elected representatives will adhere to a defensible normative account of criminalisation, one that gives full and proper weight to the human rights of all citizens. The difficulty here is that we may have little choice but to accept some democratic determination (perhaps by a supermajority?) of the rights scheme that the criminal law is, in part, designed to secure. Even the experts cannot agree about the specific rights that all individuals possess, their relative importance, and their limits. These matters will have to be decided democratically, which means that the cornerstone of the criminal justice system—the set of rules defining criminal conduct—cannot be entirely turned over to experts.

Third, some role for public input into a society's sentencing scheme might be envisioned. Tonry (1993) claims that we would be better off having sentencing schemes determined by individuals who are thoroughly schooled in the empirical evidence about legal punishment and who have an articulate grasp of such notions as proportionality, harm, and culpability. When it comes to matters of ordinal proportionality—that is, the rank ordering of crimes and efforts to ensure that more serious ones are punished more harshly than less serious ones—considerable deference ought to be paid to those who have thought long and hard and carefully about such matters. Against this, Paul Robinson (this volume) argues that there is clear evidence that the public's ranking of crimes and appropriate punishments is anything but daft, especially if those rankings are generated in carefully controlled experimental settings. If the public can be trusted to rank crimes and punishments sensibly, permitting it to play some role in devising sentencing schemes will help ensure the legitimacy of those schemes. In addition, with respect to cardinal proportionality, which concerns the overall harshness or mildness of sentencing schemes, it is widely acknowledged that there are fewer clear answers dictated either by the evidence or the various rationales for legal punishment (Matravers, this volume; Ryberg, 2004; von Hirsch, 1993; von Hirsch and Ashworth, 2005). If cardinal proportionality is not an area in which expertise is decisive, it might be appropriate for public beliefs and preferences about how harsh or mild sanctions should be overall to have some influence. Again, however, how those beliefs and preferences should have such influence is not obvious. One possibility is for there to be elected citizen representatives on the sentencing commissions that devise or revise sanction schemes. Although such representatives might know little about sentencing matters to begin, they could gradually acquire more familiarity with them after exposure to others on the commission who are there because they are deemed experts and so appointed to their posts (perhaps by elected officials).[15]

In short, it can be conceded that in these and other ways, citizens in democratic societies ought to have input into the structure and operations of the criminal justice system without this input extending to anything more than indirect or diffuse control over criminal prosecutions. True, some of the actors high in the criminal justice hierarchy should have to answer to the electorate. But these might be officials who have little role in making the numerous small but vital decisions about the prosecution of criminal offences that are the daily fare of prosecutors' offices.

REFERENCES

Bassiouni, M. C. 1992–1993. 'Human Rights in the Context of Criminal Justice: Identifying International Procedural Protections and Equivalent Protections in National Constitutions.' *Duke Journal of Comparative and International Law* 3: 235–297.

Bibas, S. 2004. 'Plea Bargaining Outside the Shadow of Trial.' *Harvard Law Review* 117: 2463–2547.

Bordenkircher v. Hayes 434 US 357 (1978).

Bowers, J. 2007. 'Punishing the Innocent.' *University of Pennsylvania Law Review* 156: 1117–1179.

Christiano, T. 1996. *The Rule of the Many: Fundamental Issues in Democratic Theory.* Boulder, CO: Westview.

Davis, K. C. 1969. *Discretionary Justice: A Preliminary Inquiry.* Urbana: University of Illinois Press.

Estlund, D. 2009. *Democratic Authority: A Philosophical Framework.* Princeton, NJ: Princeton University Press.

Fischer, F. 2009. *Democracy and Expertise: Reorienting Public Policy Inquiry.* Oxford: Oxford University Press.

Frase, R. S. 1990. 'Comparative Criminal Justice as a Guide to American Law Reform: How Do the French Do It, How Can We Find Out, and Why Should We Care?' *California Law Review* 78: 539–683.

Gold, R. M. 2011. 'Promoting Democracy in Prosecution.' *Washington Law Review* 86: 69–124.

Heumann, M. S. 1977. *Plea Bargaining: The Experiences of Prosecutors, Judges, and Defense Attorneys.* Chicago: University of Chicago Press.

Langer, M. 2004. 'From Legal Transplants to Legal Translations: The Globalization of Plea Bargaining and the Americanization Thesis in Criminal Procedure.' *Harvard International Law Journal* 45: 1–64.

Laudan, L. 2006. *Truth, Error, and the Criminal Law.* Cambridge, UK: Cambridge University Press.

Lefstein, N. 2004. 'In Search of Gideon's Promise: Lessons from England and the Need for Federal Help.' *Hastings Law Journal* 55: 835–929.

Leipold, A. D. 1996. 'Rethinking Jury Nullification.' *Virginia Law Review* 82: 253–324.

Lippke, R. L. 2010. 'Punishing the Guilty, Not Punishing the Innocent.' *Journal of Moral Philosophy* 7: 462–488.

Lippke, R. L. 2011. *The Ethics of Plea Bargaining.* Oxford: Oxford University Press.

Ma, Y. 2002. 'Prosecutorial Discretion and Plea Bargaining in the United States, France, Germany, and Italy: A Comparative Perspective.' *International Criminal Justice Review* 12: 22–52.

Pizzi, W. T. 1993. 'Understanding Prosecutorial Discretion in the United States: The Limits of Comparative Criminal Procedure as an Instrument of Reform.' *Ohio State Law Journal* 54: 1325–1374.

Roberts, J. 2008. *Punishing Persistent Offenders: Exploring Community and Offender Perspectives.* Oxford: Oxford University Press.

Ryberg, J. 2004. *The Ethics of Proportionate Punishment: A Critical Investigation.* Dordrecht, The Netherlands: Kluwer Academic.

Sherry, S. 2006–2007. 'Democracy and the Death of Knowledge.' *University of Cincinnati Law Review* 75: 1053–1070.

Stuntz, W. J. 2001. 'The Pathological Politics of Criminal Law.' *Michigan Law Review* 100: 505–600.

Tonry, M. 1993. 'Sentencing Commissions and Their Guidelines.' *Crime and Justice: A Review of Research* 17: 137–195.

Tonry, M. 2004a. *Thinking about Crime: Sense and Sensibility in American Penal Culture.* New York: Oxford University Press.

Tonry, M. 2004b. 'Why Aren't German Penal Policies Harsher and Imprisonment Rates Higher?' *German Law Journal* 5: 1187–1206.

von Hirsch, A. 1993. *Censure and Sanctions.* Oxford: Clarendon.

von Hirsch, A., and A. Ashworth. 2005. *Proportionate Sentencing: Exploring the Principles.* Oxford: Oxford University Press.

Vorenberg, J. 1981. 'Decent Restraint of Prosecutorial Power.' *Harvard Law Review* 94: 1521–1573.

Wright, R. F. 2008–2009. 'How Prosecutor Elections Fail Us.' *Ohio State Journal of Criminal Law* 6: 581–610.

Wright, R. F., and M. L. Miller. 2010. 'The Worldwide Accountability Deficit for Prosecutors.' *Washington & Lee Law Review* 67: 1587–1620.

NOTES

1. I am grateful to the other contributors to this volume for their helpful comments and suggestions during the discussion of our respective chapters in Copenhagen during the fall of 2012.

2. This figure comes from Ronald F. Wright and includes only prosecutors in state criminal justice systems (2008–2009, p. 589). It does not include federal prosecutors, who are not in any case elected.

3. For extended analysis and critique of trial penalties, see Lippke (2011, chapters 1 and 2).

4. We might also permit crime victims (or their surviving family members) to petition the courts in cases in which they believe that prosecutors have exercised their discretion not to charge or to undercharge in ways that thwart justice. This is common practice in European countries (see Ma, 2002). A record of such petitions could be made available to the voting public.

5. It should be acknowledged, however, that there is considerable debate about how much comparative justice in sentencing is desirable or attainable.

6. As Wright and Miller note, it is important to know not only what cases prosecutors pursue but which ones they decline to pursue, and why (2010, p. 1597).

7. Amongst the barriers cited by Wright (2008–2009) are that local defence attorneys who challenge a sitting prosecutor and lose might worry about how they will fare in subsequent plea negotiations conducted with the victorious incumbent prosecutor. Subordinate prosecutors will also be reluctant to challenge their bosses.

8. Wright (2008–2009) suggests that the ACLU and victims advocacy groups might help with the processing of information about the performance of a chief prosecutor's office. I wonder if such groups will offer balanced and comprehensive analyses of the kinds that will be helpful to citizens.

9. This possibility was suggested by Paul Robinson during the conference at which the chapters of this book were discussed by the book's collaborators.

10. See Tonry where he writes, 'No legislative delegation of rule-making authority to administrative agencies can forever or completely insulate policy from partisan influence, nor should it' (1993, p. 175).

11. Notice, here, Tonry's assumption that the public's emotions and myopic focus incline it towards supporting harshly punitive criminal justice practices. Yet there is nothing about the emotions or short-sightedness which necessitates such an outcome. Our concern should not be with the public's emotional responses per se but with whether and to what extent those responses are based on evidence and sound arguments.

12. How we are to weight nonpunishment of the innocent against punishment of the guilty is a matter of some controversy. For further discussion, see Lippke (2010).

13. Specifically, there is no generally agreed-upon account of what substantive human rights individuals possess, although there is considerable overlap amongst many of the competing accounts. It also is not clear how far any such account can take us towards defending the specific rules and standards of criminal procedure.

14. Another concern, suggested by David Estlund's discussion of 'epistocracy' is that an educated elite might not have much experience of social deprivation or exclusion, and so the policies it adopts or actions it undertakes might not be properly informed by such experiences (2009, chapter 11). One way to address this problem would be to encourage or enable more individuals from the excluded groups to gain legal education or admission to prosecutorial bureaucracies.

15. Another possibility, suggested by Julian Roberts would be to have sentencing commissions poll the public on sentences to find out whether there is sufficient support for the sentencing scale and, if not, to alter it (2008, p. 85).

9

Stakeholder Sentencing

Thom Brooks

Recent years have witnessed increasing interest in how to provide new avenues for incorporating a greater public voice in sentencing (see Roberts & Hough 2005; Ryberg 2010). This development is the product of a widely perceived growing crisis concerning the lack of public confidence in sentencing decisions. One important factor is negative media headlines that draw attention to cases that contribute to feeding a culture of sentencing disapproval by the public where punishments are believed to be undeservedly lenient. A second factor is the recognition that victims should have greater involvement in the criminal justice system, including sentencing decisions. But how might we improve public confidence and provide a greater voice for victims without sacrificing criminal justice in favour of mob rule?

These developments concerning the relation of public opinion and punishment raise several fundamental concerns. How much voice, if any, should the public have regarding sentencing decisions? Which institutional frameworks should be constructed to better incorporate public opinion without betraying our support for important penal principles and support for justice?

This chapter accepts the need to improve public confidence about sentencing through improving avenues for the public to possess a greater and better informed voice about sentencing decisions within clear parameters of justice. I will defend the idea of *stakeholder sentencing*: those who have a stake in penal outcomes should determine how they are decided. This idea supports an extension of restorative justice that I will call *punitive restoration* where the achievement of restoration may include a more punitive element, including imprisonment. My argument is that the idea of stakeholder sentencing offers a compelling view about public opinion and might be incorporated into sentencing that better promotes a coherent and unified account of how punishment might pursue multiple penal goals, including improving public confidence in sentencing.

1. THE PROBLEM OF THE PUBLIC

A powerful argument against greater incorporation of public opinion in sentencing decisions is that a larger public voice would contribute to disproportionate punishments. Justice is best served by ensuring that punishments are proportionate and not by tailoring outcomes to those more favoured by the public.

The idea that the public might be more likely to endorse disproportionate punishments, especially overly severe sanctions, is understood to be a compelling reason why the criminal law has endorsed victim displacement. The concern is that punishments would become too harsh and injustices practised if the victims determined the appropriate punishments for their offenders. This runs together separate issues that may bear on how we determine sentencing: the first is the voice of victims, and the second is the input by the general public. If the general public should be able to have some input on sentencing, it is often submitted that victims in particular should have a voice rather than remain silent (O'Hara, 2005).

Victims were traditionally displaced from decisions about sentencing to best promote justice through a better guarantee of consistency and proportionality:

> We seem to have lost sight of the origins of the criminal law as a response to the activities of *victims*, together with their families, associates and supporters. The blood feud, the vendetta, the duel, the revenge, the lynching: for the elimination of these modes of retaliation, more than anything else, the criminal law as we know it today came into existence. (Gardner, 1998, p. 31)[1]

Victim displacement helped end the private pursuit of justice against offenders by private citizens and promote the rule of law. We should not serve as judges in cases where we have an interest in the outcome, for John Locke, because of the danger that victims will be 'partial to themselves and their friends' at the expense of others (2004, p. 275). Decisions should be impartial to secure justice. This may be best guaranteed by ensuring that those with a special interest in sentencing decisions should not possess much influence over how these decisions are made.

The concern that a greater public voice would contribute to overly severe sanctions is thought to receive support from populist proposals, such as California's 'Three Strikes And You're Out' law where offenders convicted of a third strike-eligible crime face a minimum twenty-five years in prison (Cullen, Fisher, & Applegate, 2000; Zimring, Hawkins, & Kamin, 2001). These proposals have proven counterproductive from the perspective of effective criminal justice policy. Studies have concluded that California has benefited from, at best, a negligible deterrent effect of 2 per cent or less alongside an explosion in the prison population and associated costs.[2] If this is the kind of criminal justice policy the public most wants, it may lead to a far more expensive system for little, if any, effect on crime reduction and improved public safety.

But must a greater public voice result only in support for overly harsh sentencing? It is not inconceivable to imagine popular celebrities commanding wide support for a more lenient sentence or perhaps a pardon. The core issue is not that the public might support more punitive sentences but that sentencing decisions may become more arbitrary and less uniform where similar cases may be treated too differently and, thus, unfairly. The claim that the public are more likely to endorse disproportionate punishments is a statement about the failure of the public to properly account for proportionality more generally. This may be explained by the fact that the public may often have an inaccurate, perhaps even irrational, fear about crime and likely future victimhood (Cook & Lane, 2009; Hutton, 2005; Lai, Zhao, & Longmire, 2012; Roberts, Stalens, Indermaur, & Hough, 2003). The public is also often mistaken about the potential benefits of more punitive penal policies (Williams, 2012). If the public has inaccurate or incomplete information about relevant factors, it cannot be expected to arrive at any satisfactory judgement in sentencing matters. And yet criminal justice must command public confidence if it is to command satisfactory legitimacy and be effective. Otherwise, the public might turn to 'take the law into their own hands' and undermine the rule of law.

The *problem of the public* is that we must secure public confidence despite the fact that the public possesses deep epistemic problems. A greater public voice might only secure higher confidence at the cost of abandoning evidence-based sentencing policy on how crime reduction and other penal goals might be achieved. How might we achieve public confidence without falling into this trap?

I believe that this trap may be avoided. We should first recognise that the issue is not whether public opinion matters but rather how much it should matter. This is because the idea that the public should have a voice in sentencing is deeply entrenched in its democratic institutions. The public indirectly exercises its voice on the criminal law through electing political leaders that help shape the future contours of the criminal law and the criminal justice system more generally.[3] The public has a more direct voice as lay magistrates or juries. Many countries have long-established practices where the public may participate in sentencing decisions. One example is the use of lay magistrates in the United Kingdom to determine the punishment of less serious criminal offences (Darbyshire, 2002, Grove, 2003, Roberts, Hough, Jackson, & Gerber, 2012). Several Continental jurisdictions allow for the sentencing of more serious offences to be determined by lay magistrates sitting alongside professional judges. In addition, the use of civilian juries to determine monetary awards and offender punishment after a conviction is secured is also well established in many jurisdictions (Brooks, 2004a, 2004b, 2009). Juries are often used in trials concerning more serious offences. Juries in the United States are also entrusted with determining sentences in capital trials, including whether a convicted offender should be executed.[4] Furthermore, judges are increasingly permitted to consider victim impact statements in determining penal outcomes. These statements are presented in court and detail how a crime has affected victims and their relations. Victim impact statements have had an awkward reception by the courts where the impact on victims may be relevant in sentencing but victims' opinions about sentence preferences are not considered relevant (Brooks, 2012a, pp. 72–73).[5]

These examples confirm that the idea that the public should have a voice about sentencing is widely entrenched through democratic institutions. This fact does not render the idea uncontroversial. The issue is not whether public opinion should be less but rather whether it should be more. It is widely held that public confidence in the criminal justice system is an important source of democratic legitimacy (Bennett, this volume). This does not require that every outcome receives popular approval but rather that the overall system has satisfactory public support. This is because citizens are governed by the rule of law rather than the tyranny of the majority. So the lack of public confidence may represent a problem of legitimacy concerning sentencing outcomes.

While there is no argument for *reducing* the public voice, it is questionable whether it could be less than it is. Relatively few cases ever proceed to trial, perhaps no more than 5–7 per cent (Brooks 2004a, p. 201). Fewer receive decisions by juries on verdicts. Some populist policies, such as California's three strikes law, have become enacted due to popular support. However, it remains unclear how close the link is between public favour and penal policy outcomes. The public may favour more punitive sanctions, but it also supports crime reduction which may be undermined by increasing penal severity. This gap between public favour and public expectation is a problem for politicians trying to win both public support and crime reduction.[6]

Consider attempts to address this gap in the United Kingdom. The British government has planned to implement greater usage of community sentences and restorative justice with tough sounding rhetoric about 'breaking' reoffending cycles and community 'pay back' in an effort designed primarily to generate significant savings as alternatives to hard treatment and its much higher costs (Ministry of Justice, 2010, 2012a). These plans are correct to claim public support for criminal justice measures that are effective at crime reduction but overlook the lack of public support for measures leading to reduced punitiveness (Dawes, Harvey, McIntosh, Nunney, & Phillips, 2011). These plans are an example where securing public confidence has importance, but it does not drive policy change. This case illustrates how the indirect expression of public opinion on sentencing matters through democratic institutions does not confirm a strong link. So perhaps a reason why there is little argument for *reducing* the public voice in sentencing matters is because the public exercises relatively modest impact.

It does not follow that the public voice should be *increased* to improve public confidence and democratic legitimacy (Thomsen, this volume). The most powerful criticism is that further inclusion of public opinion may undermine just punishment. The problem is that public disapproval about sentencing decisions is known to decrease where the public has better information (Roberts et al., 2012). One approach to improve public confidence is to increase public knowledge: the problem is not how criminal justice is conducted but how little the public understands it. We require improved public education about sentencing to overcome the present crisis of low public confidence. So judges should not tailor sentencing decisions to better cohere with public opinion, but the public should be better educated about how these decisions are made for the public to support judges and not vice versa (de Keijser, this volume). So the solution to the problem of the lack of public confidence in sentencing decisions might be found in improved public knowledge. Our task might be to better shape public opinion to support current sentencing decisions rather than to create a larger space for the public voice. Improving public confidence need not require us to increase the influence of public opinion.[7] If successful, this approach might secure greater public confidence without sacrificing consistency and proportionality.

2. IN DEFENCE OF PUBLIC OPINION

Increasing the impact of public opinion on sentencing outcomes faces several important challenges. The first problem is that the public lacks satisfactory information to form a justifiable judgement. The greater influence of public opinion may open the door to disproportionate punishments based upon inaccurate or incomplete relevant knowledge. A second problem is that sentencing decisions might become more arbitrary. Like cases may not be treated similarly if outcomes were less under the control of professional judges and trained lay magistrates. The third problem is that the public may be more likely to support greater sentence severity which may undermine penal goals, such as proportionality, improving crime reduction, and offender rehabilitation. Public confidence is important to secure legitimacy, but increasing the impact of public opinion on sentencing outcomes presents us with more problems than prospects.

Overcoming these three problems requires institutional reforms where a greater public voice is exercised within clearly set parameters ensuring satisfactory consistency across similar cases. It would also entail the public gaining opportunities to acquire relevant knowledge to better inform their decisions, or what we might call the creation of an 'ontologically thick public opinion'(Dzur, this volume). How to avoid arbitrariness while getting the criminal law to better track public opinion?

Restorative justice helps us identify the way forward (Braithwaite, 2002, Brooks, 2012a, pp. 64–85). Restorative justice is an approach that offers an alternative to the criminal trial. Trials are adversarial and combative. In contrast, restorative justice aspires to create mutual understanding and reconciliation between offenders, their victims and the wider community. Criminal trials take place in courtrooms, but restorative justice is practised through a mediated conference. While trials are thought to produce winners and losers, restorative justice seeks to promote healing and a 'restoration' of damaged relationships.

The restorative justice conference often takes the form of either a meeting between the victim and offender or in some cases inclusive of victims' families and community representatives. Both settings are mediated by a trained facilitator operating under a professional body, such as the Restorative Justice Council. Offenders retain access to legal representation but must admit their guilt prior to participating in a conference and offenders are expected to speak for themselves. The conference is designed to create a structured dialogue aimed at improving understanding. A standard scenario is that the facilitator begins by clarifying the meeting parameters. The victim next explains the impact a crime has inflicted on him or her. The offender then accounts for his or her crimes. This usually includes an apology to the victim. Offenders are believed to benefit from a better understanding about how their crimes have impacted their victims and the wider community. Victims are believed to benefit by hearing the offender apologise for his or her crimes in person (and not through legal counsel), gaining greater clarity about the offender and his or her reasons for offending and having a voice on the post-conference contract the offender is expected to accept.

Restorative justice is an example about how the problem of the public may be overcome. First, there are clearly set parameters for restorative conferences that help ensure consistency (Ormerod, 2012, Restorative Justice Council, 2011a). Conferences are facilitated by trained mediators ensuring a structured dialogue where like cases are treated similarly. Restorative conferences have the advantage of greater flexibility over the range of penal options to best fit the specific needs of offenders. Conference participants agree contracts in about 98 per cent of cases (Shapland et al., 2006, 2007, p. 27). Standard outcomes include requirements that offenders attend treatment to overcome substance abuse or problems with anger management, training to improve employability and life skills, and participation in community services. These are each believed to promote the 'restoration' of an offender's public status as an equal citizen.[8] If offenders fail to satisfy the terms of their contract, a more burdensome contract may be offered or the offender can face a possible trial and a potential criminal record.

Second, members of the public that participate in restorative conferences are able to acquire relevant knowledge to help inform their decisions about contractual outcomes. Outcome decisions might benefit from operating with a more robust view about specific offences within the terms of the personal and wider 'social context', including a more robust account of desert (Roberts, this volume). Desert is often understood within the framework of legal moralism: punishment is justified where offenders are culpable for moral wrongdoing. The more wrong the crime is, the greater the punishment deserved. This understanding about desert and morality has received much criticism for its potential arbitrariness and potential incompatibility with the criminal law (Brooks, 2012a, pp. 20–26). Desert enjoys central importance for most, if not all, sentencing guidelines. We require a more compelling account that overcomes these problems. One alternative is 'empirical desert', an idea championed by Paul Robinson that identifies 'the community's intuitions of justice' discovered through 'empirical research into those factors that drive people's assessment of blameworthiness'(2008, p. 149).[9]

Restorative justice is able to provide an account consistent with empirical desert. Conference participants work together to clarify shared intuitions about desert concerning a specific offender. The structured setting of a restorative conference helps avoid the problem of relying on any one contested moral view about an offender might deserve in his restorative contract. Conference participants are also able to avoid the influence of media manipulation concerning relevant facts through direct engagement with the offender.

Restorative justice indicates how the problem of the public may be overcome. The first problem is that the public lacks satisfactory information to form a justifiably informed judgement. This is overcome through the constructive dialogue designed to generate improved understanding between victim, offender and the community. This avoids the concern that outcomes might be based on inaccurate or incomplete relevant knowledge. The second problem is that sentencing decisions would become more arbitrary if the public voice held greater weight. This problem is overcome through the

structured conference setting facilitated by a trained mediator where contracts for the offender are tailored to his or her particular circumstances.
The third problem is the worry that the public, if granted a greater say on
outcomes, are more likely to support greater sentence severity that may
threaten other penal goals. Instead, this has not been the case with most
available studies about restorative justice in practice (Braithwaite, 2002;
Doak & O'Mahoney, 2006).

Restorative justice is an approach that promotes improved public confidence while reducing offending and at reduced costs. Both victims and
offenders report high satisfaction with participation in restorative conferences (Sherman, Strang, & Newbury-Birch, 2008, pp. 25–26). It might be
likely that further use of restorative conferences will contribute to contin-
ued satisfaction by future participants. Restorative justice has also been
found to contribute to 25 per cent less reoffending than alternatives while
saving £9 for every £1 spent (Shapland et al., 2008; Restorative Justice
Council, 2011b).[10] If we want to improve public confidence without sacrificing crime reduction efforts and other penal goals, restorative justice is an
approach that we must take seriously.[11] Restorative justice indicates how
public opinion may be brought back into criminal justice and overcome the
problem of the public.

3. SENTENCING BY STAKEHOLDERS

Restorative justice is hamstrung by several limitations. Restorative justice
can overcome these challenges without sacrificing its attractiveness through
recommended revisions that I will indicate in this section.

The first problem concerns a fundamental question about 'restoration'.
Restorative justice aims at the restoration of offenders, victims, and the
community. The idea is that criminal offending has damaged the relationship between them. We require a process that may help restore the shared
bonds of association through constructive dialogue that will yield a mutu-
ally satisfactory outcome for the relevant parties. The problem is identifying
the relevant community members. Some argue, such as Andrew Ashworth,
that 'the concept of restoring the community remains shrouded in mystery,
as indeed does the identification of the relevant "community"'(2010, p. 94).[12]
He says elsewhere:

> If the broad aim is to restore the 'communities affected by the crime', as well
> as the victim and the victim's family, this will usually mean a geographical
> community; but where an offence targets a victim because of race, religion,
> sexual orientation, etc., that will point to a different community that needs to
> be restored (Ibid., p. 583).

So the first problem is identifying the community members to be restored through restorative justice.

A second problem with restorative justice concerns conference membership. Restorative justice aims to restore the damaged relationship between victim, offender, and the community. Let us suppose each party is known so we do not face the first problem of not knowing the persons to be restored. Problems remain where one or more parties are unable or unwilling to participate in a restorative conference. In practice, these conferences may proceed without the victim where he or she chooses not to attend. This is because, in part, restorative justice requires the active consent of participants: none should be coerced as this would undermine restoration. Conferences may proceed for the additional reason that some positive conclusion may result nonetheless. Perhaps the relation between victim and offender remains damaged, but there may be benefits still where offenders acknowledge their guilt and seek restoration with the community. The problem of who is a relevant member of 'the community' will remain. A related concern is in cases where the victim is murdered and unable to participate. Conference membership has central importance as these are the parties that need to be engaged for restoration to be achieved. It is a serious problem where we cannot identify whose participation is required.

The third problem is limited applicability. Most proponents of restorative justice defend the approach as alternative to imprisonment. Restorative justice as an approach to punishment seeks to engage participants outside the courtroom through constructive dialogue and mutual understanding that will lead to outcomes which avoid hard treatment.[13] The rejection of imprisonment by restorative justice restricts its applicability. The concern is that the public may not support alternatives to imprisonment, such as the use of restorative conferences, for offenders guilty of the more serious violent crimes (Kahan, 1996; Khan, 2011; Spiranovic et al., 2011). The practice of restorative justice has been generally limited to cases involving youth offenders and minor offences. Its limited applicability raises further questions about whether it can offer a theory of punishment because it may only apply to some, but not all or even most, cases.

These three limitations can be addressed together. The first challenge concerns the problem of identifying the community to be restored. I believe that we should be guided by an important principle of stakeholding: *that those who have a stake in penal outcomes should have a say in decisions about them.* Stakeholding is an idea that originates in the literature about business ethics and corporate governance (Hutton, 1998; Plender, 1997; Prabhaker, 2004). It is meant to offer a model that improves transparency and accountability through shared responsibility and communicative dialogue. Stakeholding has direct relevance for sentencing policy. Stakeholders are those individuals with a stake in penal outcomes. These persons will include victims, if any, and members of their support networks and the local community. Each marks him- or herself out as a potential stakeholder in virtue of his or her relative stake. Stakeholders will also include offenders because they, too, have a stake in penal outcomes.

The restorative justice conference setting is a useful model for working out how stakeholding might take shape. Conference proceedings aim to achieve restoration though dialogue and the offender satisfying contractual conditions that participants agree. The idea is that the expression of apology by the offender, improved mutual understanding, and completion of specified terms yields 'restoration', but we might better understand this process as promoting stakeholding. Some commentators refer to participants as 'stakeholders', and there is overlap between my account of stakeholder sentencing and standard views about restorative justice (Braithwaite, 2002, pp. 11, 50, 55). Nonetheless, the differences are crucial and reveal how restorative justice might be transformed into a more compelling account of punishment that better incorporates public opinion.

A focus on stakeholding clarifies who should be included in conference proceedings: those that have a stake in penal outcomes. This will involve those directly affected, such as the victim and his or her support network.[14] Stakeholders bear the costs and are most affected by penal outcomes. Together, they should determine what these outcomes are within prescribed limits acceptable to the general public.

It is crucial to highlight that this focus on stakeholder decision making does not exclude the general public. So while it is clear that members of the public may be stakeholders as victims and offenders, general public is also a stakeholder. Stakeholding is not about the expression of the general public's judgement nor is this often possible if thought desirable (Brooks, 2012a, pp. 10–22; Hart, 1968, p. 161). Stakeholding is instead about giving special attention to those who have a greater stake in outcomes. The general public constrains the actions of stakeholder sentencing by setting the parameters for permissible penal procedures and outcomes. So conferences are mediated by a trained facilitator to ensure procedures are sufficiently robust, and offenders are entitled to legal representation as a further guarantee.[15] Furthermore, the general public might also participate as local community members or as members of a victim's support network. Neither the victim, his or her family or support network, the offender, or others have the only say on penal outcomes. Neither does the general public. Stakeholding is about bringing these different interests together in a structured way to determine penal outcomes.

If the general public is a relevant stakeholder, it might be argued that it should have a say. The problem is that this might justify mob rule whereby penal outcomes are determined by popular vote. But not all stakeholders are similarly situated, and some have a greater stake than others. For example, victims and those directly affected by crimes and their outcomes will have a larger stake and, thus, should be included in stakeholder conferences. The general public should also be included but principally through representation, such as a few persons. So the stakeholder conference may somewhat resemble a jury in membership size. It will remain essential that its size is relatively small to better facilitate constructive dialogue and to keep focused on the needs of those with the largest stakes.[16] This position broadly supports the widely used restorative conference model instead of victim-mediation meetings.[17] This is because the latter excludes community representation. The victim may have a larger personal stake than other individuals in penal outcomes, but this does not negate the stake held by the community. Both categories of stakeholders can be accommodated through the restorative justice conference. This model has proven practically workable with the additional benefit that it promotes stakeholding.

The stakeholder model broadens the applicability of the restorative conference model to endorse what I call *punitive restoration*. This is the idea that penal outcomes arising from the conference model need not always exclude imprisonment.[18] While it is clear that incarceration often makes successful crime reduction efforts more difficult, it is also clear that prisons can and should be transformed to improve their disappointing results (Liebling, 2006). For example, restorative justice contracts often include an obligation on offenders to engage in developing employability and life skills and treatment for any drug and alcohol problems (Brooks, 2012a, pp. 66–67, 73–75).[19] There is no reason to accept that these activities could never be successfully delivered within prisons. Perhaps imprisonment should be used sparingly. This is not an argument for never using custodial sentences. It is conceivable and possible that a secure facility, such as a prison, may prove the best environment for some offenders in select cases (Perez & Jennings, 2012). Furthermore, prison officers might receive additional training to become Personal Support Officers (Chapman & Smith, 2011, p. 228). These officers have most frequent contact with imprisoned offenders and the trust that builds over time could be put to more effective use where officers provided improved pastoral support. There are then several ways in which the prison might be restructured in ways that would better enable it to foster a more conducive environment for the rehabilitation and restoration offenders than found in most prisons today. These reforms may require additional resources, but they may prove cost effective over time in the likely, although no means certain, result of improved crime reduction.

The idea that we should make more effective use of prisons does not ignore evidence that prisons often undermine offender rehabilitation.

Short-term imprisonment is often linked with high recidivism rates. This is a significant problem because most offenders receive sentences of less than twelve months and about 60 per cent reoffend within weeks of their release.[20] There is no confirmed link between reductions in recidivisms and increased penal tariffs. In the words of Prime Minister's Strategy Unit: 'There is no convincing evidence that further increases in the use of custody would significantly reduce crime' (Carter, 2003, p. 15; also see Langan & Levin, 2002, p. 2). The prison has been considered by some to be 'criminogenic' because it may contribute to more likely criminal activity post-release than if an offender had received an alternative punishment (Tonry, 2011, pp. 138, 140–141).

The lack of reformatory efforts for those serving less than twelve months sentences is a major contributing factor to the high recidivism.[21] Brief intensive interventions have been employed to address problems associated with drug use and offenders were found to benefit from 'significant gains in knowledge, attitudes, and psychosocial functioning'(Joe et al., 2012). These sessions were corrections-based treatment of moderate (thirty outpatient group sessions three days per week) or high intensity (six-month residential treatment) has been found to yield cost savings of 1.8 to 5.7 the cost of their implementation (Daley et al., 2004). Such policies indicate that prisons may be reformed to better support offender rehabilitation and improve post-release crime reduction efforts without sacrificing cost effectiveness.

These reforms towards punitive restoration are important. This is because it is possible that the punishment of offenders guilty of more serious crimes may require more punitive outcomes than currently available to most restorative justice conferences. For example, current practice rejects the permissibility of including the threat or imposition of imprisonment in restorative contracts. In contrast, punitive restoration might find offenders in a position where they might agree to treatment and community service plus a suspended sentence that could be imposed if contractual terms are not satisfied. This option would extend the flexibility of restorative justice to address a greater range of offences in a restorative context and bypass the need for a criminal trial. Stakeholder sentencing can then identify how a restorative model might be transformed and overcome the problem of limited applicability.[22]

This transformation might be objected to on the grounds that imprisonment, even for a few days, is a major curtailment of individual liberty. Such a sanction requires special safeguards that only the courtroom can satisfy. The problem with this objection is that the overwhelming majority of offenders—as many as 97 per cent in Scotland—never go to trial. Most cases end in plea bargains with a judge or magistrate.[23] If it remains acceptable for more serious crimes to be punished after this process, the stakeholder model should be an attractive alternative. This is because punitive restoration would have a trained facilitator not unlike a lay magistrate conducting criminal proceedings but with the advantages of victims gaining the satisfaction of an apology from their offender, the promotion of greater mutual understanding amongst stakeholders, and penal outcomes better targeted to address the specific needs of offenders. Perhaps it may be contended that facilitators should receive additional training or that their role is performed by magistrates. We should also expect that, if this extension of restoration justice can continue to earn victim satisfaction, it will build and support public confidence, too (Gromet, Okimoto, Wenzel, & Darley, 2012). The stakeholder model of punitive restoration can deliver a more satisfactory outcome for victims, offenders, and the wider community than the less transparent proceedings that often lead to plea bargaining.

It might be objected that punitive restoration has limited applicability even if it may be applied to far more cases than restorative justice. This is because the public will not permit its use in all cases, such as trials for murder, treason, or serious sex offences. There is an increasing amount of work that argues in favour of restorative justice in cases like these (McGlynn, 2011; Mills, 2003). If punitive restoration improves public confidence in the punishment for most, if not all, crimes, it represents a compelling alternative demanding greater engagement. The evidence already noted may be indicative, but it represents encouraging support for such policies that appear likely to grow as further studies are performed.

It might be further objected that stakeholder sentencing through punitive restoration would fail to treat like cases alike. The concern is that offenders convicted of similar crimes might receive different penal outcomes. If similar cases have different outcomes, penal justice may be undermined. This objection can be met because stakeholder sentencing is about determining outcomes that better address the needs of stakeholders. There will be differences between similar cases that the restorative conference setting can discover and better target through the greater flexibility available to it. Alternatives appear more consistent at the high price of their inability to address offender needs, for example, with the outcome flexibility of punitive restoration.

Much of my argument for stakeholder sentencing above is that it is compelling because it is an improvement over alternatives. Stakeholder sentencing is also a more powerful view about the justice of punishment. So this model offers not only a compelling way to better incorporate public opinion into sentencing decisions, but also a more compelling view about justice addressing issues of both theory and practice. Thus, stakeholder sentencing may overcome concerns that misinformed public opinion is driving criminal justice policy (Page & Shapiro, 1983). Stakeholder sentencing develops an important revision of restorative justice through the restorative conference model that extends its applicability and flexibility of outcomes in a way that is likely to improve public confidence, reduce reoffending, and be cost effective.

Stakeholder sentencing also represents a compelling view about penal justice. Punishment is often justified through its justifying aim or purpose, such as retribution, deterrence, or rehabilitation. Philosophers have long disagreed on which principle of sentencing is best although there is general agreement that hybrid theories aiming to endorse two or more principles often suffer from inconsistency (see Brooks 2012a, pp. 89–100). Stakeholder sentencing is one form that a *unified theory of punishment* might take because it is able to pursue multiple penal goals within a unified and coherent account.[24] For example, desert is satisfied because offenders must accept guilt prior to participation. The penal goals of crime reduction (including the goal of protecting the general public) and enabling offender rehabilitation are achieved through the restorative conference from the available evidence on restorative justice outcomes. Restoration is secured through the high satisfaction of participants in restorative conferences, including both victims and offenders. Stakeholder sentencing, as a unified theory of punishment, need not prioritise one penal goal over others, but it may facilitate the pursuit of several goals together. It must be emphasised that the pursuit of these goals transpires within an overall restorative framework that helps avoid conflict between principles.

4. CONCLUSION

Recent years have seen a growing interest in securing a greater incorporation of public opinion in sentencing decisions. This effort is thought to help produce improved public confidence about penal outcomes. This development has alarmed some because of the fear that a greater role for the public's collective voice will lead to disproportionate and overly harsh punishment. While it has been clear that public confidence in the criminal justice system is important to secure and sustain, it is much less clear how this might be achieved without sacrificing important penal principles and the rule of law.

I have argued that this problem of the public may be addressed through stakeholder sentencing. The central idea is that sentencing decisions should be made collectively by those who have a stake in penal outcomes. This model supports a greater incorporation of public opinion within specified parameters that avoid the concerns flagged by critics. Stakeholder sentencing sheds light on one way that public confidence might be secured without undermining the legitimacy of sentencing decisions. This approach is a revised and expanded account of restorative justice in what I have called punitive restoration.

The ideas of stakeholder sentencing and punitive restoration represent an important model for how we might bring the victim and others with a stake in penal outcomes back into the criminal justice system. Nils Christie rightly says, 'The victim is a particularly heavy loser. . . . Not only has he suffered, lost materially or become hurt, physically or otherwise. . . . But above all he has lost participation in his own case'(1998, p. 314). Stakeholder sentencing helps correct this unjust imbalance. If we wish to incorporate a greater voice for the public without sacrificing judicial standards, the idea of stakeholder sentencing deserves greater attention.[25]

REFERENCES

Ashworth, Andrew. 2002. 'Responsibilities, Rights and Restorative Justice.' *British Journal of Criminology* 42: 578–595.

Ashworth, Andrew. 2010. *Sentencing and Criminal Justice.* 5th ed. Cambridge, UK: Cambridge University Press.

Ashworth, Andrew, and Mike Redmayne. 2005. *The Criminal Process.* 3rd ed. Oxford: Oxford University Press.

Braithwaite, John. 2002. *Restorative Justice and Response Regulation.* Oxford: Oxford University Press.

Brooks, Thom. 2003. 'T. H. Green's Theory of Punishment.' *History of Political Thought* 24: 685–701.

Brooks, Thom. 2004a. 'The Right to Trial by Jury.' *Journal of Applied Philosophy* 21: 197–212.

Brooks, Thom. 2004b. 'A Defence of Jury Nullification.' *Res Publica* 10: 401–423.

Brooks, Thom, ed. 2009. *The Right to a Fair Trial.* Aldershot, UK: Ashgate.

Brooks, Thom. 2010. 'Punishment and British Idealism'. In Jesper Ryberg and J. Angelo Corlett (eds.), *Punishment and Ethics: New Perspectives.* Basingstoke, UK: Palgrave Macmillan, 16–32.

Brooks, Thom. 2011a. 'Punishment: Political, Not Moral.' *New Criminal Law Review* 14: 427–438.

Brooks, Thom. 2011b. 'Is Bradley a Retributivist?' *History of Political Thought* 32: 83–95.

Brooks, Thom. 2011c. 'What Did the British Idealists Ever Do for Us?' In Thom Brooks (ed.), *New Waves in Ethics.* Basingstoke, UK: Palgrave Macmillan, 28–47.

Brooks, Thom. 2012a. *Punishment.* New York: Routledge.

Brooks, Thom. 2012b. 'Hegel and the Unified Theory of Punishment.' In Thom Brooks (ed.), *Hegel's Philosophy of Right.* Oxford: Blackwell, 103–123.

Carter, Patrick. 2003. *Managing Offenders, Reducing Crime: A New Approach.* London: Prime Minister's Strategy Unit.

Christie, Nils. 1998. 'Conflicts as Property.' In Andrew von Hirsch and Andrew Ashworth (eds.), *Principled Sentencing: Readings on Theory and Policy.* Oxford: Hart, 312–316.

Cook, Carrie L., and Jodi Lane. 2009. 'The Place of Public Fear in Sentencing and Correctional Policy.' *Journal of Criminal Justice* 37: 586–595.

Cullen, Francis T., Bonnie S. Fisher, and Brandon K. Applegate. 2000. 'Public Opinion about Punishment and Corrections.' *Crime and Justice* 27: 1–79.

Daley, M., C. T. Love, D. S. Shepard, C. B. Peterson, K. L. White, and F. B. Hall. 2004. 'Cost–Effectiveness of Connecticut's In-Prison Substance Abuse Treatment.' *Journal of Offender Rehabilitation* 39: 69–92.

Darbyshire, Penny. 2002. 'Magistrates.' In Mike McConville and Geoffrey Wilson (eds.), *The Oxford Handbook of the Criminal Justice Process.* Oxford: Oxford University Press, 285–309.

Dawes, William, Paul Harvey, Brian McIntosh, Fay Nunney, and Annabelle Phillips. 2011. *Attitudes to Guilty Plea Sentence Reductions.* London: Sentencing Council.

Doak, Jonathan. 2005. 'Victims' Rights in Criminal Trials: Prospects for Participation.' *Journal of Law and Society* 32: 294–316.

Doak, Jonathan. 2011. 'Honing the Stone: Refining Restorative Justice as a Vehicle for Emotional Redress.' *Contemporary Justice Review* 14: 439–456.

Doak, Jonathan, and David O'Mahoney. 2006. 'The Vengeful Victim? Assessing the Attitudes of Victims Participating in Restorative Youth Conferencing.' *International Review of Victimology* 13: 157–177.

Durlauf, Steven N., and Daniel S. Nagin. 2011. 'Imprisonment and Crime: Can Both Be Reduced?' *Criminology and Public Policy* 10: 13–54.

Edwards, Ian. 2002. 'The Place of Victims' Preferences in the Sentencing of "Their" Offenders.' *Criminal Law Review* 2002: 689–702.

Edwards, Ian. 2006. 'Restorative Justice, Sentencing and the Court of Appeal.' *Criminal Law Review* 2006: 110–123.

Estlund, David M. 2008. *Democratic Authority: A Philosophical Framework.* Princeton, NJ: Princeton University Press.

Feinberg, Joel. 1970. 'The Expressive Function of Punishment.' In *Doing and Deserving: Essays in the Theory of Responsibility.* By Joel Feinberg. Princeton, NJ: Princeton University Press, 95–118.

Gardner, John. 1998. 'Crime: In Proportion and in Perspective.' In Andrew Ashworth and Martin Wasik (eds.), *Fundamentals of Sentencing Theory: Essays in Honour of Andrew von Hirsch.* Oxford: Clarendon, 31–52.

Gromet, Dena M., Tyler G. Okimoto, Michael Wenzel, and John M. Darley. 2012. 'A Victim-Centered Approach to Justice? Victim Satisfaction Effects on Third-Party Punishments.' *Law and Human Behavior* 36: 375–389.

Grove, Trevor. 2003. *The Magistrate's Tale: A Front Line Report from a New JP.* London: Bloomsbury.

Hart, H. L. A. 1968. *Punishment and Responsibility: Essays in the Philosophy of Law.* Oxford: Clarendon.

Hibbing, John R., and Elizabeth Theiss-Morse. 2002. *Stealth Democracy: Americans' Beliefs about How Government Should Work.* Cambridge, UK: Cambridge University Press.

Hutton, Neil. 2005. 'Beyond Populist Punitiveness?' *Punishment and Society* 7: 243–258.

Hutton, Will. 1998. *The Stakeholding Society: Writings on Politics and Economics.* Cambridge, UK: Polity.

Joe, George W., Kevin Knight, D. Dwayne Simpson, et al. 2012. 'An Evaluation of Six Brief Interventions that Target Drug-Related Problems in Correctional Populations.' *Journal of Offender Rehabilitation* 51: 9–33.

Kahan, Dan M. 1996. 'What Do Alternative Sanctions Mean?' *University of Chicago Law Review* 63: 591–653.

Khan, Sadiq, ed. 2011. *Punishment and Reform: How Our Justice System Can Help Cut Crime.* London: Fabian Society.

Lai, Yung-Lien, Jihong Zhao, and Dennis R. Longmire. 2012. 'Specific Crime–Fear Linkage: The Effect of Actual Burglary Incidents Reported to the Police on Residents' Fear of Burglary.' *Journal of Crime and Justice* 35: 13–34.

Langnan, Patrick A., and David J. Levin. 2002. *Recidivism of Prisoners Released in 1994.* Washington, DC: Bureau of Justice Statistics.

Latimer, Jeff, Craig Dowden, and Danielle Muise. 2005. 'The Effectiveness of Restorative Justice Practices: A Meta-Analysis.' *Prison Journal* 85: 127–144.

Liebling, Alison. 2006. 'Prisons in Transition.' *International Journal of Law and Psychiatry* 29: 422–430.

Lippke, Richard L. 2011. *The Ethics of Plea Bargaining.* Oxford: Oxford University Press.

Locke, John. 2004. *Two Treatises of Government.* Edited by Peter Laslett. Cambridge, UK: Cambridge University Press.

McGlynn, Clare. 2011. 'Feminism, Rape and the Search for Justice.' *Oxford Journal of Legal Studies* 31: 825–842.

Miller, Susan. 2011. *After the Crime: The Power of Restorative Justice Dialogues between Victims and Violent Offenders.* Oxford: Oxford University Press.

Mills, Linda G. 2003. *Insult to Injury: Rethinking Our Responses to Intimate Abuse.* Princeton, NJ: Princeton University Press.

Ministry of Justice. 2010. *Breaking the Cycle: Effective Punishment, Rehabilitation and Sentencing of Offenders.* London: Her Majesty's Stationary Office.

Ministry of Justice. 2012. *Punishment and Reform: Effective Community Sentences.* London: Her Majesty's Stationary Office.

Myers, Bryan, Allison Roop, Deorah Kalnen, and Andre Kehn. 2013. 'Victim Impact Statements and Crime Heinousness: A Test of the Saturation Hypothesis.' *Psychology, Crime and Law* 19: 129–143.

National Offender Management Service. 2012. *Better Outcomes through Victim–Offender Conferencing (Restorative Justice).* London: NOMS.

O'Hara, Erin Ann. 2005. 'Victim Participation in the Criminal Process.' *Journal of Law and Policy* 13: 229–247.

Ormerod, David. 2012. 'Editorial: Getting It Right for Victims and Witnesses.' *Criminal Law Review* 5: 317–319.

Page, Benjamin I., and Robert Y. Shapiro. 1983. 'Effects of Public Opinion on Policy.' *American Political Science Review* 77: 175–190.

Perez, Deanna M., and Wesley G. Jennings. 2012. 'Treatment Behind Bars: The Effectiveness of Prison-Based Therapy for Sex Offenders.' *Journal of Crime and Justice* 35: 435–450.

Plender, John. 1997. *A Stake in the Future: The Stakeholding Solution.* London: Nicholas Brealey.

Prabhaker, Rajiv. 2004. 'Whatever Happened to Stakeholding?' *Public Administration* 82: 567–584.

Restorative Justice Council. 2011a. *Best Practice Guidance for Restorative Practice*. London: Restorative Justice Council.

Restorative Justice Council. 2011b. *What Does the Ministry of Justice RJ Research Tell Us?* London: Restorative Justice Council. http://www.restorativejustice.org.uk/assets/_ugc/fetch.php?file=21w6_ministry_of_justice_evaluation_of_restorative_justice.pdf

Robert, Julian V. 2009. 'Listening to the Crime Victim: Evaluating Victim Input at Sentencing and Parole.' *Crime and Justice* 38: 347–412.

Roberts, Julian V., and Mike Hough. 2005. *Understanding Public Attitudes to Criminal Justice*. Maidenhead, UK: Open University Press.

Roberts, Julian V., Mike Hough, Jonathan Jackson, and Monica M. Gerber. 2012. 'Public Opinion towards the Lay Magistracy and the Sentencing Council Guidelines.' *British Journal of Criminology* 52: 1072–1091.

Roberts, Julian V., Loretta J. Stalens, David Indermaur, and Mike Hough. 2003. *Penal Populism and Public Opinion: Lessons from Five Countries*. Oxford: Oxford University Press.

Robinson, Paul H., and John M. Darley. 1997 'The Utility of Desert.' *Northwestern University Law Review* 91: 453–499.

Robinson, Paul H., and John M. Darley. 2007. 'Intuitions of Justice: Implications for Criminal Law and Justice Policy.' *Southern California Law Review* 81: 1–68.

Robinson, Paul H. 2008. 'Competing Conceptions of Modern Desert: Vengeaful, Deontological, and Empirical.' *Cambridge Law Journal* 67: 145–175.

Robinson, Paul H., Geoffrey P. Goodwin, and Michael Reisig. 2010. 'The Disutility of Injustice.' *New York University Law Review* 85: 1940–2033.

Ryberg, Jesper. 2010. 'Punishment and Public Opinion.' In Jesper Ryberg and J. Angelo Corlett (eds.), *Punishment and Ethics: New Perspectives*. Basingstoke, UK: Palgrave Macmillan, 149–168.

Schumpeter, Joseph A. 1942. *Capitalism, Socialism and Democracy*. New York: Harper Perennial.

Shapland, Joanna, Anne Atkinson, Helen Atkinson, et al. 2006. *Restorative Justice in Practice: The Second Report from the Evaluation of Three Schemes*. Sheffield, UK: Centre for Criminological Research, University of Sheffield. http://www.shef.ac.uk/polopoly_fs/1.783!/file/RestorativeJustice2ndReport.pdf

Shapland, Joanna, Anne Atkinson, Helen Atkinson, et al. 2007. *Restoratice Justice: The Views of Victims and Offenders*. London: Ministry of Justice.

Shapland, Joanna, Anne Atkinson, Helen Atkinson, et al. 2008. *Does Restorative Justice Affect Reconviction? The Fourth Report from the Evaluation of Three Schemes*. London: Ministry of Justice.

Sherman, Lawrence W., Heather Strang, and Dorothy Newbury-Birch. 2008. *Restorative Justice*. London: Youth Justice Board.

Spiranovic, Caroline A., Lynne D. Roberts, David Indermaur, Kate Warner, Karen Gelb, and Geraldine Mackenzie. 2011. 'Public Preferences for Sentencing Purposes: What Difference Does Offender Age, Criminal History and Offence Type Make?' *Criminology and Criminal Justice* 12: 289–306.

Tonry, Michael. 2011. 'Less Imprisonment is No Doubt a Good Thing: More Policing is Not.' *Criminology and Public Policy* 10: 137–152.

Towl, Graham J. 2006.'Drug-Misuse Intervention Work.' In G. J. Towl (ed.), *Psychological Research in Prisons*. Oxford: Blackwell, 116–127.

Twist, Steven J. 2003. *Rights of Crime Victims Constitutional Amendment: Hearing on H. J. Res. 48, Before the Constitution Subcommittee of the Committee on the Judiciary, House of Representatives*, US Congress (30 September 2003). http://www.judiciary.house.gov/legacy/twist093003.pdf.

Williams, Monica. 2012. 'Beyond the Retributive Public: Governance and Public Opinion on Penal Policy.' *Journal of Crime and Justice* 35: 93–113.

Zimring, Franklin E., Gordon Hawkins, and Sam Kamin. 2001. *Punishment and Democracy: Three Strikes and You're Out in California*. Oxford: Oxford University Press.

NOTES

1. See Doak (2005) and for criticisms see Edwards (2002).
2. See Durlauf and Nagin (2011, p. 28) and also *Brown v. Plata*, 563 US (2011).
3. This view supports the observation by Joseph Schumpeter that democracy is not rule by the people but rather rule by politicians elected by the citizenry (1942, pp. 284–285).
4. See *Ring v. Arizona* (2002), 536 US 584, 122 S.Ct. 2428.
5. There are exceptions for some US states where victims are permitted to offer sentencing recommendations. On victim rights and US states, see Twist (2003) citing Ala. Const. amend. 557; Alaska Const. art. I, Sec. 24; Ariz. Const. art. II, 2.1; Cal. Const. art. I, 12, 28; Colo. Const. art. II, 16a; Conn. Const. art. I, 8(b); Fla. Const. art. I., 16(b); Idaho Const. art. I, 22; Ill. Const. art. I, 8.1; Ind. Const. art. I, 13(b); Kan. Const. art. 15, 15; La. Const. art. 1, 25; Md. Decl. Of Rights art. 47; Mich. Const. art. I, 24; Miss. Const. art. 3, 26A; Mo. Const. art. I, 32; Mont. Const. art. II, sec. 28; Neb. Const. art. I, 28; Nev. Const. art. I, 8; N.J. Const. art. I, 22; New Mex. Const. art. 2, 24; N.C. Const. art. I, 37; Ohio Const. art. I, 10a; Okla. Const. Art. II, 34; Or. Const. art. I, sec. 42; R.I. Const. art. I, 23; S.C. Const. art. I, sect. 24; Tenn. Const. art. I, 35; Tex. Const. art. I, 30; Utah Const. art. I, 28; Va. Const. art. I, 8-A; Wash. Const. art. 2, 33; and Wis. Const. art. I, 9m.
6. While some argue that victim impact statements *might* influence juries to support harsher sentences (Myers, Roop, Kalnen, & Kehn, 2013), there is convincing evidence that sentencing *does not* become more punitive with victim impact statements (Roberts, 2009).
7. It is controversial whether popular decision making is likely to lead to unsatisfactory public policy outcomes. For a powerful counterargument, see Estlund (2008). Furthermore, the idea that citizens should devote greater efforts to become better educated about criminal justice matters to improve public confidence may rest on an idealistic view about civic participation unlikely to be achieved (Hibbing & Theiss-Morse, 2002).
8. See Ashworth (2002) and Brooks (2012a, Chapter 4) for doubts about whether restorative justice achieves its aims.
9. See Robinson and Darley (1997, 2007), Robinson, Goodwin, and Reisig (2010), and Robinson (this volume).
10. See Latimer, Dowden, and Muise (2005) on empirical studies confirming the effectiveness of restorative justice practices in reducing reoffending.
11. See National Offender Management Service (2012).
12. See Edwards (2006).

13. Restorative justice is practised in different ways. My focus is on its use as a view about punishment and not its use post-conviction. See Miler (2011) for an insightful account about restorative justice post-conviction and McGlynn (2011) for an approach more closely related to my defence of punitive restoration below.

14. Other relevant stakeholders will include the offender and any support network. In practice, restorative conferences often include friends and family of the victim and of the offender, respectively, in 73 per cent and 78 per cent of cases examined in one study (Shapland et al., 2007, p. 20). Interestingly, the same study found that parents were far more likely to attend restorative conferences (50 per cent of offenders and 23 per cent of victims) than partners (3 per cent of offenders and 5 per cent of victims; ibid.).

15. The involvement of legal representation might suggest the need for a judge to serve as an adjudicator. This is not current practice, but my defence of punitive restoration—administered by a trained facilitator—is not inconsistent with the facilitator's role being served by a legal professional.

16. The general public has a stake in outcomes and so should exercise a voice. The model advocated here justifies inclusion of persons serving as representatives of the general public perhaps drawn from the local community, a common practice in restorative conferences at present. This permits members of the general public to be included while keeping conference membership to a size that is large enough to include persons with largest stakes and representative membership of the general public and small enough in size to best facilitate constructive dialogue.

17. For a brief overview of different restorative justice models, see Restorative Justice Council, 'RJ Models: Models of Restorative Justice': http://www.restorative-justice.org.uk/resource/rj_models/.

18. Punitive restoration is a revision of restorative justice models that does not rule out the permissibility of incarceration under specified conditions where restoration would not be undermined. Punitive restoration may also be commensurate with further revisions of the mechanics of restorative justice, including improving the therapeutic potential of restorative justice (Doak, 2011).

19. See Towl (2006) on prison-based programmes designed to better tackle drug and alcohol abuse.

20. See Ministry of Justice's website: http://open.justice.gov.uk/home/.

21. The lack of these efforts is a major contributing factor, but I do not suggest that it is the sole or primary factor for unsatisfactory reoffending rates.

22. The UK's Ministry of Justice has published recent proposals that aim to further embed restorative justice within the criminal justice system includes the aim for greater usage between conviction and sentencing (2012, p. 5). Punitive restoration can fulfil this aim and provide a means for determining a greater variety of sentencing outcomes.

23. See Lippke (2011) for an authoritative critique of plea bargaining and Ashworth and Redmayne (2005, pp. 6–7).

24. There are several ways such a theory might be constructed, but the one I have favoured is to view crime as a harm to individual rights and punishment as 'a response' to crime with the purpose of the protection and maintenance of rights

protected by the criminal law. This model rejects the view that penalties and hard treatment have different justificatory foundations, but rather penal outcomes share a common source of justification: the protection of rights (see Feinberg, 1970). The model is then able to address the fact that penal outcomes are often multidimensional and include punitive and financial elements. The idea that those who have a stake in penal outcomes should have a say is consistent with this rights-based framework. See Brooks (2012a, pp. 123–148) for a defence of the unified theory of punishment. See Brooks (2003, 2010, 2011a, 2011b, 2011c, 2012b) for further discussions of the unified theory of punishment.

25. This chapter benefited enormously from the comments on earlier drafts by fellow contributors to this book, especially Richard Lippke and Paul Robinson. I am further grateful to Julian Roberts and Jesper Ryberg for additional written comments.

10

Repellent Institutions and the Absentee Public: Grounding Opinion in Responsibility for Punishment[1]

Albert W. Dzur

> One way of defining democracy would be to call it a political
> system in which people actively attend to what is significant.
> –Robert Bellah et al.

Contributors to this volume have explored a range of approaches to incorporating public opinion into sentencing policy and practice. This chapter questions some fundamental assumptions by targeting a certain reform-oriented picture that holds that if public opinion can be educated, it is safe for it to influence criminal justice institutions. By contrast, I argue that contemporary institutions themselves ought to be seen as problematic because of the ways which they repel public responsibility for punishment and general awareness of its moral complexity, harmful effects, and deeply biased implementation. In search of a remedy, I discuss the potential for citizen action and reflection within criminal justice institutions such as a revitalised jury system, restorative justice programs, and community policing and the possibilities available for sobering up to the reality of punishment within primary education institutions and through everyday networks of communication.

1. THE PRIORITY OF RESPONSIBILITY TO RATIONALITY

Recent academic discussions of the relationship between public opinion and punishment gravitate around what can be called the rationality problem, the alleged gap between what the lay public knows about punishment and what experts and officials know. Presumably unproblematic when criminal justice is left to the professionals, this apparent knowledge gap causes trouble when sentencing policy, amongst other matters, is influenced by popular pressure. Such is the case in the United States, where many prosecutors and judges are elected and where legislators and executive branch officials at the state and national levels struggle to show themselves 'tough' enough on crime to satisfy a concerned and distrustful electorate (see Lippke, this volume). As a solution, some scholars have proposed greater insulation between policymakers and the public—by forming sentencing committees set apart from electoral politics, for example, or by nurturing tighter professional cultures of expertise amongst court professionals and criminal justice administrators that could counteract politicisation of these roles (Lacey, 2008, p. 192; Pettit, 2004, p. 55; Zimring, Hawkins, & Kamin, 2001, p. 214). At least in the United States, however, where there is little public faith in expertise and centralised state authority, such measures are unworkable both normatively and practically.[2]

Yet perhaps the rationality problem is not so great as to warrant buffers and other distancing mechanisms between policy elites and the public. Procedural justice studies and related public opinion research consistently show that public attitudes are more complicated and less punitive than contemporary 'get tough' political rhetoric and legislation aimed to appeal to the public would suggest (Freiberg, 2001; Tyler & Boeckmann, 1997). When the context of offences is made evident and detailed descriptions of offenders are provided, survey respondents tend to be more moderate in their choices of appropriate punishment than when little context and few descriptions are provided (Doble, 2002; Roberts, Stalans, Indermaur, & Hough, 2003). 'Members of the public', writes Roberts, 'have often been asked to make snap decisions about complex subjects such as mandatory sentencing, parole, or prison conditions. The consequence has been a systematic distortion of the nature of public attitudes, which are less punitive when people are provided with sufficient information about a case with which to make an informed decision' (2011, p. 105).[3]

Thus the pressing question might appear to be not how best to keep the public at bay but how to create the kind of reflective conditions so that reasonable public opinion could be brought into the criminal justice process. Along these lines, some scholars have advocated forums such as deliberative polls and citizens' juries in which representative samples of people discuss punishment policy in a structured and informed fashion, while others recommend large-scale public education campaigns (Green, 2006, 2008). In Section 4 I share some thoughts about the conditions required to accomplish this task, but I want to focus now on something that the rationality problem obscures, which is the question of whether the contemporary public can be held responsible for the punishment enforced in its name. The underlying assumption is that if and when public opinion can be educated, it is safe to bring it to bear in a humane way in and on criminal justice institutions, but what if these institutions are resistant to their part in such an education?

Prior to asking whether and how public opinion can be safely incorporated into the punishment process, we need to examine the problem that we believe the public should have a more educated opinion about. Is it a public problem? Is it a matter about which lay citizens can form reflective opinions? In Section 2 I will argue, descriptively, that because punishment is the product of public institutions it counts as a public issue, yet because the institutions that produce punishment repel public participation and reflection, it is something that is very difficult to form reflective opinions about. Indeed, because of these repellent factors, it is very difficult even for professionals such as legislators, judges, prosecutors, or prison wardens to form reflective opinions.[4] So rather than seeing public opinion as the problem to be resolved, as if it is the public's irrationality that is concerning, I view the amoral and irrational institutional conditions as the problem. This raises the bar for possible solutions, as the current institutional context renders deliberative polls, citizens' juries, and public education simply inadequate for the task. Only when the public plays a more vital role in mainstream institutions, in fact, will the proper grounds for public opinion be laid.

In Section 3, I will argue, normatively, that public responsibility for the institutions that produce punishment is an underappreciated requirement. This is akin to but also different from a legitimacy argument, which stresses consent, for my argument emphasises a broader attunement to the ways public institutions create us as a people and reflect or fail to reflect what it is we stand for. To be responsible—as opposed to wanton, careless, and unthinking—is to steer our public institutions rather than be steered by them and to own up to the kind of people that our institutions are helping to shape.

Placing emphasis on responsibility brings into focus dimensions of both the problem and the possible solution. One of the most troubling aspects of punishment in the United States is how invisible it is, how people only seem to care about criminal justice when victimised or a heinous act is broadcast on the news. Public life is saturated with criminal justice: the human beings affected by it, the conflict between the amount and degree of punishment and our core political and social values, and the amount of public funding devoted to the penal economy. Yet all these staggeringly obvious social facts, facts that serve to construct the public world all around us, enter our conversations only rarely. They are not on standard lists of concerns at the national level (Currie, 2009).[5] They are not part of a broad political discourse at the state level, where the bulk of punishment occurs in the United States; even as the faltering economy pressures state legislatures to find ways to trim prison spending, the reforms to probation and sentencing considered inside government generate scant discussion outside. They are not part of any meaningful court professional reform discourse, either; although frustrated judges do speak out, there is little organisational momentum for change (Gottschalk, 2006, 2007). This *invisibility* of the problem of punishment, this collective *nonseeing* or *disengagement*, has to be dealt with before we can come to grips with the role of public opinion, for it implicates the very grounds of reflection or, in this case, nonreflection.

Consider an anecdote. One of the first news stories I heard upon returning to the United States from sabbatical was about an Illinois prison inmate selected for early release. While in nursing school at the age of twenty-three, Savina Sauceda was arrested for delivering a felony quantity of cocaine. Sauceda, who had not even incurred a traffic ticket before this arrest, had started selling drugs to pay off her school and credit card debts. She received a five-year prison sentence. But the Illinois department of corrections, housing forty-five thousand prisoners with an additional thirty thousand on parole at a cost of over a billion dollars a year, had become a target for budget cuts during the depths of the Great Recession. Here is how the story was framed on National Public Radio, known for its reflective and progressive reporting:

> With budget crises to solve, many states have decided that reducing their prison populations is a good way to save money. Illinois is one example. Under its new early release program, as many as 1,000 non-violent offenders will be able to finish their sentences at home or at other locations approved by prison officials.
>
> Corrections costs are typically a major component of state budgets. So as burgeoning prison populations blow holes through those budgets, more states are looking to cut costs and change policies. (National Public Radio, 2009)

The narrative relates a wise economic decision under straitened budgetary circumstances to release a nonviolent offender with no prior criminal record after serving a year in prison.

Although this was a story of a penal regime becoming more moderate, I found it strangely depressing. Absent was any discussion of the normative goodness or badness of the fact that a nonviolent offender with no criminal record and on track for employability served a year in prison and could have served up to five years. Absent, too, was any locus of normative judgment. Could this woman really have received the following sentence: 'One to five years, depending on the state budget?' Where was the collective mind that had decided that five years was right at time-1 and then changed its mind at time-2? Could we speak to that mind, interview it to ask if saving state dollars was a justifiable reason for the difference between Sauceda being in or out of prison? This story has gnawed at me because it indicates a missing moral force—an absentee public, a 'we' for which a punishment like Sauceda's makes sense. How could a person's fate be so capriciously determined by institutional imperatives only loosely coupled to the very set of normative values that justify the institution?

We are not thinking when we sentence Sauceda to one to five years, and we are still not thinking when we send her back home with an electronic ankle monitor after serving only one year. Someone else is not thinking either. Rather, the thinking and the responsibility for thinking are diffuse and incredibly difficult to trace, to get a hold of. The way to explain this is by seeing punishment as a peculiar institution, both public and repellent to the public.

2. PUNISHMENT AS A REPELLENT PUBLIC INSTITUTION

Let us follow Garland's lead in conceiving of punishment as 'a distinctive and rather complex social institution that, in its routine practices, somehow contrives to condense a whole web of social relations and cultural meanings' (1991, p. 157). It is 'an institution through which society defines and expresses itself at the same time and through the same means that it exercises power over deviants' (ibid., p. 161). To see something as an institution is to recognise that it is more than an instrument that serves a fixed purpose but instead is a semiautonomous domain with a history and an organisational density that make it difficult for those outside the domain—or in one corner of it rather than another—to understand. Moreover, an institution works on us even as we work within it and through it; institutions are significant forces in our lives.

Sociologists and others who study institutions think of them as stable arrangements that guide action and comport with communal values. 'The function of institutions is always the same', writes Parsons, 'the regulation of action in such a way as to keep it in relative conformity with the ultimate common values and value-attitudes of the community' (1990, p. 331). Institutions emerge to accomplish tasks that would be difficult to manage in a more inchoate or ad hoc fashion, such as to execute and regulate the consequences of norm breaking, but they do so in a way that inevitably reflects the normative commitments of the social order in which they are embedded. 'To institutionalize', writes Selznick, 'is to infuse with value beyond the technical requirements of the task at hand' (1992, p. 233). Marriage and family life, the practice of medicine, the meting out of justice, and the education of the next generation, amongst many other undertakings, are all institutionalised, and they all reflect social norms regarding proper relationships, roles, and interactions; they exist to make certain actions easier and others harder.

Even though most institutions are public to some degree, in that they are socially embedded, we can differentiate some as *public* institutions when they produce nondivisible common goods such as public safety, are supported by public revenues, and are managed by people held publically accountable. Private institutions, by contrast, produce private goods—as when a private security force protects only certain individuals—paid for and held accountable primarily to a subgroup, although of course also constrained by the legal system. That an institution is public places a special burden on it to install and heed public procedures of accountability that can determine whether the institution is, in fact, infused with public values.

However, the special burden tends to be rather lightly felt. A persistent theme in the sociology of institutions concerns the way that the rules and offices that impose useful regularity can also conflict with the values intended. Michels's famous study of covert oligarchical tendencies in overtly democratic organisations, for example, pointed to the ways institutional imperatives can lead to delegation of authority and divisions of labour that, in turn, can lead to concentrations of power that violate the values of the groups. 'Who says organization', Michels wrote, 'says oligarchy' (1962, p. 365). Michels thought these power-concentrating tendencies of institutions strong enough to call them 'iron laws', although contemporary scholars dispute both their strength and universality.[6] Yet even if they are not iron or ever present, the tendencies of institutions to serve internal rather than external purposes are powerful and common enough to pose problems.

Even more troublesome than the chronic potential for institutions to violate their own core values are the barriers institutions place on thought. Because of our own dependence on institutions, it is hard to even see what they are doing. While it is true that institutions are social creations, it is also true that they powerfully shape how we think about them and, indeed, who we are. This is not a matter of nefarious or underhanded or corrupt institutions or power-hungry elites, it is standard operating practice. 'How can we possibly think of ourselves in society', writes Douglas, 'except by using the classifications established in our institutions?' (1986, p. 99). 'They fix processes that are essentially dynamic, they hide their influence, and they rouse our emotions to a standardized pitch on standardized issues' (ibid., p. 92). This is just what institutions are for: they label, classify, and rank order; they think for us. As Douglas puts it, 'The instituted community blocks personal curiosity, organizes public memory, and heroically imposes certainty on uncertainty' (ibid., p. 102).

Especially important for the topic of punishment is how institutions can think for us in ways that extract normative elements and replace them with sheer process, thus deflecting concern for others. They can strip away aspects of human beings that make a person familiar, replacing them with other features that make it harder for those responsible for their welfare inside and outside the institution to recognise and act on that responsibility. Bauman has written aptly of the 'management of morality' that can occur in modern institutions through the 'social production of distance, which either annuls or weakens the pressure of moral responsibility', the 'substitution of technical for moral responsibility, which effectively conceals the moral significance of the action', and through 'the technology of segregation and separation, which promotes indifference to the plight of the Other which otherwise would be subject to moral evaluation and morally motivated response' (1989, p. 199).

What Bauman is concerned about occurs quite straightforwardly in criminal justice institutions. People are distanced from the 'law abiding' and treated in a technical rather than moral fashion as soon as they are suspects, a process that continues as defendants are given a case number and finally compelled to wear orange jumpsuits and shackles in court. Such management of morality is normal for institutions that handle a large volume of human business: complex men and women turn into *clearances*, *caseloads*, and *dockets*. The very 'language in which things happen to them', writes Bauman, 'safeguards its referents from ethical evaluation' (1989, p. 103). Both linguistic and material forces of separation are even stronger with respect to human beings accused of harming others. By the very accusation they have already become a candidate for expulsion from the warm 'circle of proximity where moral responsibility rules supreme' (ibid., p. 195).

In addition to doing our thinking for us and shaping how we perceive those they have a hold of, criminal justice institutions repel public examination and participation in three distinct ways. First, the work they do is physically removed from both the lay public and the officials not directly involved. Goffman (1962) called prisons 'total institutions' because they are separate and complete worlds for those inside; communication and interaction with those outside, indeed even visibility, are all tightly circumscribed and controlled. The work of criminal justice administration, which handles the content of probation orders amongst other tasks, is normally conducted outside the public by-ways. Courses on 'life skills', 'anger management', and the like are held in mirrored glass or blasé concrete block buildings— sometimes lacking exterior signs communicating what happens inside. The court process leading to prison or probation is decreasingly public and increasingly technocratic. Plea bargaining's dominance means very few public trials: around 1 to 4 per cent of state and federal criminal cases go to trial (Galanter, 2004; Ostrom, Strickland, & Hannaford-Agor, 2004). Even when there are trials, moreover, a fair number of jurors find them offputting, convoluted, and oddly disempowering (Burnett, 2001).[7]

Criminal justice institutions repel, second, because of their sheer complexity. As Zedner points out, the common phrase 'criminal justice system' should be resisted 'on the grounds that this label masks its plural, disparate, even chaotic, character' (2010, p. 71). What is really a 'series of largely independent organizations with differing cultures, professional ethos, and practices' is not easy even for practitioners to come to grips with, much less members of the lay public (ibid., p. 72). In his critique of the failure of democratic governance that permitted America's steep rise in incarceration, Stuntz indicates how the many-handedness of the criminal justice decision making process thwarted the assessment of responsibility:

> Where state and local officials alike were responsible for rising levels of imprisonment, neither was truly responsible. Prosecutors sent more and more defendants to state prisons in part because state legislators kept building more prison cells. . . . For their part, the legislators kept adding to their state's stock of prison beds because local prosecutors kept sending defendants to state prisons: if they're coming, you must build it. Neither set of officials fully controlled the process by which those prison beds were made and filled, so neither was able to slow or reverse that process. And the voters with the largest stake in that process—chiefly African American residents of high-crime city neighborhoods—had the smallest voice in the relevant decisions. (2011, p. 255)

Thus, even the officials and professionals involved in specific decisions at one level cannot be said to plan, intend, or even fully comprehend the cumulative institutional consequences of their actions.

Third, and most subtly, criminal justice institutions repel public awareness and involvement because they perform and characterise tasks in ways that neutralise the public's role. It has long been restorative justice doctrine that criminal justice institutions 'steal conflicts' and have 'a monopoly on justice' (Christie, 1977, p. 2; Zehr, 1990, p. 121). These are perhaps only dramatic ways of saying something quite uncontroversial, namely, that institutions take up social problems and grow their budgets and their authority to the extent that they can show that they can do *health care, justice, information gathering*, or *education* better than any alternative mode. Institutions are constantly in competition with noninstitutional modes of accomplishing the same goals and thus have a tendency to characterise social problems in the ways that they can manage them. State institutions in particular, by monopolising coercive force, can make it seem that they are the difference between disorder and order, yet they are not. The 'vast majority of crime problems', as Lacey puts it, are handled through 'social policy and social institutions beyond the criminal process' (2001, p. 9). Informal social control is far more important than the formal coercive measures criminal justice institutions deliver and yet our public discourse—influenced, of course, by the ways our institutions think for us—construes courts, prisons, and probation officers as the active agents and families, neighbourhoods, and civil associations as passive recipients of crime control benefits produced by institutions.[8]

3. RECLAIMING THE NORMATIVE

Could we not just shruggingly acknowledge the ways criminal justice institutions think and act for us as simply part of modern life? We are surrounded by complex and quasi-autonomous systems, so why is it surprising or troubling that criminal justice institutions are also complex and quasi-autonomous? Here we must draw a normative distinction between institutions that require greater public monitoring and steering and those that do not. Some institutions have clearly defined and uncontroversial objectives, the pursuit of which is easily monitored. Civil engineering agencies that plan and build highways, sewers, or airports may not require significant public engagement. Other institutions are charged with tasks that do not have discernable, long-lasting, negative effects on human lives. The Bureau of Weights and Measures no doubt influences how we count and calculate but does not appear to hold much risk of impairing people's lives. By contrast, it should be obvious that criminal justice institutions lack clearly defined, uncontroversial, and easily monitored objectives and at the same time pose enormous risks for impairing human development.

A striking feature of criminal justice policy in the last generation is its detachment from a consistent and coherent normative framework. As Stuntz has remarked, 'American criminal law's historical development has borne no relation to any plausible normative theory—unless "more" counts as a normative theory' (2001, p. 508). Punishment in the United States has been marked by two different kinds of dramatic inconsistency. One has to do with severity: from a relatively lenient status quo, at least in the North, the United States rapidly moved in the mid-1970s to a condition of 'hyperincarceration' (Wacquant, 2010). In 1972, for example, sixty-four out of every one hundred thousand citizens in the state of New York were incarcerated, a ratio consistent with the previous hundred years; by 2000 this figure had risen to 383 out of one hundred thousand, in keeping with the even higher national trend over the same thirty-year period (Stuntz, 2011, p. 33). Another has to do with the justificatory reasons decision makers and others favour: we have moved from institutional commitments to rehabilitation as a background objective for serious punishment to 'just deserts' retribution and now to something closer to deterrence and incapacitation as prime objectives, all in the span of one generation. The inconsistency of ideas and practices indicates deep dysfunction, namely, that the normative framing of punishment lacks grounding in the lived reality of offenders, victims, and their communities. As the incoherence of the Savina Sauceda case mentioned above indicates, instead of moral judgments, we see a series of incomprehensible institutional moves played out over and over without public justification. Indeed, the only thing that is consistently clear is that not one of the plural, disputed, and conflicting purposes of criminal justice—rehabilitation, retribution, deterrence, incapacitation—holds sway in either popular or scholarly debate and that what has substituted for sober reflection on a difficult institution are highly politicised and short-term-oriented patterns of thinking.

While the objectives of criminal justice institutions are fuzzy, the negative effects of punishment are all too sharply concrete. Most evident with the penalty of incarceration, they include shame, dehumanisation, feelings of inferiority, and physical suffering. Many of these consequences are experienced to some degree too by the spouses, children, and other close relatives of the incarcerated.[9] In most states in the United States, those convicted of a felony lose their right to vote: in forty-eight states for the duration of the imprisonment; in thirty-six, for the duration of the probation or parole period; and in thirteen, for life (Manza & Uggen, 2005). Economic consequences can also be significant, as prisoners' families struggle with lost wages during incarceration and severely impaired incomes afterwards. Western and Pettit report that 'serving time in prison was associated with a 40 per cent reduction in earnings and with reduced job tenure, reduced hourly wages, and higher unemployment' (2010, p. 13).

Alongside these negative effects are the equally troubling racial and socioeconomic biases of the current system. As Wacquant has pointed out, the current rise in incarceration in the United States should not be called 'mass' incarceration at all but rather the 'hyperincarceration' of a specific group of people: low income African American men in the inner cities. The 'cumulative risk of imprisonment for African American males without a high-school diploma tripled between 1979 and 1999, to reach the astonishing rate of 59%' (Wacquant, 2010, p. 79).[10] 'On any given day', writes Roberts, 'nearly one-third of black men in their twenties are under the supervision of the criminal justice system—either behind bars, on probation, or on parole' (2004, p. 1272).

Although complex and quasi-autonomous, criminal justice institutions could not function without taxpayer support, operate under the oversight of managers selected by officials elected in free, competitive elections, and purport to deliver the nondivisible good of public safety. Although they are resistant and repellent to public responsibility, they are nevertheless the public's responsibility. To put it plainly, the public needs to be more responsible for the work being done by criminal justice institutions because of the plural and contested nature of core values pursued by criminal justice, because of the severe negative consequences of punishment for those punished and because modern punishment is produced by institutions that depend upon the public to function. If we are to have penal institutions at all, we must hold ourselves accountable for what they do and for the reasons they do what they do.

My argument differs from similar process-oriented arguments that point to the proper groundwork for normative judgments rather than advocating a specific substantive value such as retribution or deterrence, in particular those stressing the importance of legitimacy. Legitimacy arguments valorise the normative role of consent: subjects of laws should have a concrete and not abstract or merely symbolic role in authorising those laws and should understand what they must obey (see Bennett, this volume; Waldron, 2006). Yet behind self-protection stands a broader conception of self-government that I wish to tap: the good of being able to control the powers to which you contribute and which speak and operate in your name. Because of the institutionalisation of criminal justice, citizens are indirect and often unknowing supporters of laws that affect people differently—some well, others poorly; some fairly, others unfairly. Such public ignorance, reinforced by and indeed *produced* by modern institutions, can harm one's own interests to be sure, but what I am pinpointing is the lack of concern for others that it implies.[11] In my view what is problematic is not the risk to ourselves of criminal justice institutions that we are failing to steer through deliberate choice making, but the fact that such a diffuse and quasi-autonomous system makes it difficult to hold each other accountable for our laws and the impact of the execution and adjudication of these laws on others not like us. Institutionally fostered public ignorance makes citizen-beneficiaries collaborationists.[12]

Twenty years ago, Bellah, Madsen, Sullivan, Swidler, and Tipton argued that American institutions were marked by serious dysfunction. Their subtle and underappreciated conclusion was that 'democracy means paying attention'; American democracy had not been paying much attention—to the way government, work, and even family structures had become 'corrupt; means have wrongly been turned into ends', in particular the ends of narrow economic success and individual fulfilment (Bellah et al., 1991, p. 291). Institutions bring out our best and our worst. They help us form and maintain intimate attachments, produce and deliver goods and services, and enact the very rules we live by. Yet they can also negatively influence how we do these things. If they are saturated by what Stears calls the 'transactional mindset' of the marketplace, as Bellah et al. believe American institutions are, or by patriarchy and racialism, as others argue, the families, jobs, and laws we have will be correspondingly affected (Stears, 2011). Institutions focus our attention, sometimes on the wrong things:

> We live in and through institutions. The nature of the institutions we both inhabit and transform has much to do with our capacity to sustain attention. We could even say that institutions are socially organized forms of paying attention or attending, although they can also, unfortunately, be socially organized forms of distraction. (Bellah et al., 1991, p. 256)

Bellah et al.'s argument, although rooted in descriptive political sociology, was intended to be normative: 'Because we have let too much of our lives be determined by processes 'going on over our heads,' we have settled for easy measures that have distracted us from what needs to be attended to and cared for. One way of defining democracy would be to call it a political system in which people actively attend to what is significant' (1991, p. 273). What is significant is the cultivation of fulfilling human lives and the reinforcement of the institutional scaffolding that makes that cultivation possible.

Ironically, although also fully consistent with their analysis, Bellah et al. fail to mention criminal justice institutions in their catalogue of dysfunction. On the one hand, this shows a surprising disconnection to social reality. The America of 1991, the year Bellah et al.'s book was published, had been on a fifteen-year long imprisonment trajectory that would lead to its present position at the top of the list of the world's most punitive states. Just two years later, in 1993, Washington state would escalate the trend with its turn to 'three strikes' mandatory minimum sentencing laws that ensured life imprisonment for a third felony offence, a reform made notorious by the even more severe version California voted into law in 1994. Such schemes led to foreseeable outcomes such as life sentences for nonviolent offenders, variable sentencing for those committing the same acts but in different sequences, and liability for prosecution under three strikes fluctuating widely depending on whether one committed the third offence in a liberal municipality like San Francisco or a conservative one like San Diego (Zimring et al., 2001). How could progressive thinkers like Bellah and his co-authors miss such apparent institutional corruption, such inconsistent, cruel, and massively life-altering policies?

Yet such an oversight is congruent with their argument about the ways that institutions distract, steer our attention away from what matters, and, worse yet, help us feel very comfortable not seeing. Bellah et al. are off the normative hook, since their not-noticing can be attributed to an institutional context that sweeps criminal offenders away, dehumanises them, adjudicates and punishes them all outside public, transparent, not to mention participatory domains. So what to do? Bellah et al. point in the right direction, towards more deliberative institutions that welcome citizen participation, yet as their own neglect of criminal justice shows, some institutions are so nondeliberative and nonparticipatory that profound change is required. Because, as we have seen, criminal justice institutions can make such a major impact on human lives, attention to what happens in and through them is a moral requirement of democratic publics. This moral requirement, I believe, cannot practically be discharged without power sharing that places citizens in decision-making roles.

4. PUBLIC ACTION AND PUBLIC OPINION

If these descriptive and normative arguments hold up, the question of how public opinion could become rational enough to positively influence criminal justice institutions needs to be restated as follows: how might criminal justice institutions stop thinking for us so we can begin to think for ourselves and steer them in ways that comport with a sober, reflective sense of justice? If I am right, it is not the public that needs fixing but the broken-down institutional spaces in which we instantiate ourselves as a public. What I have in mind as targets of critical analysis and reform, therefore, are spaces of load-bearing participation inside and outside criminal justice institutions in which we can come to grips with the meaning of punishment and exercise a newfound responsibility for it.[13]

Although at the moment they are underutilised and completely overwhelmed by mainstream procedures that discourage citizen participation, there are a number of internal sites available for lay public action that could be the focus of broader scholarship and activism. The first is the jury system, which, despite strong public support and deep constitutional entrenchment, is only barely used today. At one time the normal way of hearing criminal cases in the United States, jury trials have been in steep decline and now handle from 1 to 4 per cent of state and federal cases, with much of the rest discharged through plea bargaining. Historically, and even today, the jury is seen as a site of public deliberation that aims to correct institutional haste, callousness, and bias. This characterisation is most obvious in the rhetoric of those who advocate the 'nullification' by juries of unjust laws or law enforcement, but it is present, too, in the arguments of a growing number of reformers seeking a 'more active' jury by enhancing the deliberative culture of the courtroom by allowing jurors to question witnesses, to have notebooks that contain evidence and exhibits, and to deliberate throughout the trial (Butler, 2009; Conrad, 1998; Dann, 1993).

What nullification and active-jury proponents miss, however, is the fact that public action and deliberation about criminal justice in court cannot happen without trials. So the major challenge is to increase the number of trials by restricting or raising the costs of plea bargaining or by encouraging jury trials. While mainstream scholarship, court professional opinion, and political journalism still appear to view plea bargaining as a necessary evil to cope with the sheer number of cases brought forward, a rising number of voices have urged systemic change. Some have advocated bans on the use of plea bargaining, at least for certain kinds of cases, while others have sought to raise the costs of plea bargaining by mandating stricter judicial review of guilty pleas (Alschuler, 1983; Stuntz, 2011). From the other side of the ledger, reformers have suggested ways of reducing the cost of jury trials—by cutting procedural requirements that slow trials down, for example, or by employing efficiencies in the ways courts function (Langbein, 1992; Schulhofer 1992). Seemingly radical changes like these may deviate from present practice, but they are fully consistent with Constitutional doctrine and pre-twentieth century American legal practice.

Another site of lay public action is found within restorative justice programs extending across the country. Beginning in the 1970s, these programs involve offenders in structured dialogues with victims or victim surrogates and sometimes with other members of an affected community, a process typically facilitated by a volunteer mediator who is not a court professional or official (Braithwaite, 2002; Van Ness & Strong, 2010; Zehr, 1990). Present in every state in the United States, although more widely used in a handful of states, restorative justice has been one of the most successful criminal justice reform movements in the last quarter century.[14] In part this is because of its ideological expansiveness and institutional flexibility. Ideologically, it brings together faith-based and social justice advocates of a more peaceful resolution to social problems, libertarians eager to shrink state involvement, and victims' rights advocates pushing for greater voice and appreciation for victims; it has appealed to seasoned veterans within the halls of criminal justice administration and doggedly idealistic community activists. Restorative justice programs have been housed in mayors' offices, lower courts, prosecutors' offices, departments of corrections, and in nongovernmental community organisations.[15]

While the most commonly employed restorative justice program, victim–offender mediation, too closely resembles mainstream repellent institutions in its sparse use of laypeople and shallow roots in affected communities, there are other more robustly public programs in operation. Community Reparative Boards in Vermont, for example, are staffed by citizen volunteers and hold their meetings in public places like libraries, community centres, town halls, and police stations (Dzur, 2008; Karp, 2001). They conduct dialogues with offenders convicted but not sentenced for nonviolent offences like underage drinking, impaired driving, and shoplifting. They seek to communicate the meaning of the harm for the victims involved, to determine how to repair whatever damage was done, and to consider how to avoid such action in the future. The outcome of dialogues is a contract with offenders involving community service, reparation, apology, and the like.[16] Other explicitly public programs, such as those of the Community Conferencing Center of Baltimore, Maryland respond to referrals from police, prosecutors, schools, and community organisations by conducting neighbourhood dialogues concerning conflicts that have not yet become formal offences (Abramson & Moore, 2001). Such an effort is a 'highly participatory, community-based process for people to transform their conflicts into cooperation, take collective and personal responsibility for action, and improve their quality of life'.[17]

A third site of lay public action is found in advisory bodies composed of citizens who meet regularly with key criminal justice actors in an evaluative as well as problem-solving capacity. The 'community beat meetings' held by the Chicago Police Department since 1993, for example, create channels of communication between officers—who make the all-important street-level decisions that open the gates of the criminal justice process—and members of distressed neighbourhoods impacted by both crime and incarceration. Facilitated by civilians, these regularly scheduled hour-long meetings bring residents together monthly with the police officers who patrol their neighbourhoods. There, citizens can articulate their concerns about gangs, violence, theft, social disorder, dilapidated and abandoned buildings, traffic, parking, and even the competence and conduct of the police. Citizens also learn about the progress or lack of progress on previously raised issues and brainstorm ways of solving them. At its best, such participatory community policing shares the problem of social order with citizens themselves. As Skogan writes about the Chicago experience, citizens involved in beat meetings are 'setting the agenda for police and community action, monitoring the effectiveness of police responses to community priorities, and mobilizing residents to act on their own behalf' (2006, p. 142). Advisory bodies are present in other institutional locations, too, such as the 'community prosecution' efforts in Portland, Denver, Indianapolis, and elsewhere. In Denver, for example, prosecutors have formed 'community justice councils that provide direct community input into the definition and prioritisation of problems, and the development and implementation of remedies to solve those problems' (Thompson, 2002, pp. 356–357).

Jury trials, restorative justice programs, and citizen advisory bodies are promising in design and spirit, yet because of the dominance of mainstream institutions, they are simply too sparse and emaciated at present to offer the means through which the lay public can adequately learn about criminal justice while helping steer the institutions acting in their name.

Therefore, these sites need to be radicalised and dramatically expanded. For that to be possible, however, lay public action related to punishment must be fostered *beneath, outside, and all around* the channels of criminal justice institutions. In this context, two arenas in particular stand out: primary education institutions and everyday networks of communication.

Nearly a century ago Dewey argued against traditional textbook civics education that lectured students on constitutional history, the branches of government, and how bills become laws. A proper civic education, Dewey insisted, would emerge only if students were part of a truly collaborative environment at school; education for democracy requires acting democratically. To understand the meaning of core ideals of procedural fairness or political equality, for example, 'involves a context of work and play in association with others'. 'Social perceptions and interests', writes Dewey, 'can be developed only in a genuinely social medium—one where there is give and take in the building up of a common experience' ([1916] 1980, p. 368). Contemporary educational reformers who give children a steering role in shaping curricula, advising new teachers, and solving institutional problems are following in Dewey's path.[18] The education in criminal justice that I have in mind means allowing young people to make decisions early and often on how to cope with norm breaking. Such experiential learning fosters the self-realisation of being sentinels and guardians of each other—to borrow an eighteenth-century phrase used to honour jury duty.

Early experience with collective decision making may be effective even while not closely resembling either the form or the substance of typical adult adjudication. Paley, an intellectual descendent of Dewey's, noticed a recurrent problem in her primary school classroom. The most popular students had a surplus of playmates at recess while some children, much to their shame and disappointment, were constantly excluded. After repeated meetings with the children and referring to this painful, if invisible, issue through an ongoing series of animal stories, Paley and the youth formulated a simple rule: 'You Can't Say You Can't Play'. Chronically marginalised children could present this rule to those in more popular groups to gain admission to games that they would normally have to witness from the sidelines. With the rule in hand they could stand up for themselves and also have recourse with their teachers and playground monitors. By taking part in rule making and rule enforcement, these children were learning by doing important lessons in self-governance and participatory social control (Paley, 1992).

Consider a second case of early education featuring the 'Bathroom Busters,' a group of middle schoolers in a low income area of St. Paul, Minnesota, troubled by restrooms covered in graffiti, lacking in privacy because of broken stalls, and chronically short of soap and paper. They learned how to work with an inefficient school bureaucracy and to communicate with

parents, teachers, and administrators at the school and district level to gain
the resources needed to repaint walls, repair missing stall doors, and re-
plenish needed supplies.[19] Thus a problem that might normally and
straightforwardly be seen as a juvenile offence to be handled by school administrators and police officers was translated into a social problem taken
up by the students. By acting on their own the Bathroom Busters refused to
have their institutions think and act for them.[20]

Efforts in school classrooms can be paralleled by more diffuse and highly
informal interventions in the public sphere. For a country settled by law
evaders, founded by law breakers, and morally instructed by prominent in-
tellectuals and other exemplary figures whose lives were touched, if only
briefly, by incarceration, Americans talk surprisingly little about why we
punish, how we might do less of it, or how we could do it better. What might
provoke a political culture prone to evading difficult topics to change its
ways? Here Mansbridge's model of 'everyday talk in the deliberative system'
is useful: alongside formal discussions in legislatures, executive agencies,
and courtrooms are myriad informal but nonetheless political conversations taking place in kitchens, school hallways, and employee breakrooms
between friends, family, and colleagues. Concepts like patriarchy, for example, can get worked out, given practical definition, and challenged
through conversations in activist enclaves, which then percolate through to
the everyday talk of nonactivists:

> In everyday talk and action the nonactivists test new and old ideas against
> their daily realities, make small moves—micronegotiations—that try to put
> some version of an idea into effect, and talk the ideas over with friends. . . . In
> their micronegotiations and private conversations, nonactivists influence the
> ideas and symbols available to the political process not only aggregatively, by
> favoring one side or another in a vote or in a public opinion survey, but also
> substantively, through their practice. They shape the deliberative system
> with their own exercise of power and reasoning on issues that the public
> ought to discuss. The activism of nonactivists, which has its greatest effect
> through everyday talk, includes even the snort of derision one might give at
> a sexist television character while watching with friends. That snort of deri-
> sion is, in my analysis, a political act. (Mansbridge, 1999, p. 214)

Through the wide-reaching deliberative links between peoples of different
social circumstances, everyday talk sensitises us to the ways our ideals
clash with the practice of our institutions.

How might the current deliberative system in countries like the United
States, which is oblivious to the problem, come to register the importance of
mass incarceration? Loader calls on engaged scholars and criminal justice
professionals and other practitioners to challenge the 'naturalness of punishment', to 'expose the fallacies of the doxa which treats penal trends as a

reflection of crime rates', and to make clear that we are part of a public that has, unwittingly or not, '*opted* for penal over social regulation' (2010, p. 359; emphasis in original). In making such arguments in public forums like newspaper and television interviews, scholars and practitioners can tap into the considerable ambivalence most citizens have about punishment. Public opinion research shows that while wrongdoing does produce anger and resentment, punishment itself can elicit feelings of shame and regret, with many people viewing incarceration as pointless (ibid., p. 353). Getting more of the public to feel uncomfortable about what our institutions do to too many fellow citizens is an important first step.

5. CONCLUSION: THICKENING THE GROUND OF PUBLIC OPINION

I have been arguing that institutional changes must take place as a starting point for renewing public attention, deliberation, and action regarding criminal justice. Stopping institutions from thinking for us, if only on some issues, in some places, amongst some people, is fundamental. Without it, efforts to educate the public and to foster deliberation are like freewheels allowing the institutions to spin along without ever fully engaging the citizenry.

I disagree, therefore, with those who go no further than to advocate deliberative opinion polls, citizens' assemblies, citizens' juries, and similar procedures that bring groups of people together to discuss issues like punishment in an informed and self-critical way.[21] While aiming to be public in that such forums seek to involve laypeople not already active in formal politics as officials, staff members, interest group operatives, or party workers, they lack what normally constitutes publicness. They have no formal public authority because they have not been authorised by the electorate or by official bodies, and they have no concomitant public accountability. They are typically organised by academic research units and media organisations rather than broad-based community organisations. Even more troubling, deliberative polls and citizens' juries contribute little to an ongoing institutional memory because they are decoupled from the institutions doing the thinking for us. What can be called the 'ontological status' of the work done within the citizens' jury or deliberative poll is akin to that of a research subject's contribution; it exists in time and space the way survey data and research analyses exist (Dzur, 2012b).

Work on a traditional legal jury, on a restorative justice board, or in a police beat meeting may seem trivial given that the bulk of decision making in criminal justice institutions proceeds in relatively nonparticipatory fashion, but it is 'ontologically thick' in a way that being a public opinion poll respondent, or even a deliberative poll or citizens' jury participant, is not. Jurors, restorative justice volunteers, beat meeting participants, and school children repairing breaches in social order on their own have real existence in political space and time. They are load-bearing members of the institutions of criminal justice: the institutions are thinking and then acting through them. Their work exists to be judged by themselves and others over time.

Ontologically thick public opinion and action begins as early as elementary school, is called for periodically even if we have not chosen to participate, brings us into close contact with people who differ from us, refuses to segregate those judged from those judging, and fits into a large-scale deliberative system that is able to see, hear, and talk about difficult subjects. I believe what we have not been seeing has been hurting us as a polity. The institutional changes that I suggest address our morally significant nonperception: the ways mainstream practices shield the advantaged from the consequences of policies like the draconian criminalisation of certain drugs that sent Savina Sauceda to prison (Walker, 2007). No amount of education and talking on their own will foster responsibility, will fully convey that an institution is our responsibility. Normal, regular, citizen action within institutions is required for the contemporary public to soberly acknowledge and assume responsibility for penal institutions and for public opinion regarding criminal justice to be genuinely integrated into the working of these institutions.

REFERENCES

Abramson, L., and D. B. Moore. 2001. 'Transforming Conflict in the Inner City: Community Conferencing in Baltimore.' *Contemporary Justice Review* 4: 321–340.

Alfaro, C. 2008. 'Reinventing Teacher Education: The Role of Deliberative Pedagogy in the K–6 Classroom.' In J. Dedrick, H. Dienstfrey, and L. Grattan (eds.), *Deliberation and the Work of Higher Education: Innovations for the Classroom, the Campus, and the Community*. Dayton, OH: Kettering Foundation Press, 143–164.

Alschuler, A. W. 1983. 'Implementing the Criminal Defendant's Right to Trial: Alternatives to the Plea Bargaining System.' *University of Chicago Law Review* 50: 931–1050.

Bauman, Z. 1989. *Modernity and the Holocaust*. London: Polity.

Bazemore, G., and M. Schiff. 2005. *Juvenile Justice Reform and Restorative Justice: Building Theory and Policy from Practice*. Devon, UK: Willan.

Bellah, R., R. Madsen, W. M. Sullivan, A. Swidler, and S. M. Tipton. 1991. *The Good Society*. New York: Knopf.

Blaug, R. 2010. *How Power Corrupts: Cognition and Democracy in Organisations*. London: Macmillan.

Boyte, H. C. 2004. *Everyday Politics: Reconnecting Citizens and Public Life*. Philadelphia: University of Pennsylvania Press.

Braithwaite, J. 2002. *Restorative Justice and Responsive Regulation*. New York: Oxford University Press.

Burnett, D. G. 2001. *A Trial by Jury*. New York: Vintage, 2001.

Butler, P. 2009. *Let's Get Free: A Hip-Hop Theory of Justice*. New York: New Press.

Christie, N. 1977. 'Conflicts as Property.' *British Journal of Criminology* 17: 1–15.

Conrad, C. S. 1998. *Jury Nullification: The Evolution of a Doctrine*. Durham, NC: Carolina Academic.

Currie, E. 2009. 'An Unchallenged Crisis: The Curious Disappearance of Crime as a Public Issue in the United States.' *Criminal Justice Matters* 75 (March): 22–23.

Dann, B. M. 1993. '"Learning Lessons" and "Speaking Rights": Creating Educated and Democratic Juries.' *Indiana Law Journal* 68: 1229–1279.

Dewey, J. (1916) 1980. *Democracy and Education*. In J. A. Boydston (eds.), *John Dewey, The Middle Works: 1899–1924*. Vol. 9. Carbondale: Southern Illinois University Press.

Doble, J. 2002. 'Attitudes to Punishment in the US—Punitive and Liberal Opinions.' In J. Roberts and M. Hough (eds.), *Changing Attitudes to Punishment*. Cullompton, UK: Willan. 148–162.

Douglas, M. 1986. *How Institutions Think*. Syracuse, NY: Syracuse University Press.

Dzur, A. W. 2008. *Democratic Professionalism: Citizen Participation and the Reconstruction of Professional Ethics, Identity, and Practice*. University Park: Penn State University Press.

Dzur, A. W. 2011. 'Restorative Justice and Democracy: Fostering Public Accountability for Criminal Justice.' *Contemporary Justice Review* 14: 367–381.

Dzur, A. W. 2012a. 'Participatory Democracy and Criminal Justice.' *Criminal Law and Philosophy* 6: 115–129.

Dzur, A. W. 2012b. *Punishment, Participatory Democracy, and the Jury*. New York: Oxford University Press.

Freiberg, A. 2001. 'Affective Versus Effective Justice: Instrumentalism and Emotionalism in Criminal Justice. *Punishment & Society* 3: 265–278.

Galanter, M. 2004. 'The Vanishing Trial: An Examination of Trials and Related Matters in Federal and State Courts.' *Journal of Empirical Legal Studies* 1: 459–570.

Garland, D. 1991. 'Sociological Perspectives on Punishment.' *Crime and Justice* 14: 115–165.

Gastil, J. E., P. Deess, P. J. Weiser, and C. Simmons. 2010. *The Jury and Democracy: How Jury Deliberation Promotes Civic Engagement and Political Participation*. New York: Oxford University Press.

Goffman, E. 1962. *Asylums: Essays on the Social Situation of Mental Patients and Other Inmates*. Chicago: Aldine, 1962.

Gottschalk, M. 2006. *The Prison and the Gallows: The Politics of Mass Incarceration in America*. Cambridge, UK: Cambridge University Press.

Gottschalk, M. 2007. 'Dollars, Sense, and Penal Reform: Social Movements and the Future of the Carceral State.' *Social Research* 74: 669–694.

Green, D. A. 2006. 'Public Opinion versus Public Judgment about Crime: Correcting the "Comedy of Errors"' *British Journal of Criminology* 46: 131–154.

Green, D. A. 2008. *When Children Kill Children: Penal Populism and Political Culture*. Oxford: Oxford University Press.

Karp, D. 2001. 'Harm and Repair: Observing Restorative Justice in Vermont.' *Justice Quarterly* 18: 727–757.

Lacey, N. 2001. 'Social Policy, Civil Society and the Institutions of Criminal Justice.' *Australian Journal of Legal Philosophy* 26: 7–25.

Lacey, N. 2008. *The Prisoners' Dilemma: Political Economy and Punishment in Contemporary Democracies.* Cambridge, UK: Cambridge University Press.

Langbein, J. H. 1992. 'On the Myth of Written Constitutions: The Disappearance of Criminal Jury Trial.' *Harvard Journal of Law & Public Policy* 15: 124–125.

Loader, I. 2010. 'For Penal Moderation: Notes Towards a Public Philosophy of Punishment.' *Theoretical Criminology* 14: 349–367.

Loader, I., and R. Sparks. 2011. *Public Criminology?* New York: Routledge.

Loader, I., and R. Sparks. 2012. 'Beyond Lamentation: Towards a Democratic Egalitarian Politics of Crime and Justice.' In T. Newburn and J. Peay (eds.), *Policing: Politics, Culture and Control.* Oxford: Hart, 11–41.

Mansbridge, J. 1999. 'Everyday Talk in the Deliberative System.' In S. Macedo (ed.), *Deliberative Politics: Essays on Democracy and Disagreement.* New York: Oxford University Press, 211–239.

Manza, J., and C. Uggen. 2005. *Locked Out: Felon Disenfranchisement and American Democracy.* New York: Oxford University Press.

Mauer, M. 2006. *Race to Incarcerate,* 2nd ed. New York: New Press.

Michels, R. 1962. *Political Parties: A Sociological Study of the Oligarchical Tendencies of Modern Democracy.* Glencoe, IL: Free Press.

National Public Radio. 2009. 'States Release Inmates Early To Cut Prison Costs.' *Weekend Edition Sunday,* December 13.

Ostrom, B. J., S. M. Strickland, and P. L. Hannaford-Agor. 2004. 'Examining Trial Trends in State Courts: 1976–2002.' *Journal of Empirical Legal Studies* 1: 764–770.

Paley, V. G. 1992. *You Can't Say You Can't Play.* Cambridge MA: Harvard University Press.

Parsons, T. 1990. 'Prolegomena to a Theory of Social Institutions.' *American Sociological Review* 55: 319–333.

Pettit, P. 2004. 'Depoliticizing Democracy.' *Ratio Juris* 17: 52–65.

Roberts, D. E. 2004. 'The Social and Moral Costs of Mass Incarceration in African American Communities.' *Stanford Law Review* 56: 1271–1305.

Roberts, J. 2011. 'The Future of State Punishment.' In M. Tonry (ed.), *Retributivism Has a Past: Has It a Future?* New York: Oxford University Press, 101–129.

Roberts, J., L. Stalans, D. Indermaur, and M. Hough. 2003. *Penal Populism and Public Opinion: Lessons from Five Counties.* Oxford: Oxford University Press.

Schulhofer, S. J. 1992. 'Plea Bargaining as Disaster.' *Yale Law Journal* 101: 1979–2009.

Selznick, P. 1992. *The Moral Commonwealth: Social Theory and the Promise of Community.* Berkeley: University of California Press.

Sirianni, C. 2009. *Investing in Democracy: Engaging Citizens in Collaborative Governance.* Washington, DC: Brookings Institution.

Skogan, W. 2006. *Police and Community in Chicago: A Tale of Three Cities.* New York: Oxford University Press.

Stears, M. 2011. 'Everyday Democracy: Taking Centre–Left Politics beyond State and Market.' London: Institute for Public Policy Research.

Stuntz, W. J. 2001. 'The Pathological Politics of Criminal Law.' *Michigan Law Review* 100: 505–600.

Stuntz, W. J. 2011. *The Collapse of American Criminal Justice*. Cambridge, MA: Harvard University Press.

Tetlock, P. E. 2005. *Expert Political Judgment: How Good Is It? How Can We Know?* Princeton, NJ: Princeton University Press.

Thompson, A. C. 2002. 'It Takes a Community to Prosecute.' *Notre Dame Law Review* 77: 321–372.

Tyler, T. R., and R. J. Boeckmann. 1997. 'Three Strikes and You Are Out, but Why? The Psychology of Public Support for Punishing Rule Breakers.' *Law & Society Review* 31: 237–265.

Van Ness, D. W., and K. H. Strong. 2010. *Restorative Justice: An Introduction to Restorative Justice*. 4th ed. New Providence, NJ: Bender.

Wacquant, L. 2010. 'Class, Race and Hyperincarceration in Revanchist America.' *Daedalus* 139(3): 74–90.

Waldron, J. 2006. 'The Core of the Case against Judicial Review.' *Yale Law Journal* 115: 1345–1406.

Walker, M. U. 2007. *Moral Understandings: A Feminist Study in Ethics*. 2nd ed. New York: Oxford University Press.

Western, B., and B. Pettit. 2010. 'Incarceration and Social Inequality,' *Daedalus* 139(3): 8–19.

Zedner, L. 2010. 'Reflections on Criminal Justice as a Social Institution.' In D. Downes, D. Hobbs, and T. Newburn (eds.), *The Eternal Recurrence of Crime and Control: Essays in Honour of Paul Rock*. London: Oxford University Press, 69–94.

Zehr, H. 1990. *Changing Lenses: A New Focus for Criminal Justice*. Scottdale, PA: Herald.

Zimring, F. E., G. Hawkins, and S. Kamin. 2001. *Punishment and Democracy: Three Strikes and You're Out in California*. Oxford: Oxford University Press.

NOTES

1. Research included in this chapter was done in partnership with the Kettering Foundation. Special thanks go to Christopher Bennett, Julian Roberts, and Jesper Ryberg for very helpful comments on earlier drafts and to fellow participants in the Copenhagen workshop for a robust and insightful conversation about popular punishment.

2. See Dzur (2012b) for the argument that insulation is a normative and practical mistake. Loader and Sparks (2011) have made a similar argument in the UK context.

3. Roberts calls this 'one of the most robust and often–replicated findings in the field' (2011, p. 105).

4. Discussions of public ignorance all too frequently imply that there is an identifiable circle of experts or officials somewhere who know more or who are more kind or able judges. Yet this implication is false, as studies of expert opinion reveal (Tetlock, 2005). Ignorance of contemporary institutions is a great leveller and includes even the well born and well educated.

5. Currie writes about the 'paradoxical complacency' about criminal justice in the United States: 'Crime in its most serious forms, as well as the adverse impact

of mass incarceration, has become increasingly concentrated amongst people—and in places—that tend to be relatively invisible to most better–off Americans and almost wholly lacking in significant political influence or even voice. Last year, 67 per cent of people who lived in Philadelphia thought that crime was the number one problem facing the city. In national opinion polls the proportion of the general population who feel that way is generally in the single digits' (2009, p. 23). The 'concentration of concern' about both violent crime and mass incarceration in urban areas like Philadelphia, Detroit, and Baltimore does not impact the political discourse at the state or national level because of the political weakness of those most affected, many of whom do not vote.

6. Blaug (2010) convincingly argues that conventional treatments of organisations in Michels (1962) and elsewhere have mistakenly naturalised hierarchy and have failed to capture its destabilising and nonfunctional characteristics.

7. Burnett's (2001) experience was bureaucratic and disempowering, but the large-scale survey research of Gastil, Deess, Weiser, and Simmons (2010) found that jurors are more likely to have a positive civic experience when they deliberate more, when the case they are adjudicating is complex, and when they are treated well by the court.

8. As Zedner puts it, 'To assume that crime control is the prerogative of criminal justice agents and institutions obscures the role played in controlling crime by informal sources and institutions of social order—not least the family, the school, religious institutions, and the community. Such ability as criminal justice institutions have to tackle crime relies heavily upon these informal sources of order and their interdependent relationship with them' (2010, p. 73).

9. 'Children whose parents are imprisoned are likely to experience feelings of shame, humiliation, and loss of social status,' writes Mauer. 'They begin to act out in school or distrust authority figures. . . . In far too many cases, these children come to represent the next generation of offenders' (2006, p. 204).

10. The class dimensions of these data are borne out by the fact that 'the lifetime chance of serving time for African American men with some college education *decreased* from 6 percent to 5 percent' over the same period (Wacquant, 2010, p. 79; emphasis in original).

11. Such concern has a prominent place in democratic egalitarian and social democratic political theory. My process-oriented account can be seen as rooted in that theoretical tradition, but it also seeks to appeal to those attached to other political world-views. See Loader and Sparks (2012) for a discussion of democratic egalitarian criminal justice institutions.

12. See Dzur (2012a) for a discussion of how social movements are sometimes energised by citizen disgust over the realisation that they are indirectly supporting and thus collaborating in unjust institutions.

13. See Dzur (2012b) for more on the concept of 'load-bearing participation.'

14. California, Pennsylvania, Minnesota, Texas, Colorado, Arizona, New York, Ohio, and Alaska have the highest numbers of restorative justice programs, while some other states are experimenting with only a few small-scale programs (Bazemore & Schiff, 2005, p. 105).

15. On restorative justice as a social movement, see Dzur (2008, 2011).

16. http://doc.vermont.gov/justice/restorative-justice/

17. http://www.communityconferencing.org/index.php/about/vision_mission/
18. For an example of student participation in steering classroom requirements, see Alfaro (2008); Sirianni (2009) describes a high school in Virginia where student advisory boards produced training manuals for new teachers.
19. See Boyte (2004) for the case of the Bathroom Busters. It should be noted that the Bathroom Busters were coached by undergraduates from the University of Minnesota involved in the Public Achievement program sponsored by the Center for Democracy and Citizenship.
20. The idea that a primary school can serve as locus of community dialogues on topics other than specific curricular and administrative matters has a long history in the United States and in other countries.
21. Green, for example, recommends using deliberative polls and citizen juries as 'alternative public spaces' to discuss criminal justice (2008, p. 268). Such spaces might very well be beneficial if more ontologically thick public action was also occurring. Without it, however, the public is not even left on the sidelines; it is on an entirely different playing field than normal institutional action altogether.

11

Clarifying the Significance of Public Opinion for Sentencing Policy and Practice[1]

Julian V. Roberts

What is the appropriate role for public opinion in sentencing policy and practice? To date, no satisfactory or consensual answer to this question has appeared—hence the need for this volume. Chapter 1 noted three alternative positions: (a) allow public views to determine sentencing policy and practice; (b) allow limited public input into sentencing while retaining control of policy and practice within a professionalised system; (c) determine sentencing practice and policy without any recourse to community consultation. Inflexible positions—for example, that the public should *always* or *never* have input—seldom make sense in criminal justice; crime and justice are generally more complex and nuanced. In addition, the first position would lead to chaotic, unprincipled sentencing; few would advocate such an approach, and it is therefore not discussed further in this essay. This leaves the middle ground in which public opinion plays a restricted role and which will be the principal focus of this chapter.

To anticipate my conclusion, I believe that *limited* public input into sentencing policy and practice is desirable, a conclusion which differs from the positions advocated by some other contributors to this volume. The justifications for community opinion arise from instrumental and retributive perspectives; the justifications for limits on this input reflect a desire to ensure a principled approach to sentencing. I also want to discuss the specific ways in which public views can be incorporated into sentencing practices. What lessons should agencies concerned with shaping sentencing practices—sentencing guidelines bodies—draw from the literature and arguments discussed in this volume? Should they pay heed to community values when determining the factors considered by courts at sentencing or the levels of severity for individual offences? These practical questions need to be addressed. Towards the end of the essay I consider some recent proposals to promote the voice of the public in sentencing, including 'stakeholder sentencing' and sentencing by juries (rather than by professional judges).

1. OVERVIEW OF ESSAY

Public opinion could be canvassed on a variety of levels relating to sentencing policy and practice. For example, particular punishments (such as capital or corporal punishment) might be employed or prohibited in the face of strong public support or opposition. The nature of sentencers might be determined by consulting the public—would they prefer lay adjudicators, professional judges or some hybrid model as is found in Italy and other European jurisdictions? It might also be reasonable for a democratic legislature to canvass its citizenry to determine the levels of support for potentially conflicting sentencing philosophies. The statutory sentencing purposes—deterrence or rehabilitation—might be determined in part to reflect relative levels of community support.[2] However, to constrain the debate, in this essay I focus on the role of public opinion in influencing sentencing practices. I review the principal justifications for considering public opinion at sentencing, beginning with the utilitarian perspective.

2. THREE CONDITIONS: JUSTIFICATION, METHODOLOGY, MECHANISM

Before public opinion is allowed to determine or influence sentencing policy or practice, three elements need to be in place. First, it is necessary to demonstrate the normative significance of community views: why, exactly, are they relevant to the state punishment of offenders? If a satisfactory justification is established, the second requirement is an adequate methodology for establishing the nature and strength of community views. Consider the classic case of capital punishment: how are we to determine the nature of public opinion on this or other sentencing issues? Assuming that we agree that public views are relevant, are there methodological criteria that need to be fulfilled? For example, we might argue that a representative sample of the public is used and that this sample be given ample time and information on the issue to come to judgment—to dispel transitory or unstable opinions. Or should we simply follow the opinions emerging from polls which provide a snapshot of mass opinion? Finally, if we have resolved this issue, we then need a mechanism for shaping sentencing policies or practice in a way consistent with community views. Should the community be directly involved in sentencing—for example, by replacing professional judges with juries drawn from the community? Or should some independent institution—a sentencing guidelines authority—serve as a filter to determine which public opinions are 'actionable' for the purposes of sentencing?

3. JUSTIFYING PUBLIC INPUT INTO SENTENCING: THE NORMATIVE ARGUMENTS

Enhancing Deterrence

If deterrence—general and specific—is the overarching goal of sentencing, as Golash and Lynch (1995) note, there is little need to assess public perceptions of the relative seriousness of crimes. However, it will be necessary to evaluate the perceived severity of assigned sentences. Imagine a sentencing system based on deterrence and where (a) sentences are imposed in secret; (b) where all punishments are derisory in severity, or (c) where sentences of custody are always immediately suspended—to save costs. In the first example, only a small number of legal professionals (and the offenders actually sentenced) would be aware of the actual severity of penalties; potential offenders would not be deterred because they would have no clear idea of the penal consequences of offending—vague threats are unlikely to deter offenders. (Unless everyone assumed that severe punishments would ensue—even if they had no idea about the actual severity of punishments—no deterrence would be achieved). In the second and third examples, potential (and actual) offenders would not be deterred because the penalties would be insufficiently aversive to discourage offending. Deterrence advocates would argue that penalties need to be sufficiently severe to deter members of the public, and this necessitates research into public ratings of sentence severity and the calibration of actual severity levels to ensure that they were sufficiently high to deter.[3] General deterrence, then, requires public input if it is to be effective in preventing crime.[4]

Enhancing Compliance with the Law and Co-operation with Criminal Justice

A second category of utilitarian justifications for public engagement involves compliance with the law and with the justice system. A number of interrelated arguments have been advanced.

Moral Alignment Promotes Compliance and Changes Attitudes

Paul Robinson (2009, this volume) argues that compliance with the law is more likely when legal punishments track community preferences—'empirical desert', to use his term. The Robinson model of public input into sentencing is explicitly instrumental: Robinson argues that carefully conducted research reveals a reasoned and reasonable set of sentencing principles derived from the public. Importing this model of desert into sentencing would enhance the moral alignment of sentencing with community views and lead to higher levels of compliance with the law.

This hypothesis seems reasonable; if people believe that the criminal law functions in a way which is greatly inconsistent with their expectations, confidence in and the incentive to co-operate with the criminal justice system can only be undermined. But does this provide a sufficient justification for aligning sentencing practices with community views? Should we, for example, take factor X into account at sentencing simply because the public consider this factor relevant, and excluding the factor would carry negative consequences in terms of compliance? What happens when public views assume an indefensible position? I do not share Robinson's optimism that members of the public are sufficiently sophisticated in their sentencing responses, even when their views are measured under the most careful conditions. Frej Thomsen (this volume) also expresses scepticism with respect to the epistemic quality of public opinion. The empirically derived desert model of sentencing seems unchallengeable on theoretical grounds (see Matravers, this volume). If I am right, shaping sentencing practices to accord with community views will result in unprincipled sentencing outcomes and, possibly, with little benefit in terms of enhanced compliance. Robinson concedes that intuitions of justice may on occasion be immoral. If this is true, implementing empirical desert principles and practices will produce injustice. Robinson's solution to this problem would be some form of deontological 'override': 'A deviation [from empirical desert] may be justified if the community's shared intuitions of justice are clearly unjust' (2009, p. 9).[5] This statement suggests some principled limits on the empirical desert model. However, determining whether a public view is unjust surely leads us back to the point of departure: how to decide whether a given policy or practice is normatively justifiable? How to establish that intuitions are unjust?

Perceived Legitimacy Promotes Compliance and Co-operation with Criminal Justice Agencies

A related perspective concerns community perceptions of legitimacy. Hough and his colleagues (e.g. Hough & Kirby, 2013; Jackson et al., 2012)[6] argue that legal compliance, co-operation with criminal justice, and respect for the law are affected by *legitimacy*: if people perceive the system to be legitimate, they are more likely to co-operate with the system and comply with the law. Hough and Kirby claim: 'The closer the fit between sentencing outcomes and public perceptions, the more secure will be the legitimacy of the justice institutions and the greater people's commitment to the law' (2013, p. 145). This suggests a link exists between perceptions of the sentencing process and willingness to co-operate with the system: people who believe that courts impose appropriate punishments following appropriate principles (i.e. those to which the community subscribe) may be more likely to assist the system by serving as witnesses or submitting victim impact statements at sentencing and so forth. It is worth noting, however, that the claim assumes that legitimacy arises from or is defined by, the degree to which an authority represents or expresses the views of the community. But legitimacy can be defined in many ways and an alternate interpretation would be that the perceived legitimacy of courts rests on a different perception, namely that judges are not representative of any element of the community or the community itself but rather are impartial arbiters who act on legal argument and reasoning (see discussion in Sharpe, 2013).

My objection to these various but interrelated arguments in favour of public input is twofold. First, the heightened legal compliance as a result of moral alignment—through the adoption of empirical desert findings—is likely to be negligible; the extent to which people perceive the courts to sentence consistent with their views probably explains little variance in compliance behaviour. Moreover, the hypothesis that moral alignment or perceived legitimacy promotes compliance and co-operation has yet to be adequately tested, let alone convincingly demonstrated. It is unclear why people who perceive that sentencing practices conform to their views of sentencing would therefore be more likely to comply with the law. Compliance is affected by many factors, including the perceived legitimacy of the justice system, individual morality, the democratic nature of the society, an individual's stake in that society, and many other variables. Whether a person perceives the sentencing system to be in moral alignment with his or her views of punishment seems an unlikely predictor of whether he or she decides to offend or declines to participate in the criminal justice system or to comply with the law. In addition, as Kolber points out, the hypothesis that people prefer a sentencing system which privileges community perceptions has not been adequately tested: 'If lay intuitions better comport with the deontological approach, then laypeople may find unattractive a criminal justice system that is based on empirical desert' (2009, p. 42). Nevertheless, if the alignment-compliance hypothesis was borne out empirically, it would constitute a reason for at least considering adjustments to sentencing practice to reap any benefits of enhanced compliance levels.

Public Confidence

Another claim for public input into sentencing rests upon the need to maintain public confidence. The importance of public confidence in the courts is often asserted by courts and some scholars simply as a good in its own right. Yet there must be some identifiable benefit of high levels of confidence—or some clear problem with low levels; otherwise, it would be tantamount to promoting confidence in the medical profession without caring whether physicians were effective in responding to disease.[7] As Ryberg (2010) notes, we need to do more than simply assert that there is a problem; a utilitarian analysis would need to identify the specific adverse consequence associated with low confidence levels and then possibly set against this any costs in adopting policies or modifying policies with the explicit goal of promoting confidence. Imposing very punitive sentences may promote public confidence in sentencing but at the cost of much higher correctional budgets, not to mention many other adverse effects on the lives of offenders and their dependents.[8]

Confidence is a somewhat different concept from perceived legitimacy or a belief that the system is morally aligned with the views of the community; it suggests an expectation that the system will effectively act in ways deemed to be appropriate to the community—although clearly this may invoke a reflection on the degree of fit between judicial practice and community views. Confidence levels may be affected by many influences—because sentencing is conducted by high-status professionals, because sentencing is seen as too lenient, and other grounds. Promoting public confidence might therefore constitute another legitimate consideration at sentencing, with consequences for sentencing practices. Some minimal level of confidence in the sentencing process is surely necessary. If people have no confidence in sentencing, adverse consequences may well include disengagement with the system—a refusal to co-operate with a justice system, the final stage of which enjoys no public confidence. One way of promoting public confidence is to ensure some degree of concordance between community views and sentencing practices. Low confidence may well be a consequence of totally decoupling sentencing practices from community views.

The conclusion that I would draw is that while compliance with the law, co-operation with the criminal justice system, or confidence in sentencing may increase if people see the system as imposing punishments consistent with their own views, these are insufficient justifications for *determining* punishments with this objective in mind. Reshaping sentencing practices to ensure a tighter fit with community values may carry some minor benefits in terms of compliance and confidence, but this cannot justify direct public control over sentencing. Against any putative benefits with respect to compliance and confidence must be set the possible burdens—for example, adopting sentencing policies or practices which are popular but unprincipled.

Finally, shaping sentencing to reflect community views is one of several potential ways of enhancing public confidence and, ultimately, compliance with the law. Other strategies may be more or equally effective and without the potential disadvantages of privileging community views of punishment. For example, advocates of problem-solving courts such as drug treatment and community courts claim that these innovations enhance public confidence (for discussion, see Nolan, 2009, p. 199). If the goal of incorporating public views is to enhance perceptions of legitimacy or levels of confidence, the full range of options to achieve these objectives should be canvassed; we should not simply leap to the conclusion that aligning sentences with the public is the most appropriate or effective strategy.

Role of Public Opinion in a Proportional Sentencing System

When the primary sentencing rationale is retributive, privileging proportional sanctions, the role of public opinion is less apparent and the grounds for considering public opinion when determining whether, and how much, punishment is justified need evaluating. The general argument would be that cultural values constitute a legitimate influence over the definition of a crime and the nature of an appropriate punishment. Proportionality is not a culturally invariant concept but one which reflects a societal element. Community views influence the ascribed seriousness of criminal acts and ascriptions of blameworthiness; these concepts do not exist in a vacuum without some reference to the community in which such judgements are set. If this is the case, some mechanism for incorporating community views is necessary.

Within this perspective there may be a range of views: The extreme position is that community values should determine whether conduct is criminalised; the more modest position is that public opinion can influence levels of punishment—even if it plays no role in defining that conduct as criminal in the first place.

Public Opinion and Criminalisation

Criminalisation offers an example of the influence of cultural values as expressed in public opinion. A populist approach to criminalisation that can be readily rejected would argue that any conduct attracting a consensual condemnatory response from the community should be criminalised.[9] We obviously need a more stringent set of criteria to guide the decision to criminalise behaviour, and over the years several have been offered. Is public opinion engaged by any of these principles? Conceptual frameworks for criminalisation generally articulate some guiding principle to determine whether conduct should be subject to penal sanctions. The most well known is the harm principle, articulated by Mill (1859) and refined by various scholars including Feinberg.

According to the original formulation, criminalisation should not occur absent a need to prevent harm to others; it is hard to see how public opinion could serve as a reliable guide to determining whether a given action harms the interests of others. The tightly drawn harm principle is loosened by theorists such as Feinberg, and more recently, Simester and von Hirsch (2011) who discuss the criminalisation of offensive conduct. Consistent with a liberal approach to the issue, they caution against criminalising conduct merely because it may offend: 'It is not enough that the conduct displeases; grounds must be provided why that conduct is wrongful, in the sense of treating others in a manner that is grossly inconsiderate or disrespectful' (Simester & von Hirsch, 2011, pp. 106–107). They assert that offensive conduct must fulfil a wrongfulness requirement—an independent, normative argument which articulates why conduct X is wrong and sufficiently wrongful to warrant criminalisation.

One potential justification for the criminalisation of particular conduct is that it constitutes a sufficiently flagrant violation of community standards. Many such examples exist. Until ruled unconstitutional by the Supreme Court, burning the US flag constituted a federal offence; many Americans regarded this act as sufficiently reprehensible to justify criminalisation. Prominent display of images associated with the Nazi regime or denials of the Holocaust may be considered by some countries to justify state condemnation by means of a criminal statute. These laws demonstrate an empirical link between criminal justice and culture but will be seen by some as illiberal corruptions of sound criminalisation principles. Determining the extent to which these acts violate standards of community acceptance—and whether the additional requirements of criminalisation are met—requires measuring public opinion.

In practice, then, community values seem to influence criminalisation, but should they? Violation of community standards alone surely cannot justify criminalisation; if it did, a wide range of otherwise legal conduct would become criminal. We need to demonstrate that conduct constitutes some demonstrable harm for which the criminal sanction is therefore justifiably invoked. The fact that conduct violates community standards is insufficient justification for criminalisation; the role for public input here is therefore very limited, at best. This argument demonstrates the effect of public views (and legislators' sensitivity to these views) but provides no justification for acting upon them.

Sentencing

Moving to sentencing, the argument would be that community views may play a role in determining which factors are taken into account at sentencing or sentencing levels. If the determination of crime seriousness and offender culpability were left entirely to individual sentencers to resolve, sentencing would surely become less consistent; appellate review might rectify the most egregious inconsistencies between courts, but perceptions of what is relevant to harm and blame vary widely, even amongst a relatively homogenous bench of professional judges. A better approach involves a careful review of factors and features of crimes and offenders which in the eyes of the community may indicate greater or less harm and culpability—an exercise undertaken by a number of guidelines authorities. In the United States, sentencing commissions rank order offences according to their relative seriousness and then assign rank-ordered punishments to each rank of seriousness.[10] Sentencing is not a technical matter governed by physical laws, but rather a cultural exercise in the expression of collective disapprobation (see Garland, 1991). If this is the case, some degree of public input may be desirable.

Enhancing Penal Censure

Public input may also be relevant to ensure effective penal censure. The most influential retributive theories today are censure based. They are communicative theories of punishment: a message of reprobation is communicated to the offender in the hope that a moral transformation will occur (e.g. von Hirsch, 1993). It may well be the case that when censure fails—because the censuring agent is perceived to lack legitimacy for example—no moral transformation occurs, and reoffending is the result; this is a consequentialist outcome. But a failure to convey censure represents a breakdown of the communication essential to censure-based theories. Von Hirsch (1993) argues that hard treatment is a necessary element of censure-based sentencing: without this element, punishments would lack the necessary prudential disincentives to offending. The reprobative power of sentencing would stand or fall on the degree to which offenders believed they were being legitimately censured, and the community's view of the same issue. Effective censure assumes the existence of some degree of legitimacy on the part of the censuring agent. The most effective censure, whether interpersonal, professional, or penal derives its effectiveness from the high standing of the censuring agent.[11]

Censure without Sanction and Sanction without Censure

A sentencing system which involved state reproof without hard treatment would consist of *censure without sanction* and would fail to contribute to the crime preventive function of the criminal law. Yet with no link between the sentencing process and public views, the system would lose its power to censure—a case of *sanction without censure*: offenders would feel punished in ways that had no moral element. Without hard treatment, a sanction would lose its power to contribute to the crime preventive objective of the model.[12] Without some concordance between social context and the sentence, the system would lose its power to censure which is the means by which a moral transformation of the offender is achieved.

Retributive theories offer only limited support for considering public opinion. Rankings of crime seriousness and hierarchies of penalty severity may need some adjustment to reflect perceptions of gravity and severity, but public views alone should not determine rankings. The fact that the public believe that factor X should mitigate does not justify mitigation on this ground, any more than public support for criminalising conduct Y makes it criminal. However, the seriousness of particular acts reflects to some limited degree cultural values; in addition, the censuring power of the criminal sanction may be undermined if the public believe that courts sentence according to very different criteria from the community standards. As with the claims made by advocates of compliance and confidence, the retributive justification is limited in scope.

Justifying Public Input: Summary

To summarise, a sentencing system which ignored public views entirely might ultimately suffer from lower compliance, diminished confidence, less co-operation and weaker penal censure, although the exact consequences of these trends remains unknown. Sentencing should at least prevent full-scale public antipathy, and this justifies some rapprochement between community views and sentencing practices. In short, and to return to the options which began this essay, limited public input seems preferable to direct importation or total exclusion of public views.

Second Condition: Determining the Nature of Public Opinion

If justifications for public input into sentencing policy and practice can be found, we can turn to the second condition for incorporating community views, namely the need for an appropriate measure of public opinion. The critical choice is between 'mass' or 'informed' opinion, the former derived from polls and the latter from more educated samples of the public. Research has convincingly demonstrated that people have little accurate idea of the relative seriousness of different crimes, the moral significance of particular sentencing factors and principles, or, as noted earlier, the objective severity of various sanctions (Hough & Roberts, 1998; Roberts & Hough, 2005). These empirical findings constitute an important restriction on the use of public opinion at sentencing, or at least require a decision as to whether mass or informed views are to be followed.

De Keijser (this volume) identifies a 'damned if you do, damned if you don't' paradox: the public are ill informed about sentencing, and so incorporating their views would result in unprincipled and capricious sentencing. However, if given more information, these people become unrepresentative of the general public, and no additional legitimacy will be generated by heeding their views. De Keijser criticises the use of an informed sample on the grounds that it is elitist and that the informed public is unrepresentative of the community as whole, most members of which may be deemed less well informed.

It is well documented in the field that when public opinion is measured by means of simple questions on polls, responses are relatively punitive (see discussion in Green, 2006). This is not surprising; public judgements about many issues tend to be more reasoned and sophisticated when people are given sufficient time and information to reach a reasoned judgment. Adopting a purely populist approach—deciding sentencing policy or practice by reference to polls—would result in chaotic and punitive outcomes. The single-minded pursuit of populism for its own sake would have disastrous consequences. People must be given information about the issue and then allowed time to reflect. Is this position elitist? Possibly, but given a choice between informed but elite views and uninformed but representative views, the former is surely preferable. Public criticism of this 'informed' public consultation should be met by noting that in all areas of public policy, including criminal justice, public consultation is of an informed rather than mass nature.

Third Condition: The Mechanisms Permitting Public Input

Having established a justification for limited public input into sentencing practices and a methodology for measuring community views (those of an informed rather than mass public), it is necessary to determine how, in practical terms, these views might be incorporated. One possibility is through direct engagement with the sentencing process, for example by using lay decision makers in the determination of sentence. The alternative is to measure public views but then filter these opinions through some professional authority such as a sentencing commission or council. I favour the latter approach for reasons which will become clear.

4. DIRECT PUBLIC INPUT

In terms of direct input, or increased democratisation of state punishment, a range of options have been proposed. But what exactly is the added value of increased democratisation, and what forms might it assume? Albert Dzur (this volume) makes an important point about the way that the public has been distanced from the machinery of legal punishment. This isolation from the suffering inflicted on offenders has many adverse consequences which need addressing. My view, however, is that it is preferable to sensitise the community to the punishments being inflicted in their name, rather than incorporating the public directly into the determination of sentencing practices. With respect to direct input, I will briefly comment on one proposal and discuss a second at greater length. Thom Brooks (this volume) advocates some form of 'stakeholder sentencing forum' along the lines of a restorative justice program.

This proposal would clearly promote a more communitarian approach to sentencing. All parties with a stake in the offence would convene to work towards a solution, and only defendants who accept responsibility for the offence would be eligible. Evaluation of this proposal must await a more detailed description. Much would need to be resolved, however, and there are problems associated with such an approach, not the least of which is the potential loss of consistent and principled sentencing outcomes as criminal charges are resolved by such local meetings. Surely the outcomes of stakeholder forums would reflect the interests of the local parties, rather than established national standards? This particular problem could be addressed by providing the stakeholder fora with guidance on sentencing principles and practices, but this returns us to the question of whether we are going to shape this guidance to reflect public views—the fundamental question explored in this volume. Another obvious difficulty with this approach is in defining the stakeholder parties: who has standing besides victims and offenders? Local community representatives? Individuals representing the state prosecution branch? Reaching an accommodation with a diverse collection of stakeholders will be challenging. Finally, this solution would need to consider the advantages and disadvantages of restorative solutions which have been explored at length in the restorative justice literature[13], and will not be discussed further here.

Another strategy to increase the democratic nature or oversight of sentencing is much closer to current practice and therefore holds greater promise as a solution, if only because implementation would be more likely.

Sentencing by Juries

Chris Bennett (this volume) and Albert Dzur (2012) advocate the use of juries to determine sentence. This proposal has attracted increasing interest from scholars as a way of promoting democratic values or enhancing the role of the community in the criminal justice system (e.g. Hoffman, 2003). A number of benefits have been claimed for sentencing by juries rather than professional judges. Jury sentencing is said to be more democratic than sentencing by judges who are appointed from (and by) the elite, to result in sentences which attract more support from the community, and to result in better sentences since jurors may be more capable of making subtle distinctions amongst cases than professional judges, who are inured to sentencing after many years on the bench. Jury sentencing will appeal to those who favour community input of an informed, deliberative, and responsible nature. After all, jurors are screened to exclude individuals prejudiced in favour of one party; they swear an oath which will encourage a responsible approach to their decision making, and they deliberate after evaluating testimony rather than responding with their unreflective intuitions. In this sense juries represent an elite incarnation of community input—in contrast to the views expressed by members of the public in response to opinion surveys.

The claims made on behalf of jury sentencing by advocates of this approach are amenable to proof; research evidence will demonstrate the extent to which these benefits exist and any potential countervailing costs. In fact, the claim is twofold: first, that sentencing by juries would become more principled and more consistent as a result of greater public involvement having replaced (or supplemented) a judicial officer by a panel of laypersons; and, second, that jury sentencing would address the 'democratic deficit' and result in greater satisfaction with sentencing outcomes and enhanced perceptions of the legitimacy of the sentencing process.

Sentencing by Jury: The 'Principle Deficit'

Considering sentencing by juries broadens the debate about the role of community in state punishment. A number of authors have explored the consequences for increased legitimacy or democratic involvement; yet when discussing these proposals, it is important not to lose sight of the object of state punishment: the offender. Any sentencing reform proposal, including jury sentencing, should promote, or at least not undermine, important principles of sentencing or unfairly infringe the liberty interests of defendants. Sentencing by juries carries a significant risk of exactly this happening.

Principled sentencing requires the decision maker to apply principles such as equity, proportionality and restraint equally across cases. Sentencing authorities—whether judges or juries—need to distinguish probative information (e.g. the offender had no previous convictions) from prejudicial facts (he or she has an unsympathetic character). Why would a group of laypersons be better equipped than a highly trained legal professional to distinguish relevant from extralegal sentencing factors?[14] Although there is a wealth of evidence showing that the public can (and do) make sophisticated and theoretically consistent judgments about crime seriousness, this is usually only the case when people are given information and sufficient time in which to reflect on their responses. Members of the public serving as jurors would inevitably revert to intuitive judgments—they would probably disregard some important sentencing factors and ascribe undue weight to factors of tangential relevance. They may also be influenced by particularly emotional testimony to a greater degree than professional adjudicators who are trained to seek probative information and disregard prejudicial material with no probative value. Victim impact evidence is just one example of testimony which is often a complex cocktail of probative and prejudicial information, and professional judges are surely better equipped to distinguish the evidential wheat from the chaff.

The public are less able than professional judges to make subtle distinctions between offenders of varying culpability. Imagine a jury has just convicted a defendant of a serious crime of violence: how much weight, if any, would jurors give to an appeal, at sentencing, for mitigation on the basis that this was his or her first offence? Yet first offender discounts are an established and principled element of all sentencing schemes.[15] In the opposite direction, consider the additional quantum of punishment that jurors would inflict after learning, at the sentencing hearing, that an offender convicted of rape has previous, related convictions? It is likely that they would assign disproportionate weight to the previous convictions, thereby undermining proportionality in sentencing. In this way sentencing may become more popular (by being more populist) but only at the expense of principles.

Sentencing by Juries: The US Experience

There is a research literature on sentencing by juries, and the results offer little encouragement to jury sentencing advocates. Reviewing the considerable body of research is beyond the scope of this essay, but a few representative findings may be noted. One good illustration of the weaknesses of jury sentencing can be found in the experience with jury decision making in capital cases in the United States. The example is telling because in this context potential jurors are screened—'death qualified'—to ensure that they are impartial with respect to the decision to sentence the offender to death or life imprisonment. In this sense they constitute an 'elite' version of the jury, one that might be expected to perform more competently than juries in cases of lesser seriousness. Despite the use of procedural safeguards to ensure fair decision making, studies have shown that capital jurors are 'unreceptive to mitigation and predisposed to vote in favour of execution' (Trahan, 2011, p. 1). 'Democratic values' in this example translates to values which undermine principles of fundamental justice: Promoting democratic values may literally cost lives.

In a small number of US states, juries sentence offenders convicted of noncapital (felony) crimes. What does the experience in those jurisdictions tell us about the issue? Research by King and Noble (2004) have usefully compared the sentences imposed by a jury with sentences imposed by a judge following a bench (judicial) trial. These researchers report that jury sentences were more variable than bench trial sentences. Moreover, a careful analysis controlling for a range of potential explanatory variables found that sentence lengths imposed by juries were significantly longer—a finding which is consistent with the punitive responses to defendants in capital juries to which reference has already been made. Prosecutors in Arkansas note that the harsher sentencing 'is deterring defendants from opting for jury trial' (King & Noble, 2004, p. 51). Advocates of jury sentencing must therefore confront the likelihood that sentencing could become more punitive and more populist.

Findings from Australia

A recent and careful study by Warner and Davis (2012) conducted in Australia also sheds light on actual jurors' sentencing preferences. Although the research explored the issue of ascertaining public attitudes to sentencing by surveying jurors, this research reveals the often capricious nature of public sentencing—even by people sworn to serve as jurors. Jurors were first asked to impose sentence in a case they had just heard before the judge imposed sentence. At a later point, having been informed of the actual sentence, the same jurors were again asked what sentence they thought should be imposed. On this second occasion approximately four out of ten now favoured a *more* punitive sentence than they had previously endorsed. It is unclear why so many abandoned their first opinion so readily; what is important, however, is the volatility of jurors' reactions.

Additional insight into the alleged benefits of jury sentencing may be gleaned from a careful review by the New South Wales Law Commission. In 2005 the chief justice in that jurisdiction proposed that juries play a greater role at sentencing. Specifically, he suggested that after convicting an offender the jury would enter the judge's chambers for an *in camera* discussion about the appropriate sentence to be imposed. He argued that this reform would enhance public confidence in sentencing. The proposal was subsequently the subject of an extensive public inquiry including a public and professional consultation by the New South Wales Law Reform Commission (2006). After considerable amount of study, the report came to the following unequivocal conclusion: 'The Commission does not believe that benefits would result from consultation with jurors on matters of sentencing. It is difficult to conceive of any form of jury involvement in sentencing having advantages significant enough to outweigh the serious incursions into the integrity of the criminal justice system that would inevitably result' (New South Wales Law Reform Commission, 2007; p. 54).

Threats to Consistency

The conventional model of a criminal jury is for jurors to serve on a single trial and then be discharged, possibly never to be called for jury service again. How, therefore, can they know whether a six-year sentence is consistent with sentences imposed for similar offences in the past? Consistency would not so much suffer, as evaporate, following a series of one-off judgments.[16] Professional judges who have sentenced many previous cases or who have followed appellate judgements are far better equipped to preserve the essential principles of consistency and proportionality and to follow detailed and at times complex sentencing guidelines. As Wright (2003) noted, knowledge of sentencing practices over time which judges accumulate is the most difficult problem for jury sentencing advocates to overcome. An additional problem arises from jurors' awareness when deliberating upon the verdict that they will ultimately also impose sentence in the event that they decide to convict.[17] This knowledge may affect their decision making; in marginal cases, they may be inclined to convict and then impose a minor sentence. This is one reason why common law systems go to great lengths to ensure that the fact-finding jury is not aware of the likely sentence to be imposed in the event that the defendant is convicted.

Some of these adverse consequences of lay (jury) sentencing may be mitigated if jurors received intensive training,[18] were required to follow detailed sentencing guidelines which identified relevant (and proscribed irrelevant) factors, provided with sentencing ranges, or were assisted or directed by professional judges. A sentencing jury could be given training in sentencing and sufficient time to deliberate on the sentence to be imposed, although this could never, in practical terms, reach the level attained by a sentencing judge. But the greater the degree of professionalisation in this respect, the less likely it is that the jury's decision will reflect community values. We are back to Jan de Keijser's paradox: *intuitive* public judgments are often unprincipled; *informed* public opinions are unrepresentative of the general public.

Finally, it is perhaps worth recalling the evolution of the criminal jury in common law jurisdictions. It is not an historical accident that juries have been ascribed the task of fact finding, but not sentencing.[19] A panel of, say twelve people may be more capable than a single individual in reaching judgement about the facts of the case and of answering questions such as: which of these conflicting witnesses is telling the truth? Jurors evaluate evidence adduced at trial according to strict rules of evidence (devised by professional jurists) without having to decide whether a piece of evidence or particular testimony is admissible. However, it has long been the practice that determining admissibility or applying complex sentencing principles has been left to trained legal professionals.

Would Jury Sentences Attract More Community Support?

Even if we make the brave assumption that no adverse consequences in terms of principled sentencing would ensue, are jury sentences actually likely to attract higher public confidence than judicial decisions? Even if they did, would this confer any additional benefits in terms of increased compliance with the law? It is surprising that no one has conducted a direct empirical test of the hypothesis that jury decisions inspire more confidence than the same decision reached by a professional sentencer. Anecdotal evidence suggests that a decision is taken by a jury rather than a judge does not ensure community support. For example, in the United States, the acquittals by a jury of officers charged with assaulting Rodney King did not prevent widespread mass rioting. My guess is that any uplift in public confidence would be modest and the increase in community compliance negligible–for the reasons noted earlier in this essay.

Once again, the limited research record on this question offers no support for the claims of jury advocates. For example, public support for the courts is no higher in jurisdictions such as England and Wales where most sentencing decisions are taken by laypersons.[20] Lay magistrates are regarded by the public as just as out of touch with the community[21] as professional judges.[22] There is no evidence that the public in the United States where sentencing is determined by juries—the test case jurisdictions, if you like—are more supportive of the sentencing process. The same trends emerge in other jurisdictions. De Keijser (this volume), for example, has demonstrated that increased lay involvement in sentencing may actually undermine public confidence: the Dutch appear to prefer a professionalised judiciary which takes decisions independent of community opinion (see also Klijn & Croes, 2007). Research upon the Spanish jury system found that most members of the public believed that judges' decisions were fairer than those by juries and also expressed a preference to be tried by a professional judge rather than a lay jury (Martin & Kaplan, 2006). Fukurai and Krooth (2010) note the refusal of many Japanese citizens to participate in jury trials. Similarly, Yamamura (2009) provides public opinion data from Japan showing that approximately four-fifths of the public were unwilling to serve as lay sentencers—a curious result if lay adjudication is supposed to generate a positive response from the public.

Finally, a number of European jurisdictions utilise mixed panels of sentencers, composed of two laypersons and a professional judge. There is no evidence that this promotes more principled sentencing or higher levels of public confidence. Research has demonstrated that in practice the lay members defer to the opinion of the professional judge. Catellani and Milesi for example note that such mixed juries are 'characterised by a strong asymmetry in the influence of professional judges' (2006, p. 139). Parlak reports the same phenomenon in Polish mixed juries; she notes that lay judges serving on mixed juries 'have no chance to present or discuss their views because the professional judge authoritatively makes the decision' (2006, p. 173). These findings call into question claims for enhancing public participation in criminal justice decision making.

Taken together, these findings are hard to reconcile with the view that jury sentencing is likely to promote public confidence or enhance perceptions of the legitimacy of sentencing. At the very least, advocates of sentencing by jury need to explain these patterns of data and offer some convincing, fresh evidence that lay sentencing is superior to the professional alternative or that it carries ancillary benefits in terms of enhanced legitimacy or compliance.

Structuring Public Input into Sentencing

If direct input by means of a jury drawn from the community seems unwise, how should public opinion be incorporated into sentencing policy and practice? The model of limited public input that I advocate is indirect in nature: public views are measured and then considered by a sentencing authority when guidelines are constructed. Two obvious mechanisms for incorporating community values are through the democratically elected legislature and the sentencing guidelines authority. Parliament may place a specific sentencing factor on a statutory footing for courts to consider at sentencing. In fact, several legislatures have taken this step with respect to factors such as hate motivation or sentence reductions for a guilty plea. The support of the community for such a step is assumed within the democratic character of the elected representatives. This strikes me as a poor vehicle for public input; legislators are as likely to use public opinion to support their own pet sentencing reforms as to promote reforms which attract community support. They are also likely to misread the nature of public opinion, being more familiar with public opinion polls rather than careful academic research.

A sentencing guidelines authority represents a more promising mechanism for public consultation and input. My model envisages a sentencing authority conducting research into and then deliberating upon the role that public opinion about crimes and punishments might play. This research would explore the informed opinions of representative samples of the public with a view to identifying policies and practices where courts and community disagree. Having isolated these, the sentencing authority would determine whether the public view contained some principled basis hitherto overlooked by courts. If this were the case, practice might need adjusting—through guidelines, presumably. If the public rejected a sound sentencing principle, practice should not be adjusted; instead attempts should be mounted to educate the public about the wisdom of a sentencing practice to which they intuitively object. The sentencing authority might want to consider whether the benefits in terms of increased public acceptance of sentencing might justify deviations from a purely retributive model of sentencing.[23]

In addition to reviewing public opinion regarding sentencing factors and practices, a sentencing authority might consider public opinion as a reason to deviate from a purely proportional model. Pure retributivists who endorse a sentencing model with tight upper and lower limits on sanctions are rare. Many people, for example, might support a modest reduction in the severity of a sentence when the offender, recognising the wrongfulness of his or her conduct, reports to the police, confesses to an offence, and records an interview in which he or she expresses his or her desire to forego the right to trial and to plead guilty. (Some people would still disagree with this mitigation). Similarly, the community may favour mitigation in the case of a single mother, convicted of driving dangerously and causing the death of a passenger who happens to her own child. These two examples involve derogations from a strictly proportional sanction which are advocated in pursuit of some wider criminal justice objective such as sparing victims and witnesses from having to testify and promoting public confidence. The challenge of course is to decide which derogations are justified and to ensure that they do not individually or collectively wreck a proportionate sentencing scheme.

Establishing Sanction Severity

The sentencing authority might also investigate the relevance of public opinion for the second half of the proportionality equation within a retributive framework. The principle of proportionality requires a calibration of punishment severity with crime seriousness; public evaluations of the severity of different punishments may help to determine severity rankings. Mirko Bagaric (this volume) makes the important point that the severity of any particular sentence is best determined by the reactions of those experiencing different sanctions. This is surely true; the only way of knowing whether six months imprisonment is worse than, say, a twelve-month period of intense community supervision is to experience the two sanctions or measure the perceptions and experiences of people who have been subject to both forms of punishment.[24] Nevertheless, a severity ranking which was totally unrelated to community values would be problematic. Imagine a serious offence resulting in a penalty that the public believed to be derisory in terms of its impact on the offender—the sanctioning power of the particular sentence and of the sentencing system would falter. Yet public rankings of the severity of different sanctions cannot be determinative; people often have inaccurate views as to the actual severity of existing punishments. Indeed, the promotion of community-based alternatives has long suffered from the public misperception that they are all soft alternatives to imprisonment. The solution is to devise a severity scale which incorporates public views and more objective indicia such as the actual impact on offenders' lives and then to educate the public about the true severity of sanctions. Over time, presumably, public, professional. and subjectively experienced offender rankings of penalty severity will coalesce—particularly if efforts are made to educate the former.

5. CONCLUSION

Let me conclude this discussion of the ways that public opinion might reasonably affect sentencing by reiterating the two principal reasons for *constraining* the influence of the public upon sentencing policy and practice. First, the social component of crime seriousness cannot alone justify the imposition of punishment; punishing X with Y severity because the public believe this is the appropriate response is unprincipled. Public opinion cannot therefore constitute a foundational basis for incorporating factor X or excluding factor Y. If it were, all manner of illogical and unprincipled factors would be incorporated into sentencing practices. We have seen too many examples of intuitive *injustice* over the years. Simons puts the case well when he concludes:

'The depth and pervasiveness of moral indignation at a criminal act are relevant data in assessing the punishment that the act justly deserves . . . Nevertheless, the social context in which the public develops its retributive reactions may understandably lead to prejudice, misunderstanding, and ill-considered, volatile judgments. To those who suffer criminal punishment . . . we owe a more principled explanation and justification' (2000, p. 667).

Second, the utilitarian justifications for heeding the community—to preserve public confidence and encourage public compliance—probably generate only a very modest uplift in both, even assuming one accepts that these goals justify assigning punishments in the first instance.

REFERENCES

Bagaric, M., and R. Edney. (2004). 'The Sentencing Advisory Commission and the Hope of Smarter Sentencing.' *Current Issues in Criminal Justice* 16: 125–139.

Catellani, P., and P. Milesi (2006). 'Juries in Italy: Legal and Extra-Legal Norms in Sentencing.' In M. Kaplan and A. Martin (eds.), *Understanding World Jury Systems through Psychological Research*. New York: Taylor and Francis.

Diamond, S. (1990). 'Revising Images of Public Punitiveness: Sentencing by Lay and Professional English Magistrates.' *Law and Social Inquiry* 15: 191–221.

Dzur, A (2012) *Punishment, Participatory Democracy, and the Jury*. New York: Oxford University Press.

Fukurai, H., and R. Krooth. (2010). What Brings People to the Courtroom? Comparative Analysis of People's Willingness to Serve as Jurors in Japan and the US.' *International Journal of Law. Crime and Justice* 38: 198–215.

Garland, D. (1991). 'Sociological Perspectives on Punishment.' In M. Tonry and N. Morris (eds.), *Crime and Justice*. Chicago: University of Chicago Press.

Golash, D., and J. Lynch. (1995). 'Public Opinion, Crime Seriousness, and Sentencing Policy.' *American Journal of Criminal Law* 22: 703–732.

Green, D. (2006). 'Public Opinion Versus Public Judgment about Crime: Correcting the Comedy of Errors.' *British Journal of Criminology* 46: 131–154.

Hoffman, M. (2003). 'The Case for Jury Sentencing.' *Duke Law Journal* 52: 951–1010.

Hough, M., B. Bradford, J. V. Roberts, and J. Jackson. (2013) *Attitudes to Sentencing and Trust in Justice: Exploring Recent Trends from the Crime Survey of England and Wales*. London: Ministry of Justice.

Hough, M., and A. Kirby. (2013). 'The Role of Public Opinion in Formulating Sentencing Guidelines.' In A. Ashworth and J. V. Roberts (eds.), *Sentencing Guidelines: Exploring the English Model*. Oxford: Oxford University Press.

Hough, M., and J. V. Roberts (1998). *Attitudes to Punishment: Findings from the British Crime Survey*. Home Office Research Study No. 179. London: Home Office.

Husak, D. (2008). *Overcriminalization. The Limits of the Criminal Law*. New York: Oxford University Press.

Jackson, J., M. Bradford, A. Myhill, P. Quinton, and T. Tyler. (2012). 'Why Do People Comply with the Law? Legitimacy and the Influence of Legal Institutions.' *British Journal of Criminology* 52: 1051–1071.

Kalven, H., and H. Zeisel. (1966). *The American Jury*. Chicago: University of Chicago Press.

King, N., and R. Noble. (2004). 'Felony Jury Sentencing in Practice: A Three-State Study.' *Vanderbilt Law Review* 57: 885–962.

Klijn, A., and M. Croes. (2007). 'Public Opinion on Lay Participation in the Criminal Justice System of the Netherlands.' *Utrecht Law Review* 3: 157–168.

Kolber, A. (2009). 'Compliance-Promoting Intuitions.' In P. Robinson, S. Garvey, and K. Ferzan (eds.), *Criminal Law Conversations*. Oxford: Oxford University Press.

Martin, A., and M. Kaplan. (2006). 'Psycological Perspectives on Spanish and Russian Juries.' In M. Kaplan and A. Martin (eds.), *Understanding World Jury Systems through Psychological Research*. New York: Taylor and Francis.

Nagin, D. (2013). 'Deterrence in the Twenty-First Century: A Review of the Evidence.' In M. Tonry (ed.), *Crime and Justice: A Review of Research*. Chicago: University of Chicago Press.

New South Wales Law Reform Commission. (2006). *Sentencing by Jury*. Issues Paper 27. Sydney: New South Wales Law Reform Commission.

New South Wales Law Reform Commission. (2007). *Role of Juries in Sentencing*. Report 118. Sydney: New South Wales Law Reform Commission.

Nolan, J. (2009). *Legal Accents, Legal Borrowing. The International Problem-Solving Court Movement*. Princeton, NJ: Princeton University Press.

Parlak, D. (2006). 'Social-Psychological Implications of the Mixed Jury System in Poland.' In M. Kaplan and A. Martin (eds.), *Understanding World Jury Systems through psychological research*. New York: Taylor and Francis.

Petersilia, J., and E. Deschenes. (1994). 'Perceptions of Punishment: Inmates and Staff Rank the Severity of Prison versus Intermediate Sanctions.' In J. Petersilia (ed.), *The Prison Journal* 74: 306–328.

Roberts, J. V. (2002). 'Public Opinion and Sentencing Policy.' In S. Rex and M. Tonry (eds.), *Reform and Punishment: The Future of Sentencing*. Cullompton, UK: Willan.

Roberts, J. V. (2010). 'Re-Examining First Offender Discounts at Sentencing.' In *The Role of Previous Convictions at Sentencing: Theoretical and Applied Perspectives*. Oxford: Hart.

Roberts, J. V. (2013). *Sentencing Guidelines: The Role of Research into Public Opinion*. Paper presented to the Drapkin International Seminar, Jerusalem, March 2013.

Roberts, J. V., and M. Hough, (2005). *Understanding Public Attitudes to Criminal Justice*. Maidenhead, UK: Open University Press.

Roberts, J. V., L. S. Stalans, D. Indermaur, and M. Hough, (2003). *Penal Populism and Public Opinion*. Oxford: Oxford University Press.

Robinson, P. (2009). 'Empirical Desert.' In P. Robinson, S. Garvey, and K. Ferzan (eds.), *Criminal Law Conversations*. Oxford: Oxford University Press.

Robinson, P., S. Garvey, and K. Ferzan (eds.). (2009). *Criminal Law Conversations*. Oxford: Oxford University Press.

Ryberg, J. (2010). 'Punishment and Public Opinion.' In J. Ryberg and A. Corlett (eds.), *Punishment and Ethics: New Perspectives*. Basingstoke, UK: Palgrave MacMillan.

Sharpe, R. (2013). *Are Courts Representative Bodies? A Canadian Perspective*. Oxford, UK: Foundation for Law, Justice and Society. http://www.fljs.org/sites/www.fljs.org/files/publications/Sharpe.pdf

Simester, A., and A. von Hirsch. (2011). *Crimes, Harms, and Wrongs. On the Principles of Criminalisation*. Oxford: Hart Publishing.

Simons, K. (2000). 'The Relevance of Community Values to Just Deserts: Criminal Law, Punishment Rationales, and Democracy.' *Hofstra Law Review* 28: 635–667.

Trahan, A. (2011). 'In Their Own Words: Capital Jurors Reactions to Mitigation Strategies.' *IJPS* 7: 1–16.

Tyler, T. (2006). *Why People Obey the Law.* Princeton, NJ: Princeton University Press.

Tyler, T. R. (2007). *Legitimacy and Criminal Justice.* New York: Russell Sage Foundation.

Tyler, T. R. (2010). *Why People Cooperate? The Role of Social Motivations.* Princeton, NJ: Princeton University Press.

Victoria Sentencing Advisory Council (2012). *Community Attitudes to Offence Seriousness.* Melbourne: Victoria Sentencing Advisory Council.

von Hirsch, A. (1993). *Censure and Sanctions.* Oxford: Clarendon.

von Hirsch, A., Roberts, J. V., Bottoms, A. E., Roach, K., and Schiff, M. (eds.) (2003). *Restorative and Criminal Justice. Competing or Reconcilable Paradigms?* Oxford: Hart Publishing.

Warner, K., and J. Davis. (2012) 'Using Jurors to Explore Public Attitudes to Sentencing.' *British Journal of Criminology* 52: 93–112.

Wright, R. (1999). 'Rules for Sentencing Revolutions.' *Yale Law Journal* 108: 1355–1387.

Yamamura, E. (2009). 'What Discourages Participation in the Lay Judge System (Saiban'in Seido) of Japan? Interaction between the Secrecy Requirement and Social Networks.' MPRA Paper No. 17197. http://mpra.ub.uni-muenchen.de/17197/

NOTES

1. I am very grateful to the participants at the seminar held in Copenhagen in October 2012 and in particular Jesper Ryberg and Jan de Keijser for feedback on earlier drafts of this essay.

2. For example, if the public were adamantly opposed to, say, retributivism, it would make little sense for the legislature to direct courts to privilege this perspective by placing the principle of proportionality on a statutory footing.

3. This research would employ representative samples of the public to measure general public reactions to sentences; the goal would be to understand mass rather than elite expectations of sentence severity. In addition to measuring public perceptions to determine the level of severity necessary to deter, it would also be necessary to survey the public to measure levels of awareness of the penalty structure and perceptions of the likelihood of punishment if a crime is committed.

4. I leave aside here the literature on the effectiveness of general deterrence which is far from encouraging (for a review, see Nagin, 2013).

5. See Robinson (2009) for further discussion and Robinson, Garvey, and Ferzan (2009) for some responses to the empirical desert model.

6. See, more generally, Tyler (2007, 2010).

7. Witch doctors are an example of individuals generating high levels of community confidence but in the absence of any evidence of effectiveness.

8. In calculating the costs and benefits of various solutions to the problem of low confidence in the courts, it will be necessary to select the strategy which achieves the most effective uplift in confidence levels—and this may mean educating the community rather than making punishments harsher—modifying the views of the public rather than the practice of the courts (see Ryberg, 2010).

9. Recent events in England suggest that some courts regard mere offensiveness as justifying not just criminalisation but the imposition of custody. In one case an individual was sentenced to two months custody for a supposedly amusing twitter message about the murder of a child; in a second an offender was sentenced to four months in prison for wearing a t-shirt with an offensive message directed at the police. Neither example would come close to fulfilling the criminalisation prerequisites proposed by Husak (2008) or Simester and von Hirsch (2011).

10. For an example of a recent and sophisticated analysis of community perceptions of crime seriousness see Victoria Sentencing Advisory Council (2012).

11. Many examples may be offered in support of this proposition. Punishments by occupying forces during a time of war inflict suffering yet without conveying censure. On a more mundane level, the reaction of some adolescents to court-imposed punishments such as England's antisocial behaviour orders reveals the same phenomenon: even restrictive conditions carry no censure from the perspective of the individual on whom they are imposed because the authority lacks the standing to act (in the eyes of the offender).

12. Similarly, penalties designed to shame the offender, whether in a positive (restorative) or a condemnatory (exclusionary) way will only be effective if the authority imposing the penalty carries legitimacy and the community agrees that the penalty attracts shame to the individual on whom it is imposed.

13. See the competing perspectives discussed in von Hirsch et al. (2003).

14. In this respect I am in agreement with Bagaric and Edney (2004) who argued that sentencing requires expertise, in the same way that designing a car requires training and expert knowledge.

15. See discussion in Roberts (2010).

16. Bennett (this volume) suggests a six-month term for jurors; while this may be better than a one-off role, they would still acquire very little experience in sentencing a range of different offences; their sentencing decisions would reflect their knowledge of the specific facts before them in any particular case.

17. In some jurisdictions such as Canada judges adjudicate and sentence the offender they have just convicted, yet unlike jurors they are trained to ensure that their verdicts are unaffected by the knowledge that they will also ultimately impose sentence.

18. Although as Kalven and Zeisel noted in their classic study of the jury, 'The perennial amateur, layman jury cannot be so quickly domesticated . . . it remains susceptible to stimuli which the judge will exclude'. (1966, p. 498).

19. Hoffman (2003) alludes to the apparent paradox of entrusting the most important part of a criminal trial—the determination of guilt—to members of the public serving as jurors but then excluding them from sentencing. The explanation for this is that the guilt phase is essentially a question of fact-finding, whereas the determination of sentencing invokes more complex questions of legal principle.

20. The latest representative survey in England and Wales found that approximately three quarters fully of the general public held the view that sentencing was too lenient (see Hough et al., 2013). This is comparable or higher than the percentage of the public holding this view in the United States, Australia, or

Canada, where sentencing is conducted by professional judges (with the exception of the US states noted earlier in this essay; see Roberts & Hough, 2005).

21. One explanation for this finding is that ironically, lay magistrates may be less, not more inclined than professional judges to reflect community views, and juries may also adopt this approach: Diamond (1990) reported that legally trained magistrates were more likely to take the views of the community into account and more likely to agree that these views should be taken into account.

22. Analysis of the British Crime Survey found that the percentage of the public believing lay magistrates were 'out of touch' with community values was almost as high as the percentage that held this view of professional judges: 74 per cent of the sample thought lay magistrates were out of touch; 82 per cent held this view of judges (see Hough & Roberts, 1998).

23. This approach is broadly followed by the Sentencing Council of England and Wales which conducts research into public attitudes to issues such as sentence reductions for a guilty plea. The results of this research are then considered when the council issues guidelines for courts to follow at sentencing. For example, prior to issuing a guideline on the appropriate reductions that should be awarded defendants who plead guilty, the council will determine the nature of public attitudes to such sentencing discounts. For example, the consequences of widespread and intense public opposition to sentence reductions can then be considered by the council as a factor to be set against the benefits of reductions (such as reducing the costs of criminal justice); see Roberts (2013) for discussion.

24. Research has demonstrated significant differences in rankings of severity derived from the people on whom punishments are imposed and those from criminal justice professionals or the public (e.g. Petersilia & Deschenes, 1994).

INDEX

advisory bodies or panels: citizen, 11, 218; sentencing, 2, 251n10

American Law Institute, 65, 179

anchor(ing) points or effects, 7–8, 36, 40–42, 51n7, 60–61, 84, 130, 142n6, 152

arguments: consequentialist (*see* consequentialism); deontological (*see* deontology); desert-based, 7, 17, 103–104, 231; epistemic, 10, 126, 128–133, 138, 231; institutional, 10, 126–127, 133–134, 138; instrumental, 10–11, 103–104, 126–127, 134, 136, 231; process-oriented, 214; public opinion-based, 3–4; punishment-of-the-innocent (*see* punishment: of innocent)

Ashworth, A., 39–40, 84–85, 87, 93–95, 190

Australia, 3, 77–78, 100n17, 106, 242–243, 251n20

authority, 59, 149–150, 154, 158, 169, 209, 221, 232; sentencing (guidelines), 246–247

Bagaric, Mirko, 6, 9–10, 110, 115, 124–125, 247, 251n14

Barry, Brian, 35, 43–44, 53n17

Bauman, Z., 210

Bedau, Hugo Adam, 45

Begle, Angela, 91

Bellah, R., 204, 214–215

Bennett, C., 10–11, 44, 240, 251n16

Benn, S., 33

Bentham, J., 4, 6, 35, 52n13, 83, 121

blameworthiness, 48, 60–64–67, 71–72, 75, 82, 92–93, 104, 109, 189, 234

'Bloody Code', 38

Bordenkircher v. Hayes (1978), 166

Bottoms, Anthony, 4

Brooks, Thom, 11, 239

brutality, 41, 55

Canada, 3, 13n3, 83, 251n17, 252n20

capital punishment. *See* death penalty

censure, 7, 11, 15, 43, 45, 81–82, 104, 114, 136, 236–237, 251n12, 236–237, 251n11, 251n12

China, 55, 70–73

Christiano, T., 175–176

Christie, N., 197

common law, 62, 243–244

community: defined or identified, 62, 190–191; judge or magistrate and, 1–2, 10, 116, 231, 244, 252n21, 252n22; views or values (*see* public opinion; sentiments; values)

256

Index

Finland, 78
France, 113

gap, punitiveness, 3, 6, 10, 15,
    101–102, 109–111, 114–115,
    204, 231
generality assumption, 20–21,
    25–29, 31–32n10
Germany, 46, 78, 85, 175
Goffman, E., 210
Great Britain, 3, 106, 112, 186
guidelines, 2, 10, 12, 18, 84, 147,
    158–160, 189, 228, 230, 236,
    243, 245–246, 252n23
guilty, plea of, 2, 165–167, 172–173,
    245, 252n23

Hanson, R., 91
Harding, C., 83
hard treatment, penal, 34, 186, 191,
    203n24, 236–237
harm, 5, 18–19, 42, 54, 75n1, 81,
    87–89, 92–93, 100n16, 134,
    152, 179, 235
Hegel, G. F. W., 4, 35, 39, 41, 51n5
Hoare v R, 77
homicide, 37–38, 40–41, 62, 64, 67,
    91, 95, 100n17
homosexuality, 46–47, 52n8, 86
Hough, M., 106–107, 112,
    231–232
Hubel, G., 91

imprisonment, 19, 47, 86, 129, 183,
    210–211, 215, 220–221, 226n5,
    247; economic cost of, 70;
    impact on prisoners of, 94–96,
    213; life, 41, 48, 58, 60, 73, 215,
    241; proportionality and, 77,
    79, 93, 96; recidivism and, 79,
    194; restorative justice or
    punitive restoration and, 191,

193–194, 202n18; statistics on,
    79, 100n17, 213
incarceration, mass or hyper-,
    212–213, 220, 226n5
Indermaur, D., 106
information effect, 102–103,
    105, 114
innocence, presumption of,
    173, 175
insanity defence, 62, 67, 162n10
institutions, 204–222; (criminal)
    justice or penal, 11, 72, 120,
    150, 175, 204, 210–216, 219,
    221–222, 226n8, 226n11,
    231–232; democratic, 133,
    185–187; education, 11,
    204–205, 208, 219–222,
    227n20; morality or religion
    and, 15–16, 210, 226n8; public
    or social, 5, 96, 206, 208–214;
    punishment as, 5, 96, 208;
    reform or change of, 188,
    221–222; repel public, 204,
    206, 208, 210–211, 213;
    theories about or studies of,
    208–210, 214–215
intent, criminal, 18, 21, 67, 73, 87,
    92–93, 152
interests, 37–39, 41, 88–89, 95, 235
Internet, 55, 70–71, 74
intuitions, 6, 9, 32n11, 32n13, 63,
    101, 104, 107, 109, 121, 135,
    143n14, 144n16, 144n17, 243;
    defined, 31n2, 143n11; desert
    and, 60, 189, 231–232;
    generality assumption about,
    20–21, 25–26, 28, 31n10; of
    jurors, 240–241; penal theories
    and, 9, 16–29; philosophers' or
    penal theorists' moral, 16,
    21–25, 32n10, 32n14; reliability,
    validity, or injustice of, 22,